WHO BUILT SCOTLAND

Alexander McCall Smith

WHO

Alistair Moffat

BUILT

James Crawford

SCOT

A History
of the Nation
in Twenty-Five
Buildings

James Robertson

LAND

Kathleen Jamie

Published in 2017 by Historic Environment Scotland Enterprises Limited
SC510997

Historic Environment Scotland
Longmore House
Salisbury Place
Edinburgh EH9 1SH

Registered Charity SC045925

British Library Cataloguing-in-Publication Data. A catalogue record for this
book is available from the British Library.

ISBN 978 1 84917 224 0

Individual chapters remain the copyright of their respective authors:
Alexander McCall Smith, Alistair Moffat, James Crawford,
James Robertson and Kathleen Jamie

Typeset in Granjon, Didot and Gotham

Cover Design by James Keenan
Proofread by Mairi Sutherland
Indexed by Linda Sutherland

Printed and bound by Clays Ltd, St Ives plc

Supported by Creative Scotland

Contents

Introduction

Look around you, wherever you are right now. Maybe you are reading this while browsing in a bookshop in a city; or you are on a bus or train rumbling through a town centre; or you are in an armchair in a tenement flat or a semi-detached house or a cottage out on its own, surrounded by nothing but fields and stone dykes. Stop for a moment, and take in all the things you can see. There may be roads and pavements, long lines of concrete and tarmac filled with cars and pedestrians. There may be streetlights, shining down on row after row of houses, stretching off into a suburban distance. Perhaps you are in a hotel, ten storeys high, with a view that takes in a whole city, other buildings far below, thinning out towards hills and a river that widens to the sea. Maybe you are in a village on the coast – an old village with a hook of stone harbour and, beyond, out on a promontory, a tall, whitewashed tower with a spinning light, standing alone. Or you are high in the mountains, far away from any urban hum, in a basic, tin-roofed stone bothy for climbers and walkers, reading by the light of a fire you've lit yourself among the ashes of a soot-blackened hearth.

Now think – someone, at some time, built all of this. A process was started, long ago, to put things into, and on top of, the land. Permanent things. Things that might, and in many cases have, lasted far beyond the lives of their makers. In simplest terms, at some point, we stopped being just travellers, and we became builders. The fires we made to keep us warm no longer moved from place to place. We put walls around them and roofs over them. We made homes. Places for families – places to eat, work, sleep, love, fight and argue. Places to live.

You can still see some of these places today. Travel to Orkney then catch a ferry – or if you're brave, a ten-seater twin-prop plane – to the northernmost island, Papa Westray, and then head on to a place on the west coast called the Knap of Howar. There, fringed with grass and wildflowers and directly overlooking the sea, are two holes in the ground. From above, seen side-by-side, they look like two footprints: two footprints that were hidden beneath the earth until a storm in the 1930s tore at the sand and soil and exposed the tops of walls made of interlocking stone. Now you can climb down to the shore side, stoop low to pass through a doorway. It is a journey of just a few metres, but also of 5,000 years. You are inside the oldest building still standing in northern Europe. You are sheltered from the wind, but it still whips the air above you, in the empty space that once held a roof. The entry doorway frames perfectly the shore, sea and sky. The sun sets on that horizon. There is a fireplace and the remains of ancient furniture and cupboards. And as you stand there, you realise that it is not so much distance that you feel from the people who built these homes – who lived in them for generation after generation – as intimacy. Our modern living rooms and kitchens, with sofas and smart TVs and electric ovens and microwaves, aren't really so different. You can pull on the thread between now and then and feel it taut and strong.

What we build always reveals things that are deeply and innately human. Because all buildings are stories, one way or another. They each offer their own threads to pull, threads that lead you to ideas, emotions, hopes, dreams, fears and conceits. So go on, look at everything around you and think, *really think*, about how it got there. Who planned it, who designed it, who paid for it, who actually got their hands dirty making it? Who lived in it, or worked in it, or worshipped in it, or learnt in it, or was born in it, or died in it? It's a dizzying prospect, vertigo-inducing even, when you attempt to peer over the metaphorical parapet at the layers of history upon which all of our lives are built.

In this book, we have picked just twenty-five buildings to take us from a beginning to an (open) end. As a result, we will, inevitably, have missed both the obvious and the obscure. But it is the nature of the journey that is important. Starting with the earliest hearths left behind by our nameless ancestors, we will move steadily forward, and in the process tell a new history of Scotland, rooted in the roots themselves, the things that we have raised up – in stone, wood, steel, glass and concrete – and that still persist in the landscape, whether hunkered down with unshakable tenacity, or reduced to the faintest of traces. Our five authors have been all across the county in the process, from city centres to remote glens and lonely island peninsulas. They have travelled to these buildings and – where they have been able – walked inside them or through them or on top of them, to reflect on both their histories and how they relate to personal stories and experiences. This book, then, is an account of twenty-five individual journeys, which come together to form a narrative of a nation. But it is also an invitation to you, the reader, to get out and explore Scotland, to look anew at everything that you see, to reach out to the stones and feel them coarse or smooth to the touch and to find the seam that leads you onwards, on your own journey.

1

Signs and Traces
Kathleen Jamie

Geldie Burn, 8000 BC

In the beginning was a hearth, a gathering round the fire.
    In the beginning was shelter, hides stretched over wood, with water nearby.
    In the beginning was the land, not long emerged from the ice, seashores, rivers, glens and watersheds. Birch and hazel woods, the open hill.
    In the beginning was the smell of fish roasting in the cinders, of hazelnuts.

Nowadays, if you make your way to Braemar, and then to the Linn of Dee, it's possible to park a car there under the Scots pines, and walk or cycle farther into the Mar Lodge Estate, following the upper Dee by a Land Rover track through its broad strath up to White Bridge, where the Dee and the Geldie meet.

Back then, 8,000 years ago, you lived with stone and wood. With animals, birds and fish. With the seasons and the weather, with one another. You moved around the country: a season here, a gathering there. Some places were familiar; you came over and again, took what you needed. Intimately your hands knew wood, stone, bone, hide, gut, grass, bark, sinew, antler.

The bridge crosses the Dee, which would otherwise be dangerous in spate. You pass remnants of native pine wood and more modern plantations; a few ruined blackhouses. Signs direct you toward the high passes, the fabled names of the Cairngorms: the Lairig Ghru. The hills are almost free of snow. The sky is high and clear; today, white clouds are travelling eastward.

It wasn't enough to say 'bone'. Which bone? Scapula or knuckle? Which species of animal, at what age? Likewise grass. What kind was best for weaving hoods, which for fish baskets?
    You knew these things. You knew things we'd still recognise now, in our

hearts: the smell of wood smoke, faces by firelight. The stars at night. The turn-
ing seasons. A coming and going. Voices. Tasks to be done.

   A day in early summer then was just as long and as full of bright promise.

At Chest of Dee you can follow that river higher toward its source. There
is a narrow part where the water, blue *and* aquamarine, surges between
rocks so strongly it purls backward on itself. A place of recreation and soli-
tude, haunt of the long-distance hillwalker and naturalist.

   Potentially dangerous. The hills stand guard. In the clear meltwater of
the pool at the waterfall, a single fish inhabits its own world.

*At the confluence of two rivers, on a flat shingly riverbank. The water is fast
and clear – almost greenish. It's meltwater falling through a tight linn, draining
the snowfields higher in the mountains. Perhaps there are sparse stands of birch,
hazel, even pine to feed the fires. There is a camp. Tents of hide, windbreaks of
woven willow. Morning smoke. Voices. Work to be done. Around the tents are
drying racks for fish or meat, frames to stretch skins.*

   *When you arrived there were the traces of the last time you were here – bits
of stone, a midden, dark ashy patches where the fires were lit – a familiarity.
You're here for a reason, following something maybe, a herd of animals that
gather at this time of year. Or a certain wood, or a certain kind of stone. You
have followed a river well inland, almost to its source.*

The river which meets the Dee here is the Geldie. 'Geldie' is an old name
meaning clear, white, pure. The track follows the river as the Geldie trends
eastward. Today, 25 blackcock were gathered at their lek, an adder basked
on the path where the Bynack Burn joined the Geldie.

   The path rises onto heather, then narrows to a walking trail.

   The river is below on your left, meandering and looping because the
little strath is level; the hills on the south side are even, glaciated, heather
covered. There are no trees whatsoever. On the opposite bank stand the
ruins of Geldie Lodge, a nineteenth century shooting lodge; a brief intervention in the landscape, in the long scheme of things.

*You know fine well that if you follow one of the rivers, it will take you higher
into the hills. You were first taken there as a youngster – it was an adventure.
After some hours' walk you will turn westward into a higher, lightly wooded
valley, with a marshy floor. Perhaps there are deer up there, grazing quietly,
maybe even reindeer on the high slopes. Perhaps the reindeer are already gone,
they have become a story the elders tell.*

However, you've left the main camp by the waterfall and crossed the major river. Alone, or in a small gang. You follow the lesser river, keeping to its northern bank and head into the hills. There's a place you favour upstream, a good morning's walk away, where you reckon you'll stop for the night. Though it's on a small ridge, it's sheltered among spare trees. The valley it looks out upon is sedgy, with sparse birch and hazel trees. The gentle hills are green.

It was here, at about 1,500 feet, where the path crosses Caonachan Ruadha (the wee red burn) that some workers repairing the eroding footpath discovered under the peat a number of tiny flint artefacts. They saw them with a sharp eye; a hunter-gatherer's eye.

The flints comprised what the archaeologists call a 'lithic scatter'. Tiny blades, not the length of your thumbnail, flakes and off-cuts of flint and rhyolite. They lay strewn in such a way that suggested they had littered the ground around a fire within a tent of some kind. A small camp, no more than two or three people on a high route through the hills, among trees, perhaps for some special function. That was before the peat came and covered them.

Another half day's march would take you to the top of the glen. The hills, still snow-wreathed, appear to close the glen but you know there are routes between them. If you kept walking and managed some tricky river crossings, you'd find your way down into another separate river system, a whole different part of the country, maybe another kind of people. But tonight you stop.

What have you brought? You've brought some means of making fire. Hides to sleep under. Tools, knives to cut a few withies. A pouchful of nuts, pemmican of some sort. Some twigs of yew – why that? For its cleansing smoke, for tipping poison darts? Snares, which you'll set. The pelt of a hare, still in its winter whites, makes perfect mittens, baby clothes. Perhaps bow and arrows, perhaps you're waiting for migrating animals to file through the high pass.

You set the fire. Do you need to consider bears? To keep someone awake on bear-watch at night? Maybe you'll see prints in the marshy mud but they won't worry you.

The scatter of flints, a fire-scorched place, the site of what was likely a shelter. Little else is preserved in Scotland's somewhat acidic soil. The carbon dating of the hearth gave dates of 8,000 years ago; suggesting the mountains were part of people's range and resource from the earliest days of human settlement.

Why were they here?

At this time of year the nights are short but cold. Actually, they're getting colder. The elders say winters are much colder than they used to be, snow and ice are lingering longer into the year. You relish the daylight, having come through a winter lit mainly by moon and firelight, or lamps of animal fat. Here in the high glen, you use the gift of daylight. You sit on stones in the gloaming by the fire re-sharpening and re-working tools: the tiny blades and flint points which are an endless labour if they are to keep their edge. A stone in either hand, you knap carefully. The chipped-off pieces lie where they fall. The flint has come with you from the coast, but there are rhyolite outcrops up here. Perhaps you'll fetch some while you're about it. Yours are working hands: muscular, knowledgeable.

You feed the fire. When you talk, you talk about what you're doing, about each other, about weather-signs, animal-signs. Some daft adventure you recall. A story.

What do you call this place? Where did you say you were going when you set off, and why? Who might you meet up here, on the high track through the mountains?

There are Mesolithic sites all along the Dee, only now being discovered. At Chest of Dee, there were bigger sites, possibly longer lasting, repeatedly visited, with their hearths and lithic scatters. It may be that this little camp at Caochanan Ruadha is an outpost of those. You can sit here now under a bright sky and look westward up to where the river rises.

You might meet a lone walker passing, with his backpack, a portable shelter, some warm well-made clothes, some easy-to-carry food. When he speaks, you can tell where he comes from. He describes crossing a river, dangerously, water up to his waist. You exchange pleasantries, he walks on.

Your shadows are long as you walk away from camp to check your snares before the ravens get there first. The sky is clear, ashy pink in the west, a quarter moon already risen high. It all bodes well for the morrow, and the morrow. You lived lightly on the land for 4,000 years.

Imagine! Four thousand spring times. A million and a half days and nights. What did they build, our hunter-gatherer forebears? Nothing as yet discovered, if by 'build' you mean stone piled on stone. Our forebears left little trace of themselves before the transition to farming was complete. But they built a long culture, a profound knowledge communicated by memory, story, instruction by elders to youngsters.

Wind in the grasses. River-rush. Sun on your face. Silence on the hills.
  Westward, the wide glen closed by hills against a high spring sky.

*

Then came farms, beasts, crops. A few black kye grazing, a few fields of barley or bere. Still the hearth, peat-burning now though, that sweetest smoke. The year still turns, but it's the farming year, a pastoral year.

On a midsummer's afternoon in the upper reaches of a Perthshire glen, up where the burn rises, where no-one lives and few folk linger, you're exploring a cluster of ruins. Even the word 'ruin' sounds too grand for these traces of stone and turf.

You're quite alone, though it's a fine day to be outdoors and the Ben Lawers car park is full. Folk have other reasons nowadays for heading to the hills. On the summit of Ben Lawers itself – a well-worn path leads there – a gang of youngsters are trying to launch a paraglider.

If they weren't given on the OS map you might hardly notice the ruins, they are so of a piece with the landscape: same stone, same turf and moss.

But if you sit for a few minutes, getting your eye in, you can detect more and more. They're on either side of the burn, raised up on small green knolls and ridges, each within hailing distance of the next.

You creep out under the low lintel into the morning, glance at the hillsides, the sky. Perhaps cloud has lowered during the night to hide the surrounding summits; a shower dampened the turf roofs and grasses underfoot. A wee shower doesn't matter, the bothans are newly repaired.

Peat smoke from a dozen other huts is drifting over the upper glen. Peat smoke and dung: smells so familiar you don't notice them. You smell of peat smoke yourself, your clothes and hair. Later, when the sun breaks through to warm the ground, you'll catch the scent of grasses and wildflowers too.

Some are drystane enclosures with walls just knee high, others are turf, mossy and overgrown. One or two are ovals with a narrow doorway on the long side you can squeeze through. You can sit inside a little stone hut, open to the sky. Reeds and grasses now grow where people once slept. Sheep enter now too; tufts of fleece are caught on the stones. The huts seem too small inside, taking up no more ground than tents, with barely room to lie your length, never mind space for children, a fire, chattels. One or two of the huts still have a stone recess set into their end wall, a cool place to stand cheeses.

The cattle are lowing, the calves answer. Aye, better get them milked so the herds can drive them up to the day's pasture. The sheep and goats are on the steeper braes, with a few herds to guard them against foxes – or wolves, even, in the olden days. And to keep them on your lands. Or your laird's lands, rather.

The sky is high and blue. It's mid-June and the whole upper glen is silent but for pipits, and the Allt Gleann Da-Eig hastening down to join the River Lyon. There is not a human voice, not a cow or calf, but the grass still remembers to be green after all these years, enclosed and protected by the higher hills.

There are 6,200 recorded shieling sites in Scotland, reaching from Perthshire north and west to the Western Isles. An entire pastoral culture, thousands of years' worth, expressed gently in the high hills and moors, and little visited today.

Huts and shelters, cattle pens, dairies, stores. Generations of re-building and repair on the same green knoll.

Your neighbour's calling from her door; aye, it promises to be a fine day. At your own door, your goods and gear brought up from the wintertown: your churn and milk pails, maybe a spinning wheel or a distaff. There's never not work to do. You must take advantage of the long light, winter will come soon enough – darkness and firelight. But for now the season is still young. You go to the burn for water. There are bannocks to bake, the bairns need their breakfast, there's the kye to tend to, your daughter will help. You always lived with cattle. You know their ways, their needs and ailments and cures. How to milk and churn, how to make butter, how to keep cheese. You learned from your mother, she from her mother.

Who came to the shielings? Accounts vary. Fond tradition says only the women and bairns stayed for the full six weeks or so in the hills, the men-folk had work with the ripening crops below. Some sources speak of a grand procession up from the glen as entire townships made the move. Others suggest that latterly it was just the milkmaids and herds. Whatever, the annual flit to summer grazings had been happening since time out of mind. It was the custom in medieval times, for sure. Maybe its origins are much older, reaching back to the Bronze Age, even the Neolithic, when people began keeping livestock and growing crops. These are long eras of time and so not without changes. There were changes of society and politics, of land control and ownership. Populations waxed and waned. There were serious fluctuations in climate: the balmy medieval era gave way to sharp fourteenth century cooling, with associated plague. After a brief recovery came the Little Ice Age, a time of dearth.

But the shielings! Places of high days and holidays, a sense of summer freedom for women and children. The shieling of poetry and song. It's a romantic notion maybe, but why not? There is no contesting that the midsummer days were long in the north, then as now. Midsummer nights in the hills are but a few hours of cold blue before the day dawns again. Gloamings are long, the wildflowers bloom. One could gather tormentil (good for dysentery and even sunburn) and butterwort (considered a magic plant, offering protection from malevolent fairies).

You can send the bairns to pick flowers or roots, or fresh heather for your beds or the calves' beds, or lichen for dyes, maybe a handful of early cloudberries.

If days were warm, there were surely long moments of peace and ease. But then as now, hours must have been spent huddled out of the rain. So much is constant: if you live by the land in marginal places, you must grasp what the land offers, and in Highland glens it offers a few fleeting weeks of high grazing. Bringing the milch cattle up into the hills allowed the lower grazings to recuperate, and kept hooves away from tender crops.

But you can't see right down to the wintertown, because the glen turns east. For a few weeks, you are out of sight of your home. Though the days are long, they are fleeting, mind; soon the smell in the air changes, the nights darken, the mornings are cool. Harvest time is coming and needs you with the kye and the hens and the new-made cheeses and the bairns taller than when they left. Someone's belly swelling, ready for a winter birth.

Though there are old island folk who still recall being carried to the shielings as infants, for the most part the practice was over by about 1800, and for the usual reasons: sheep, potatoes, agricultural improvement and associated depopulation, clearance. The new mills and mines of the Lowlands were opening their doors. So we have these innumerable small buildings left quietly on the land: marks of the common folk, female folk, of long custom. One can barely even call them 'buildings', just a few courses of stone or turf. They are not statements, they are not possessive – that's their charm. They are cultural expressions, much as pipe music is. (Bagpipes are a pastoralist's instrument, the bag was originally sheep's or goat's stomach.) At 1,500 or 1,600 feet, halfway between the valley floor and the summits, halfway between the modern cafes and hotels, and today's windblown hillwalkers, a shieling ground carries a particular atmosphere. You can visit from one wee hut to the next, wondering who last slept there.

You sense a link to the land, though it was often a precarious and poor life. A link also to languages and music and implements and lore, to people's knowledge, their ailments and ignorances. Rightly or wrongly, shieling grounds don't speak of people torn violently from the land, but rather of the land relinquishing them, as easily as it surrenders the down of bog cotton, and – almost – awaiting their return. Mica sparkles in the hand-shifted stones, cloud-shadows pass on the hillsides. Because they were places for women and children and culture and memory, the hills are the better for the shielings.

But, for now, the sun's burning off the low cloud, and breaks through. Though there still are wreaths of snow in the high corries. You feel the heat on your face and forearms. It may be summer, but there's plenty work to be done, in the heat and sweat. There's aye work, food to win, wool to spin to weave cloth to hide your nakedness and ever the rent to be found.

Industrial Revolution. Capitalism. Landowners realising there were fortunes to be made from rough stuff under their moors and hills. Almost all you needed was labour – lots of it. And people were fleeing the land, or thrown from it, or seeking wider horizons than their native glen.

You came up when you married and became a collier's wife. A pitheadman's wife. You were both 25, and it wasn't long till the first baby arrived. The neighbours were kind, and there was no shortage of them: 400 folk crammed into a couple of squares and a few rows of houses the mine owners built.

An Ayrshire moor, on a summer's day. On the western edge of the moors above Auchinleck, at 700 feet or so. Not high, but the sense is of space and openness. You're on top of a mound that adds another 150 feet or so, and that makes all the difference. Eastward lies Airds Moss: eight miles of blanket bog, a place for birds – or it will be once the restorative work is complete.

South, the land rises again. There are still opencast mines there, trucks moving. A parade of lorries on the A70 between Muirkirk and Cumnock seems silent from up here. Westward, through, that's where the real views open out. The land falls to the coast, there's Arran. Goat Fell – in fact the whole lower Clyde. Is that Jura?

But the hill which offers this panorama is not natural. It's an old bing; the spoil from an opencast site abandoned now. At first there were pits, and after the pits were worked out, the opencast mining began. The opencast site is a cruel-looking gouge in the earth, now deeply flooded, because opencast mining also came to an end. All mining up here ended. In the space of a long century it was over and done. Rapid industrialisation, unleashed capitalism – just a flash in the pan.

Not for those who spent entire lives up here, perhaps. It must have seemed eternal.

Your mother and in-laws aren't far away. They were the ones who had come over from Ireland. From County Antrim farms to a mine. They still kept their accents. Down the row Scots names alternate with Irish: Moffat, Gormauley, McCarthy, Baxter, Stirling, Lafferty, Gemmel, Muir, McSherrie. All crammed in two rooms per family, one window. The young leaving their famished land in droves and considering themselves lucky, perhaps, to be hired.

North of the bing and the flooded opencast site stands one farmhouse, Darnconner, that looks as though it has endured since before the mining began, a link to the long centuries of farming that came before.

The bing is slowly earthing over. There are even butterflies feeding on flowers that like its dry stony ground.

Immediately north of the bing, a new wood is planted, Duncan's Wood. The young trees, native species, are still in their protective tubes.

You're no stranger to work, mind. Before you married you were in the cotton mills at Catrine, with your own meagre wage, but a wage. Now it's a job of work to keep the place decent, and the family fed and clean from coal dust and glaur. Make and mend, redd the men's clothes, bring water from the standpipe, keep the fire on. The moor's at the door, near enough. No pavements. An endless job, especially in the winter rain. And the weans: five in all, eventually, evenly spread out over fifteen years. Not bad. But you didn't live to see them grow. The firstborn was destined for the pit from the moment he was born. Wee Agnes was only five when you died. Your man James succumbed in 1917, to lung disease and heart disease.

You didn't live to see your firstborn going off to the war; you were spared that worry, at least. He lived, married a kind lassie from the Borders, had a family of seven of his own. The war was his great adventure. After that, he was a miner all his days.

You can stand on the bing and see land, but not as hunter-gatherers or pastoralists would know, to be returned to over and over in a cycle. Life here was brief, brutal and extractive. Hire labour on the cheap, and when its over, its over. Move on. 'There are no washing-houses, but several washing-house boilers have been erected. Whoever erected them forgot to build a house over them, and the women have to do their washing in the open air. There are two closets, without doors, for these seventeen families; and an open ashpit in the centre of the square was filled to overflowing and the stinking refuse strewn about for yards.' So said the report by the new National Union of Mineworkers.

It'll take an archaeologist's eye to see the shapes in the land that were railbeds and pithead works and the footings of what were houses. They were cleared, not worth saving. Homes of all those miners and their wives and families lie tangled with the roots of the young trees.

As with the Mesolithic camps, as with the Highland shielings; they are almost invisible traces of people's lives. Especially women's. In this case, a few generations doing their best to defeat the squalor of the 'raws' the mining companies provided.

There must have been more to it than just cooking and cleaning, mustn't there? More than glaur and dirt? Long summer evenings when the moor maybe wasn't too bad a place; trains and carts to take you visiting, into Ayr or even Glasgow — surely. More to life than coal, and the winning of coal. Mining places were famous for their societies, the choirs and bands, philosophical and political societies, the hobbies and associations. But maybe just for the men.

You looked after the men and the men houked the coal and the coal fired the trains and ships and factories. You built the country, though no-one ever said as much.

In years to come, if the flooded opencast pit becomes a loch, you will have a natural landscape. The young trees will maybe make a forest eventually, though there is more to a wood than the trees. You need your microbes and fungus, flowers and understorey; the insects and birds all have to establish themselves. But give it 8,000 years or so, one day a tree may blow down in a storm and some archaeologist of the future will wonder at the brick fragments exposed. A 'lithic scatter' of crushed house bricks.

You'd have liked a decent house, with a bathroom.

*

Three human landscapes, all but vanished. There are no great buildings to show for all those lives. The hunter-gatherers managed for thousands of years, living lightly on the land. Then the pastoral/farming times, more thousands of years, until its abrupt halt. Then industry, extractive and powerful, which changed the landscape and lasted not much more than a couple of centuries. The pits, the bings, the railway cuttings, opencast gouges ... and now there comes reclamation and restoration: where the miners' houses stood, a new forest grows.

Up on the moors, in the Highland glens, on shores and mountains, islands and Lowland riversides, everywhere in Scotland there is evidence of occupation. They are faint traces, some deliberately destroyed, but marks nonetheless of generations who left little of themselves behind. They are testament to ordinary people who arrived here and lived out their lives and raised families in the only context they knew, the present. They left no grand buildings, but they built Scotland.

Who built Scotland? We did, because they are us.

2

The Sky Temple
Alistair Moffat

Cairnpapple Hill, Midlothian, 3500 BC

I only knew the way because I had been before, many times. For the site
of this unique and remarkable place, there are no signs in Linlithgow or
Bathgate, the nearest towns. On the northern approach, the B road leading
to Cairnpapple Hill, there is a brown Historic Scotland sign pointing left,
but when a fork in the road is quickly reached, there is nothing to indicate
the correct choice. If I had stayed on the main road and gone left, I would
have been taken off in entirely the wrong direction. I knew to turn right up
the steeper road and after a short time found the entrance and parked in
what is little more than a passing place where another brown sign helpfully
pointed out the obvious. Unsurprisingly, no other car was parked there on
a bright and blustery April morning.

Cairnpapple is a fascinating place and the public should be shown how
to find it. It rewards the effort of a visit with unlikely insights into our
prehistory, a long period that is often relegated to a distant second place
behind the last 2,000 years of more or less recorded history. It is sometimes
seen as pre-history, somehow something less than history. This is because
it lacks stories, named individuals, recorded events such as battles, corona-
tions, invasions, elections, and yet for the 11,000 years since the pioneers
first came to Scotland after the retreat of the ice-sheets, prehistory is the
overwhelming balance of our time here, 9,000 years of experience in one
place. It is perhaps worth a road sign, or even two.

What engages my emotions and inclinations is the nature of our prehistory. Precisely because it is anonymous, it is perforce that elusive thing,
a people's history of Scotland. We do not know the names of kings or
queens, priests or warriors, and the accidents of survival mean that archaeologists have uncovered the houses of farmers at Knap of Howar, Skara
Brae and elsewhere on Orkney and the remains of magnificent religious
sites at Kilmartin and Callanish. By comparison, the last two thousand

years are well recorded, but very top heavy. Until the Statistical Accounts of the late eighteenth century and the censal returns from 1843 onwards, the voices of ordinary people are largely unheard, their actions not noted. Scotland's story is all too often told as a recital of lists: of great men, and very few women, battles won and lost, majestic ruins and the exemplary lives of saints. This shortbread tin lid version of our past with endless images of Robert Bruce, Mary Queen of Scots and Bonnie Prince Charlie is wearisome to the point of scunner as the same old episodes and the all too familiar iconography is endlessly recycled.

Prehistory is about mystery. It offers occasional glimpses of an entirely unexpected past, of people who were not like us, of another country that seems not to be Scotland. It is also more than frustrating: the gaps in knowledge centuries long and the map a series of blanks with rare splashes of light and colour. What can the stones and bones of archaeology offer except whispers from the darkness of the long past? How can we piece together fragments, make a coherent picture out of the unmade jigsaw of the millennia before Christ?

At Cairnpapple, mystery clings to the cold stones around the great cairn like morning mist, but the site is not entirely inscrutable – because it can be read, can be at least partly understood. If the visitor is willing to ignore the twenty-first century and allow this atmospheric place to speak, some flickers of why it was made and why it remained a place of profound sanctity for more than four thousand years can light up the darkness. At Cairnpapple, it is important to look but also to listen for the faint echoes of voices racing across the millennia on the windy hill.

As I pulled on a padded jacket and locked my car, I noticed a sign by the gate that told me the cost of a ticket to enter the monument is £5 and that it was 'open summer only'. And that summer in Scotland ran from April to September. Energised by such optimism, I climbed the steep steps up to the hill. The public is made to approach from the east and I had forgotten how much of the path crosses a long plateau whose edge screens the summit of the hill until the last few yards. If our ancestors took this route, and it is the most easily accessible, they would not have seen what they had come to see until they had reached the edge of the flattish summit. That late reveal might have heightened anticipation. Perhaps a procession sang and played music as it approached the hill. Those crossing the plateau would certainly have been reverent. Cairnpapple may be hard to find now, but once it was a place of great power. The name itself remembers that. The first element is obvious but the second more obscure. Versions of Papple are to be found at Bayble, Paible and Paibeil on the Isle of Lewis and in the name of the island of Papa Westray in Orkney. It derives from Papar, the Old Irish word for a priest. Cairnpapple means the Cairn of the Priests. And not only Christian priests; the building of the great cairn was supervised by priests who celebrated much older beliefs, faiths that have entirely disappeared.

When I reached the gate through the perimeter fence around the archaeology on the summit, I realised that Historic Environment Scotland's optimism about a six month Scottish summer was just that. The ticket office, a small green Nissen hut, was shuttered and I could find nowhere to make a donation of £5. Having been on the hill half a dozen times, I knew that a bright, graphic spring day should immediately be taken advantage of and I climbed to the highest point, the top of a concrete dome built at the centre of the site. The vistas are vast, breath-catching.

From this little, unexpected hill, only a thousand feet high, almost all of the geography of central Scotland is visible. Out to the east lies Edinburgh, Arthur's Seat very clear and beyond it the East Lothian coast, the outlines of North Berwick Law and the Bass Rock obvious in the late spring (or summer) sunshine. Too cold to be hazy and with the brisk breeze to keep the clouds moving, I could see the cliffs of May Island out in the Forth and the line of the Fife coast stretching away into the distance. The seamark of Largo Law and further inland the Lomond Hills were well defined, and beyond the Ochil Hills, the southern mountains of the Highland massif, made a jagged horizon. To the west lie the Campsie Fells and, using my binoculars, I reckoned I could make out the outline of Goat Fell on the island of Arran in the Firth of Clyde. That meant I could see clear across the middle of Scotland, from the east to the west coast. South of Cairnpapple the ranges of the Moorfoot Hills (the derivation of my surname) rise and, to complete the panorama, the northern edge of the Pentlands and Caerketton look over the southern suburbs of Edinburgh.

These sweeping vistas are eternal and they are what drew people over millennia to climb the hill and worship. To see it all lie before you on every side is to comprehend the majesty of creation and to know something of the scale of what the gods had made. Our ancestors did not come to the hill because they enjoyed a good view. They did not live in the canyons of cities or were hemmed in by motorways and busy streets: they were farmers and saw views every day. What made Cairnpapple singular for them was its panorama, the way it dominated the landscape even though from its summit many higher hills and mountains rise up on all horizons. And if this was the place where it was possible to see the creation of the gods and all its passing moods and seasons, then it might also be the place where men and women might be able to commune in some way with the divine, to lift their eyes and worship.

From the top of the concrete dome, it is easy to make out the layout of the site, the various versions of the temples and monuments built by our ancestors, but it is impossible to see the first marks they left on Cairnpapple. Some time around 3,500 BC, groups of people climbed up from their farms in the valleys below and lit fires. Gossamer traces of six hearths have been found where branches of oak and hazel crackled and sparked in the wind. Perhaps these were sacred woods, perhaps the fires were lit at the turning points of the year.

Two pieces of very early pottery and two axe heads were found near the hearths and they are symbolic of a new way of life. The transition from hunting and gathering to farming was the greatest, most profound revolution in human history and it took place in Scotland late, in the centuries around 4,000 BC. New people arrived from Europe and they understood how to grow crops and domesticate and husband animals. But before farms could be established, the wildwood that carpeted the landscape had to be cleared, and that made the stone axe the first and most important farming implement. And it appears to have been revered in some way as a gift from the gods.

What archaeologists found were not practical axe heads but something symbolic. Made from igneous rock and polished with abrasives to give a dark lustre, they were too smooth and small to be useful in any way. Perhaps the axe heads were exchanged as valuable gifts or used in ceremonies on Cairnpapple Hill in some unknowable role. One was produced at the great prehistoric axe quarry at Langdale in the Lake District. High up near the summit ridge of the Langdale Pikes, in difficult and dangerous places, there are ancient quarries of volcanic stone. Even though much more easily accessible and workable deposits lie further down the slopes, the prehistoric miners preferred to climb up and hack the rock for their axes out of the highest outcrops they could find. No practical reason for this puzzling choice can be deduced. Perhaps they worked on the summit ridge because it was nearer to the gods, who had possibly touched it with lightning.

The pottery was more mundane but no less important. Farming and the need to store securely its harvests and surpluses led to the manufacture of pots of varying sorts. Hunter-gatherers moved around the landscape in search of seasonal prey and the wild harvest of fruits, nuts, berries and roots; pots were of little use to them, being both heavy and fragile. But when farms made for a more settled life (not that hunting and gathering ceased), good storage was needed, well stoppered against raiding vermin, and pots that could sit and seethe by the side of a cooking fire filled with the great staple known as pottage, a stew of any and all sorts.

Around 3,000 BC a henge was built on the hill and its remains can be clearly seen. I walked around the ditch that had been dug around the highest part of the summit and in places it was still deep. Beyond its perimeter, the upcast from the ditch had been piled up to make a bank. And then at some point, twenty-four timber posts were arranged in a wide circle inside this area. The building of this temple demanded well-organised effort on the part of the community of farmers who lived in the valleys around the hill. This in turn implies a directing mind or minds, someone who introduced the idea of a henge and could unpack its religious significance. This clearly involved a central sense of a holy of holies, a closed-off inner sanctum where mystery happened. But for all its builders on the outside, the henge and its hill were visible from below: it was their cathedral and the timbers a kind of spire.

The bank and the ditch were designed to keep out the many and accommodate only a few, and the timber posts provided a further screen since they are thought to have been six or seven feet tall at least. So that they remained upright in the ever-present wind on Cairnpapple, a good deal of their length would have been planted in the ground. The henge has two gaps for entrance and exit and it seems likely that processions snaked up the hill, around and into the inner sanctum and that these were accompanied by song or chanting and music. Drums and flutes were certainly made and there may have been other instruments that have not survived. Colour may also have brightened these ceremonies. It is easy to forget that classical sculpture, all now grey marble, was painted and at the near-contemporary prehistoric temple complex at the Ness of Brodgar on Orkney, some of the stones were painted with red and yellow ochre and their mixtures.

For a thousand years, farmers climbed the hill to worship in ceremonies lost to us. But the architecture of the henge does allow some reasonable conjecture. Then, as now, what mattered most to farmers was the weather. Would it be a warm and wet spring so that the new grass would flush quickly and feed the ewes, nanny goats and cows so that their milk would be rich for new-born lambs, kids and calves? Would the sun shine in June to dry the tall grass so that good hay could be cut for winter forage, and would there be no wind and rain at harvest time? Bad weather meant hungry winter months, and good supplied surplus. Farmers every day looked to the skies to see what the day would bring and on Cairnpapple

Hill the weather over half of southern Scotland can be seen. Did these communities climb the hill to worship and propitiate sky gods? Was that why henges were built in rough circles and ovals – to imitate the courses of the sun and the moon, and more, to be open to the skies so that the gods could see the faithful pray and offer sacrifice? It seems likely.

The hill's concrete dome was built to protect perhaps the most spectacular of the archaeologists' finds. An awkward climb down a metal ladder is rewarded with the remains of three graves. Around 2,000 BC, the function of Cairnpapple changed when the henge began to fade out of use as beliefs shifted. But the sanctity of the site seems not to have diminished and for at least two and half millennia it was used for burials. The first of these is preserved under the dome. A massive upright stone, almost 8 feet tall, has been placed at one end of a rock-cut grave surrounded by an oval setting of large stones. This was a monument to a person of great importance, perhaps a king or a queen, and archaeologists found evidence of the burial ceremony. It seems that the corpse was wrapped in a shroud made from organic material, possibly grass matting. A mask of burnt wood was carefully placed over the corpse's face. Perhaps it was used to hide decay and the wood burnt as an act of purification. Next to the body, a burnt wooden club had been laid.

The most eloquent evidence was found in two beaker pots. One had a wooden lid and both were filled with food and perhaps drink. Beakers from other graves of that period contained a cereal-based alcoholic drink as well as porridge of some kind. Both the mask and the pots seem to me to imply an afterlife. The food and drink may be offerings to the gods but more likely is the sense of sustenance being supplied for the journey through the veil of death to the other side. Before a small cairn was piled over the grave, it seems that it was strewn with seasonal flowers.

It looks as though over four millennia and many millions of funerals, little has changed in the way that we bury our dead. A big tombstone was raised to mark the grave of someone important who believed in an afterlife and the mourners brought flowers and drank alcohol, perhaps in some sort of ceremony whose descendant is a modern wake.

From the dome, I could see a ring of massive kerbstones laid out in a rough circle. These formed the perimeter of the last substantial monument raised on Cairnpapple Hill, probably in the first millennium BC. This was a huge cairn, about 100 feet in diameter but not high. It covered the post holes of the timber henge, long out of use by that time, and under it two cremation burials were found. But they were not the last human remains to be interred on the hill.

To the east of the massive cairn and the dome over the huge tombstone, four graves were found cut out of the rock. Aligned east to west, these are thought to be Christian burials, perhaps dating to some time around AD 600. When I walked over to have a closer look, I could see posies of dandelions growing bright yellow along the grassy edges of the two larger graves. And for some reason, it made me smile.

On Cairnpapple, there is an extraordinary continuity of sanctity. For four millennia and more, people with differing beliefs had climbed the magic hill to look around its stunning vistas, to marvel at the beauty of creation and wonder about the unseen forces that made and changed it.

Each time I have visited the site, I have found myself alone there, and that is both a privilege and a pity. But this last time, I noticed something new. There has long been a tall radio mast to the south-west of the old henge and, painted battleship grey, it has somehow always seemed to fade to near-invisibility. However, planners have given permission for a large wind turbine to be raised to the north of the hill on its lower slopes. And because its white sails rotate in the wind, it is terribly intrusive, distracting. It is a sacrilege and should be removed. Our ancestors deserve all the respect we can give them.

Cairnpapple is a national treasure, a place where the lives of our ancestors are made vivid, a mysterious place whose uncertainties prompt endless interest and interpretation, a place that lies at the heart of Scotland. A place that should be at the heart of our sense of ourselves.

3
Who are You, and What do You Think You're Looking at?
James Robertson

Calanais, Isle of Lewis, 3000 BC

Two miles from my home in Newtyle, Angus, beside a narrow road that runs along the northern flanks of the Sidlaw Hills past East Keillor Farm, is a decorated standing stone: 'the Pictish Stone', as it is known locally. Composed of metamorphic gneiss, it is a foreigner in this land of sandstone. Either ice or humans brought it there. It is six and a half feet tall, two and a half feet wide. Big enough, yet hardly monumental, it makes a modest statement of stony fact: 'Here I am. I came here long before you and I'll be here long after you are gone.' Barring an act of extreme vandalism, an earthquake or a lightning strike, this is hardly disputable.

The stone's surface is so weathered that without the right light illuminating it from the right angle it is hard to make out the designs carved upon it. Near the top there is an animal – some authorities say a wolf, others a boar or a bear. Further down are other Pictish symbols: a double-disc and Z-rod, and concentric circles near the base which may represent a mirror. What do they mean? I have no idea, which makes me only slightly less of an authority than the authorities. For the truth is, the people who raised and inscribed this stone and hundreds like it left no explanation of what they and their markings say.

There is also great mystery surrounding the Picts themselves. Recent historical research suggests that as a people they had heartlands both north of the Moray Firth in Easter Ross, East Sutherland and Caithness, and south of it in Aberdeenshire, Angus and Fife, but a few of their symbol stones are found much further afield, in Orkney, Shetland, the West Highlands, Skye and the Outer Hebrides. However distinctive the Picts were, they must have co-existed with other people living in all of these places. And then, in about the ninth century, the Picts performed one of the great vanishing acts of history. Their entire culture seems to have been subsumed very rapidly into that of the Gaelic-speaking people of Dalriada as the latter expanded their territory eastward. From that amalgamation or incorporation or elimination – from that benign or enforced union – emerged what became the kingdom of the Scots. The Picts left a great void scattered with these enigmatic message boards, their symbol stones, a void which has been filled ever since by myth and speculation.

I run out to the stone at Keillor often. The route I take varies: sometimes I run through the woods higher up the slopes; sometimes I follow the path along a disused railway line which carried passenger and goods trains from the late 1860s until the mid-1950s; sometimes I take a path in front of Bannatyne House, where in the 1570s George Bannatyne, an Edinburgh lawyer, retreated from the plague and compiled a manuscript of Scottish poetry, without which much of the work of the Renaissance Makars would be lost to us. But whether I am only running to the Pictish Stone and back, or whether I am going further, I cannot pass it without touching it. I circle it widdershins – against the movement of the sun, which might be deemed unlucky by some but I am left-handed and it seems natural to me – and touch it, front and back, before moving on. I don't know why I do this. It is a habit born, no doubt, out of some superstition that would crumble on examination, but I have a positive feeling about this stone, and a strong desire to renew contact on each visit. I feel as if I am touching something beyond myself and my time.

In the 1830s, when it was first recorded, the stone was intact, but by 1848 it had cracked near its base, and the bulk of it was lying on the ground. Maybe lightning has struck once already. A few years later the stone was re-erected and secured in place by iron clamps, and these have held it up-right ever since. My hand, touching it, connects not only with the touch of the people who restored it, but also with people who were here thirteen centuries ago – or perhaps still further back, for St Ninian is supposed to have brought Christianity to the southern Picts in the sixth century and the stone's carvings appear to be pre-Christian. The grassy mound upon which it stands is a tumulus, or burial mound, and cists containing ciner-ary urns are said to have been dug from it in Victorian times. Perhaps the mysterious symbols relate to important individuals, long dead, burned and buried; perhaps the stone is a signpost pointing out of this world to anoth-er. Who, now, can tell?

*

Long ago there were people in this country called the Pechs; short wee men they were, wi' red hair, and long arms, and feet sae braid, that when it rained they could turn them up owre their heads, and then they served for umbrellas. The Pechs were great builders; they built a' the auld castles in the kintry; and do ye ken the way they built them? – I'll tell ye. They stood all in a row from the quarry to the place where they were building, and ilk ane handed forward the stanes to his neebor, till the hale was biggit.

The publisher Robert Chambers, in his *Popular Rhymes of Scotland* (first published in 1826), concocted this account of 'the Pechs' from different oral sources, and a fine piece of nonsense it is, with its legend of the last Pech refusing to divulge the secret recipe of heather ale, and how even as a decrepit old man he could snap an iron bar in two like a clay pipe. Chambers was echoing much earlier stories: a twelfth century Norse manuscript, *Historia Norvegiae*, described the Picts of Orkney as short stocky creatures who were phenomenal builders of walled towns in the morning, but who were overcome with weakness at midday and had to hide underground until their strength returned in the evening.

Once they had disappeared from history, then, the Picts acquired mythic, almost supernatural attributes in place of their renown as builders. Before long, if you were strong and aggressive enough, you could be a Pict almost anywhere in Scotland – even in Galloway in the south-west, where to date archaeology has revealed only one site containing genuine Pictish artefacts. When King David I invaded England in 1138, the Gallovidian soldiers in his army were referred to as 'Picts' on account of their ferocity: at the ensuing Battle of the Standard, a heavy defeat for the Scots, an English chronicler described one of these men as being stuck full of arrows like a hedgehog, yet still rushing about in blind madness alternately wounding enemies with his sword and carving the air with useless strokes.

Later, the Picts became akin to fairies or Brownies, half-seen figures in a misty landscape. In John Buchan's early short story 'No-Man's Land' an archaeologist is captured by a tribe of troll-like beings while out tramping the hills of Galloway. A fellow-academic has piqued his curiosity:

And in that very place you have the strangest mythology. Take the story of the Brownie. What is that but the story of a little swart man of uncommon strength and cleverness, who does good and ill indiscriminately, and then disappears? There are many scholars … who think that the origin of the Brownie was in some mad belief in the old race of the Picts, which still survived somewhere in the hills.

Buchan had a great appetite for fantasy but he was also a realist who understood the fragility of civilisation and the rapidity with which historical change can sweep settlements and whole societies into oblivion. Buchan saw with a kind of Presbyterian horror that nothing, however solid and immovable it may seem, is forever.

Humans have been coming to the site of the Pictish stone at Keillor for a very long time. It commands a spectacular, panoramic view of Strathmore and the Grampians beyond. To the south-west are Ben Vorlich and Stuc a' Chroin; to the north-west loom the peaks of the Ben Lawers group, and the unmistakable pyramid shape that is Schiehallion; to the north-east are the Angus glens, the big round hills of Glen Shee and the distant Cairngorm massif. If you were a Pict and wanted to put up a stone where you could mark your territory, watch for trouble or cheer coming from the north, and enjoy the scenery, this would be a good place.

Much more recently, somebody else had similar ideas. In 1752, James Mackenzie, younger brother of the Earl of Bute, bought land at Meigle and spent £10,000 on a new home, Belmont Castle. As well as being a Member of Parliament and, for forty years until his death in 1800, a Privy Councillor, Mackenzie was a keen scientist, weather-recorder and astronomer. In 1774, he built an observatory tower on Kinpurnie Hill, 1,134 feet above sea level. This was a rectangular structure, forty feet high and with walls three feet thick, with two doors, several windows, and a pitched slate roof. The roof collapsed or was removed not long after completion. Mackenzie shared his scientific interests with the then minister of Newtyle, and they are said to have spent many cold nights up at the tower studying the stars, but understandably they preferred the comforts of Belmont Castle where Mackenzie had another observatory complete with a state-of-the-art telescope. On Keillor Hill behind where the Pictish Stone stands, he erected a solid-stone pillar surmounted by a stone ball. This twenty-foot-high structure was due south of Belmont and gave Mackenzie a meridian line, which enabled him to check the accuracy of his clocks against the movement of the sun. The pillar is known as 'Privy's Prap', that is, the Privy Councillor's target or marker. With Kinpurnie Tower as his third triangulation point, Mackenzie was able to make all kinds of calculations, such as the heights and distances of hills and mountains. Today, Privy's Prap is still in very good condition, and Kinpurnie Tower, though long a roofless shell, is a highly visible landmark. Many folk who live hereabouts are reassured by regular sight of these modern standing stones. I have heard one man say of Kinpurnie Tower, 'See that, and ye ken ye're hame.'

In the nearby village of Meigle is a remarkable little museum full of

Pictish sculptured stones. There are twenty-seven of them, dating from the eighth to the tenth century, and the fact that they were all found in the kirkyard or elsewhere in the village indicates that Meigle was an important Pictish centre. Eight more stones are known to have been lost during the nineteenth century, and fragments of others are probably embedded in the walls of the church or of nearby houses. It was another local laird, Sir George Kinloch, who converted the old village schoolhouse into a museum towards the end of the nineteenth century. Partly due to the stones having been under cover ever since, and partly because of the quality of the carving, the detail they retain is astonishing. They tell of a sophisticated society in which skills in war, hunting and craftsmanship were all highly valued. Crucially, unlike the stone out on the hill, they proclaim a strong Christian faith. Whoever the Picts had been before, by the time these stones were carved they were steeped in the iconography of Celtic Christianity.

The biggest stone at Meigle is over eight feet high, a majestic cross-slab, dressed, and sculpted in relief. It, along with another large stone, previously stood in the kirkyard, on either side of a grassy mound known as Vanora's Grave. At this point myth, history and faith become thoroughly enmeshed. Vanora is another name for Guinevere, queen of King Arthur. She, so the story goes, was abducted by the Pictish king Mordred and held by him in a fort on Barry Hill, a few miles from Meigle. When she was liberated – or recaptured – she paid with her life for being a woman in a culture dominated by violent and competitive men. Found guilty of infidelity, she was sentenced to be torn to pieces by wild animals. Her remains were buried at Meigle. Vanora had no children, and local lore still maintains that any young woman who walks on her grave risks infertility.

The great stone in the museum is an elaborately carved Christian cross, its head studded with projecting bosses like a highly ornate piece of metalwork. The shaft is filled with wild animals, large and small, all intricately connected by their tongues and tails: it is as if the carvers could not bear to leave the cross unadorned, but had to show off their talents in every square inch. On the reverse of the shaft, a kind of strip cartoon in stone is presented: first, a huntsman on his horse, and alongside him two hounds and an angel; next, another rider, preceded by three mounted guards; then, the centrepiece – is it Vanora surrounded by the beasts about to dismember her, is it Daniel in the lions' den, or have these two stories become as entwined as the creatures on the front of the cross? The last two scenes depict a man-horse or centaur, with an axe in each hand and leafy branches, which he has presumably hacked through, under his arm; and another beast, like something from a painting by Hieronymus Bosch, with its jaws round an ox's head, while a man armed with a club looks on.

If, here and now in the twenty-first century, we can slip through the lattice of these strange, brutal narratives, will we find ourselves in a place we know, or will a sense of our own lost smallness simply be reinforced? We are in an ancient land, and these engrained, embedded markers make us conscious of it, and of how long humans have been treading here. At Eassie, Glamis, Cossans, Aberlemno and throughout Angus symbol stones stand in fields or kirkyards or beside roads, where they have stood for centuries. In Brechin Cathedral, the Meffan Institute in Forfar and St Vigeans by Arbroath, further collections of Pictish carved stones are now protected from the weather. We can marvel at their beauty and their survival, but do they tell us anything about who *we* are? Do they give us reassurance, philosophical resignation, a sense of belonging? Or do they remind us of our own transience, that we are at the mercy of merciless forces, and that we might at any moment find our lives and the meaning of our lives torn to pieces?

*

Not surprisingly, Scotland's standing stones have been puzzling, disturbing and inspiring the imaginations of writers for a long time. In his 1932 novel *Sunset Song* Lewis Grassic Gibbon used the gossipy, suspicious voice of the community of Kinraddie to describe a stone circle by a nearby loch:

> … *some were upright and some were flat and some leaned this way and that, and right in the middle three big ones clambered out of the earth and stood askew with flat sonsy faces, they seemed to listen and wait. They were Druid stones and folk told that the Druids had been coarse devils of men in the times long syne, they'd climb up there and sing their foul heathen songs around the stones; and if they met a bit Christian missionary they'd gut him as soon as look at him.*

Neil Gunn in his novel *The Serpent*, published a decade later, described a group of four stones in a similar way, but his character 'the Philosopher' has a more empathetic attitude than the Kinraddie folk:

> *These massive stones were prehistorically old, but age was about them in other ways. The peat had grown up past their waists; they were grouped closely together, tilted slightly, so that they were like old men, like the shoulders of squatting bodachs, held for ever in a*

last moment of meditation. He sometimes made a fifth in this eter-
nal séance and, after the labour of the climb, became as mindless as
any of them.

The work of the great Orkney writer George Mackay Brown is full of
stones, which is not surprising given the nature of the Orcadian landscape.
In one poem, 'Foreign Skipper: 17th Century', a captain who has sailed to
the islands is asked what he found there. Every response is shaped by stone;
even the wild fruits are found in 'coarse stone-scattered Grass'.

> *Were there trees?*
> *No trees. Wind cut too sharp from*
> *North and east. There were Stones.*

Asked if there were dragons, the skipper says he saw one carved on a stone.
Finally:

> *Were there stones?*
> *Everywhere, like Flowers. Stones*
> *Of great beauty, Wave-blown.*

The fertile green fields of Orkney are bound by stone dykes, and its farms
and houses are built from the same grey stone. So, too, are its 'ancient monuments'. When I first went to the islands, as a teenager, the Neolithic settlement of Skara Brae had no visitor centre attached to it, as it now does, and
little in the way of interpretative signage. If you wanted to see inside the
burial chamber of Maeshowe, you waited at a certain time and the local
farmer would arrive on his bicycle to take you inside. Plaques sternly announced that these places, along with the Ring of Brodgar and the Stones
of Stenness, were 'in the care of the Secretary of State for Scotland' but he
didn't seem to do very much and certainly, at that time, hadn't needed to
construct car parks for the occasional visitors. The people of Orkney appeared to go about their daily lives not noticing the remnants of prehistoric
culture that were all around them, but was this any more unusual than
Edinburgh folk not noticing Arthur's Seat or the Castle, or barely glancing
at their watches when the One o'Clock Gun went off? Familiarity does
not necessarily breed contempt or neglect. Sometimes it breeds nothing but
itself, an easy, incurious acknowledgement of the backdrop against which
life goes on. The fishing, crofting, small-town life of Orkney has that sense
of continuity, as if it is merely an extension of a very long story, as if it
has always absorbed and assimilated new-fangled ways; as if, though hardly noticed, the old stones are a kind of anchor against the drag of time.

George Mackay Brown understood these things, and captured them in his work.

It was Hugh MacDiarmid, however, in his long poem of 1934 'On A Raised Beach', who definitively addressed the stoniness not just of Scotland but of the planet, and drew from his contemplation a series of bleak but beautiful conclusions:

> *What happens to us*
> *Is irrelevant to the world's geology*
> *But what happens to the world's geology*
> *Is not irrelevant to us.*
> *We must reconcile ourselves to the stones*
> *Not the stones to us.*

Most tellingly, MacDiarmid makes the point that 'there are plenty of ruined buildings in the world but no ruined stones'. If water, weather or even human actions wear down a stone sufficiently, it ceases to be a stone and becomes gravel or sand. ('A bag of gravel is a history to me, and … will tell wondrous tales,' the great Enlightenment geologist James Hutton wrote in a letter to a friend, in 1772.) It is true that a standing stone which falls becomes a kind of ruin – but only because of the human intervention that once placed it upright.

Neal Ascherson, in *Stone Voices*, his meditative journey of 2002 through Scotland's cultural, historical and physical landscapes, writes persuasively about the persistent dominance of geology in shaping human life here. One outcome of that geology has been poverty, a result of the thin depth and poor quality of much of Scotland's soil. 'This has been a hard country to live in, as in many ways it still is,' Ascherson writes. 'Scottish earth is in most places – even in the more fertile south and east – a skin over bone, and like any taut face it never loses a line once acquired.'

One possible way of looking at standing stones – scattered as they are across almost every part of the mainland from Angus to Argyll, from Dumfriesshire to Caithness, and in great number too across the northern and western isles – is to see them as teeth or bones poking through tissue, symbols of the hardness of life that Ascherson describes. But these stones are not like other stones: they are not in their 'natural' places. They are geological survivors like every pebble and boulder, every scree slope and mountain ridge, but they have been appropriated by our forebears, who dug up or quarried or hauled them, then stuck them into the ground, sometimes just as they were, sometimes sculpting and dressing them. Once, perhaps, the stones were symbols of worship, deference or appeasement – to the sun, the wind or the earth itself. Now, they sometimes seem more like gestures of defiance raised to gods or powers unknown, challenges made to time or to those unimaginable inhabitants of the future, us. 'Here we are, still,' the stones say. 'Who are you, and what do you think you're looking at?'

All this is prelude or preamble or a series of steps to a journey from south to north, from east to west, from the present back through history to a time before history, across the sea to a place on the very edge of human intervention. From the west coast of Lewis in the Outer Hebrides it is six hundred miles to Iceland, two thousand to Newfoundland. Here, at this extremity, stand the stones of Calanais (or Callanish in its anglicised form). Only once have I been there before, thirty years or half my life ago, but that, however it may seem to me, is not even the first movement of a blink in geological time. The Lewisian gneiss of which these huge slabs are all composed is a hard crystalline rock that has been crushed, melted and folded over a span of 3,000 million years. When, in 1788, James Hutton wrote in his revolutionary 'Theory of the Earth' that 'time, which measures every thing in our idea, and is often deficient in our schemes, is to nature endless and as nothing', this was the scale of incomparable comparison he was describing.

The main group of stones at Calanais is the largest of some twelve similar sites in the vicinity. Some, like the rings at Cnoc Ceann a' Ghàrraidh ('Calanais II') and Cnoc Fhillibhir Bheag ('Calanais III') can be seen from Calanais ('Calanais I'), while the main group's prominent position on a long ridge makes it highly visible from various directions. That so many sites have survived suggests that, when the stones were erected between four and a half and five thousand years ago, the area was home to a well-developed culture which had these laboriously constructed formations at its heart. The climate was warmer then, the sea level lower, the sea and rivers full of fish, the land free of peat and fertile enough to support grazing cattle and sheep as well as the growing of barley. There was woodland and marshland and an abundance of birds, deer and other wildlife. A mixture of simple farming, hunting and gathering would have sustained a sizeable human population. Such a society would surely have asked the questions that humans always ask. Who are we? What are we doing here? What happens to us when we die? Looking up at the sun and the night sky, observing the seasons and the stars, are we part of something that is also beyond our reach? And, if so, does this gives us comfort or make us feel afraid?

Out of such questions, perhaps, the great stone setting at Calanais arose.

In about the year 1680, a Lewisman called John Morisone wrote of the Calanais stones that 'it is left by traditione that these were a sort of men converted into stone by ane Inchanter: others affirme that they were sett up in places for devotione.' A visitor to the island a decade later, Martin Martin, said that he had been told that Calanais 'was a Place appointed for Worship in the time of Heathenism, and that the Chief Druid or Priest stood near the big Stone in the centre, from whence he address'd himself to the People that surrounded him.' At this period the local people sometimes referred to the great stones as '*na fir bhrèige*', that is, 'the false men'. (There are three stones on the slopes of Bashaval in North Uist also called Na Fir Bhrèige.) As late as 1866 another visitor jotted down in his notebook that this name was still being used, and that the locals 'made out that they [the stones] could not be counted'. Perhaps the natives were having fun at the expense of an inquisitive stranger: by the 1860s more and more visitors were turning up, the stones of Calanais were becoming famous and attracting the attention of archaeologists and historians as well as wealthy tourists. One of the reasons for their increasing fame was that they could be more easily seen than previously, because in 1855 the owner of Lewis, Sir James Matheson, had given instructions for the peat to be cleared from around them.

Peat to a depth of some five feet was removed: it had been accumulating for nearly three thousand years, which gives an indication as to when the stones were abandoned, around 800 or 1000 BC. Some cultural change must have happened then – a belief system became redundant, or new inhabitants displaced the old, or there was a deliberate cleansing of the ancient site which, however, stopped short of toppling the stones. Whatever it was, the stones lost their meaning, becoming figures in a landscape which gradually began to cover them.

Not only did Matheson's excavation make the stones look considerably more impressive by revealing their true height, it also uncovered, beside the central monolith, a chambered cairn which the peat growth had completely hidden. The cairn was constructed, probably, about three hundred years after the stones were erected: time enough for whatever practices were formerly carried out at Calanais – spiritual, sacrificial, ceremonial, funereal or astronomical – to have changed greatly. The prehistoric history of the site, in other words, was not static. Just as the people of Scotland today are not the people of seventeenth century Scotland yet are their inheritors, so those prehistoric generations differed from one another but were also alike. After the building of the cairn, another three thousand years of continuity and change went by before the site was abandoned. Three hundred or three thousand years from now, will people still come to this place and, if they do, what will they know, or think they know, of us?

*

A ring of thirteen stones, with an enormous monolith standing in the middle but not in the true centre, is the main feature of the formation. Two long rows of stones, more or less in parallel, approach the ring from the north – or, more accurately, from the north-north-east – like an avenue. Much shorter, single rows of stones lead from the ring to the west, east and south, creating a rough 'Celtic cross' shape if viewed from above – not, of course, that this design has anything to do with Christianity, which it predates by three thousand years. Nor are the stones carved like the Pictish stones of that later age. It was work enough, perhaps, to heave these unadorned giants into place and keep them upright. The middle stone is fifteen feet high and three feet wide, and has been estimated to weigh about seven tons. Calanais, like Rome, was not built in a day.

To split these huge slabs of gneiss from a rock-face and transport them to the site would have needed the strength of many hands, and some ingenious use of log-rollers, even though the land over which they had to be dragged was drier, grassier and probably less pitted than it is today. The foundation holes dug from the clay, into which the stones were placed, were not deep. Once the stones had been heaved upright, more clay and stones were packed around their bases to keep them upright. This simple technique worked remarkably well. In 1980, during archaeological work across the whole site, a fallen stone was located under the peat at the eastern end of the east row. Careful excavation exposed the hole into which the stone had originally been placed, and when it was put back it fitted precisely into the socket, and thus regained the orientation it had been given five millennia ago.

There is a fine, new, sensitively positioned visitor centre at Calanais, with a permanent exhibition, a shop and a cafe serving excellent coffee and home-made scones. I think, when I was last here thirty years ago, there was a tea room along the road, where you could buy postcards and booklets. That was in October. The ground around the stones was boggy. On this return trip, in May, the day is hot, the sky blue, and the turf underfoot dry and obviously being well cared for. In the bright afternoon, the stones gleam and seem to be stretching like plants towards the sun. It is early in the season, and not very busy: the stones outnumber the people who have come to see them.

To walk among the Calanais stones, touching them and seeing their beautiful layers and striations and suggestive shapes – one looks like a hand held up in peace, another like a woman with a creel on her back, a third like a huge bird on its nest – is somehow an intimate experience, despite the presence of others doing the same thing. And it is an experience that people seem, mostly, to want to do on their own. Groups and couples split up and become individuals, *at one* with the place. When I step back to the western edge of the site, everybody else disappears from view behind the stones. There are sheep with new lambs in the next field, and crofts and bungalows spread across the landscape beyond: life continuing. When I walk on round the perimeter, I pass a woman quietly chanting an incantation. People come here for all kinds of reasons. Maybe for her it is the end of a pilgrimage. Maybe it is the beginning of one, or a point on some other journey. Maybe she knows something I don't.

*

Archaeology can tell us much about how people lived, but it can only guess at what they felt or thought. The folk who built Calanais did not feel or think exactly the same things as those who later lived near what they had created. People who walked among the stones, say, four thousand years ago may have done so with that mix of curiosity and wonder with which today's visitors arrive; or they may have had feelings quite lost to twenty-first century humans.

Although there is some evidence to suggest a connection between the layout of the stones and astronomical events, it is tenuous at best. Perhaps Calanais really was constructed as a kind of observatory and perhaps, as some have sought to demonstrate, there really is a connection, revealed every eighteen years, between the stones and the moon's progress over the hills to the south. But if we set aside what cannot be proven then we are left with Hutton's 'wondrous tales' of geology and archaeology, and a lot of hypotheses. Our scientific knowledge pushes into the future with more confidence than it probes the past. We can say that the main circle is not a true circle, that the alignment of the avenue is not truly north to south, that there is nothing precise about the way the stones are positioned: but none of this tells us what Calanais was actually built for.

Scientists and artists, believers and agnostics, seekers of truth and weavers of myth all can – and do – pick and choose how to interpret the stones. But an interpretation remains just that, an interpretation. As MacDiarmid wrote, we must reconcile ourselves to the stones, not they to us. The questions that all standing stones ask, relentlessly – 'Who are you, and what do you think you're looking at?' – are of our own making. They go to the heart of being human, and there are no easy or definitive answers.

4

The Stone Mother
Kathleen Jamie

Mousa Broch, 100 BC

It's half past ten at night in mid-July, and in the far north-west the sun rides low on the horizon, sinking amid sashes of ruby and crimson-tinted cloud. In the north-east, the cliff called the Noup of Noss stands silhouetted against a sky that is not quite dark.

On the pier at Sandwick waits an earnest group of about 40 people. We're almost all middle aged, almost all visitors to the islands judging by our accents and languages. Some carry digital cameras, and torches we are requested not to use. *No flash, no bright light, please keep torches pointed downward.*

But a torch is not necessary. Our eyes soon adjust to the ambivalent shifting twilight the Shetland people call the 'simmer dim'.

It's a good business for the local boatman and his crew, ferrying visitors to Mousa and back. It's only a fifteen minute crossing by motorboat. Mostly they sail by day, but for a few weeks in midsummer they offer midnight trips too. The boat is full, the water is sheeny, two dark-eyed seals watch our progress.

The island of Mousa has been uninhabited for the last couple of centuries. A couple of miles long and a mile wide, now grazed by sheep, it's tucked in against the east Shetland Mainland. When we reach its jetty and look back across the Sound, we see a few streetlights gleam, In the distance, southward, Sumburgh Lighthouse sends out its measured flash.

Having disembarked, we form a long straggle following the shore southward. As we climb over a stile, cross a burn, walk through a damp hollow, the sound of the waves seems louder than by day. Snipe are calling from the thick grasses inland. The night is strange, atmospheric. We follow the curve of a bay, then a half mile away, darker than the low land around, see our destination, the brooding tower of Mousa Broch. From that distance, and in the half-dark, it looks like something left over from the Industrial

Revolution, a structure both squat and tall – a bottle kiln perhaps. But it's not industrial, that at least is known for sure. It's Iron Age, and reputed to be one of the finest prehistoric buildings in Europe. But what exactly a broch is, or was, still remains unclear. In the twenty-first century, however, it's drawing night visitors like a congregation.

*

Brochs are a Scottish phenomenon. Hundreds have been registered by Historic Environment Scotland, almost all in the north and north-west, mostly at the coast, but most are just mounds of overgrown rubble. Only Mousa still stands complete. It's worryingly close to the shore, but the land has eroded since it was built. The land has eroded, 2,000 Shetlandic winters have blown over it, but it's still there, 13 metres high, and we're walking towards it in the middle of the midsummer night, as snipe call, and seals sing a mournful song. When we reach it, the broch seems very tall in the half-light, stolid and resolute. Its walls are beautifully made, stone on stone. Local stone, no mortar: this building is an expression of the island itself. 'I was made here of this place,' it says, but that's all it admits to. Now at just a few feet away, we can see that its ancient stones are softened by whiskery lichen, just visible in the half light.

Tall, thick, inscrutable and round. No windows, of course, but on the seaward side there is a single low and irresistible entranceway.

You have to duck, and feel your way in along a dark passageway. Halfway in are holes where a bar would have slid behind a door, and after two or three metres more you can stand, finding yourself at the bottom of a great stone well. A cylinder of stone. Just a few fellow visitors have come inside, speaking in whispers, and we're all perched on a stone bench at the edge of a central circular yard. It's gloomy, probably even in daylight, the sky is a disc of grey high above. Again, it's the stonework that amazes. Mousa has the classic broch features: its base is monumental but built on that solid foundation are double walls, one inside the other with a stack of 'galleries' running up the landward side – openings in the inner wall which lighten the structure. Up they go, eight or nine. On the ground floor are dark and eerie openings: the lower walls are so thick little rooms or cells have been built into them. There's a hearth space, a shallow tank, a smell of stone and earth, and silence. And of course, through one of the openings let into the wall, access to a tight stone stairway between the two skins, like a secret.

I'm struck by the difference to the outdoors, the world outwith the broch. Inside is silence. Not a wave, not a wind. Not a shout. You could be anywhere or nowhere. Maybe that was true in its day too. Perhaps a broch was a very different beast, depending on whether you were included or not, and that's why they've been so difficult to interpret. Read the archaeological literature, and you'll see that brochs have been all things. Strongholds, defence, posturing, protection, migrants and invaders, swagger, status and fear – since the nineteenth century all have been invoked at one time or another to account for brochs. They are like empty vessels into which we can pour our own modern anxieties. To some they are clearly defensive: thick walled and windowless, you could cram everyone and everything inside, if you had to. To others they are deterrents: proud on promontories, visible for miles by land or sea, no-one would attack a broch. To others they are simply status symbols. Who would these imaginary raiders be, they ask? Iron Age boats were shore-hugging, skin-covered craft, hardly fit for surprise attacks. It was all swagger. Maybe, but we still spend precious resources defending against foes who never come. Think of the listening and radar stations of the Cold War, abandoned on these same northern coasts.

It's novelists, of course, who have developed some of these speculations. Mollie Hunter's *The Stronghold* is a dramatic and war-like book for youngsters. Her broch was the product of a bright young mind, Coll, who sought to build something, anything, that would save his people from Roman slave hunters in their fast ships. *The Stronghold* was written in the 1970s, but more recent archaeology suggests that brochs didn't arrive suddenly, like a rash, but arose slowly, over hundred of years. The first had been built long before the Romans hove into view.

In George Mackay Brown's *Beside the Ocean of Time,* he imagines brochs as built by migrants, wealthy and powerful newcomers who had dispossessed the native people. That was also a view which had its day, in archaeological circles. But that seems odd now, to invoke incomers from the south who were much more skilled than the locals – a bit of a cringe. Some recent research contradicts that idea, saying instead that broch towers were indeed built by local folk, out of a long tradition. They developed from roundhouses, the circular stone dwellings people had used for thousands of years in the treeless north. No invaders or aristocratic immigrants required.

In Brown's imagination, the broch is a protector, a place of safety, and she is female. The novel's young hero makes a poem called 'The Song of the Broch':

'Stone mother of the Island, keep us well' he says

'Great stone mother of the headland'.

Is there anything we can say for sure? Mousa was built around 100 BC, that much seems settled. People lived here for generations, maybe hundreds of years. The last residents would have had no memory of the first. Stories maybe, but not living memory. But they might have had hereditary claims. It was maybe inhabited by a chieftain's family with other kinfolk in lesser dwellings around outside.

But how would you inhabit a stone well?

It's suggested that a wooden floor could have been laid across the diameter of the stone shell, supported by wooden posts. That would be your living room, with a hearth. Here in the basement, the now-gloomy cells might have been stalls for animals, kennels maybe. So you'd have noises and smells. I try to populate it, imagine my own extended family, dogs, furnishings, our goods and gear, a fire and bedding, all the familiar. A central fire and a few seal-oil lamps would be your lighting indoors, and summer shafts of sunlight down the long entranceway. You'd be outside most of the time anyway, but at night it would have been homely enough, secure from weather and winter dark.

And what would they have done all day, this Iron Age community? Get on with it, as everyone always has. Raised cattle and sheep, grown crops, kept dogs, snared birds, done a bit of inshore fishing. Woven textiles and baskets. Ground grain. Made pots, cooked food. Dearth and disease were your likely enemies. And if raiders did come, some summer morning? Get inside and bar the door. Lob rocks at them from the wallhead. Hell mend them.

The wallhead. Because Mousa is so complete, it's possible even now to step up into a gap between the double walls, and edge up the dark stone stair which climbs the narrow space between the walls. The steps are narrow, uneven, you feel your way up and round within the curve of the building, until abruptly the wind greets you and you're outside on the wallhead, high above the ground. Here are heightened, airy views of dark islands and sea, beacons and lighthouses. It's true, from up here, you could see anyone approach, day or summer night. And they would see you, with your commanding building. Also, you could survey your land. An island like this, with fields and grazing, fresh water and a bit of shore or cliff, this would provide almost everything: building materials, fuel, textiles, meat, plant food grown or gathered, seabirds and their eggs and inshore fish, or seals if they could be had. A stranded whale would have been a bonanza. Enviable. A broch might be an imposing home, visible from afar, which announced a high-ranking family's status and their claim. Defence, maybe, a home for sure, surveillance possibly, a symbol of wealth or owner-ship – but also a lot of show-offery.

Amid all this speculation though is a simpler practical question, now we're up high: how was a broch roofed? Was it roofed at all? You'd assume so, in this climate. And what of the smoke? To really understand a broch, you'd need to build one. And even if a replica could be built, what would it tell us of people's fears and hopes, their language or beliefs?

And here's another question that comes to me as I edge gingerly back down the stair, hands on the stone walls, hoping no-one is coming up. A stair is so obvious to us now, but was this the first building in Scotland to have a staircase? Did the tenement stair originate within the double skin of a broch?

Mousa seems to have survived because it was special even when it was built, an architectural triumph in its own time. Here the proportions are just right, the walls thick at the base but thinner as they rise, the inner court small in diameter by broch standards. Smallish, but imposing and strong on its shoreline. It was already 1,000 years old when real raiders arrived: the Vikings in their marvellous ships. By then Mousa Broch was abandoned, but still standing. We know the Vikings were familiar with Mousa because we catch a glimpse of it in the sagas. A few lines in the Orkneyinga saga, set down at the dawn of written history, tell of Erlend the Young and a certain Margaret, widowed mother of an Orkney earl. The pair took refuge here in the broch as they eloped. That was in the twelfth century. I try to imagine them, cosied up in here, but I can't really. It's the Vikings we have to thank for the names 'Mousa' and 'broch'. What the Iron Age folk called their creation, we'll never know. Mousa came from the Norse for 'mossy island', and the word 'broch' is derived from 'borg', which meant 'fort'. The ruins give little away, and the tough old Scots word 'broch' fits them well. Descending the stair, I smell earth and stone, and now a whiff of something else, another smell: funky, oily.

And there it might have remained. Mousa Broch, a survivor on the shore, a relic repaired and monitored, a visitor attraction for people who like prehistoric mysteries, who like to breathe the past. Creeping along the long passage to reach the outside again, I was almost startled to emerge among people with cameras and fancy outdoor clothing, could almost im-agine the terror we might have caused two thousand years ago, had we turned up one day with our horrible noises and gizmos, but the broch peo-ple are long gone, and we mean no harm. On the contrary, the night vis-itors are quiet and attentive, wrapped against the chill, waiting. Waiting, because whether it was a stronghold or a dwelling, a status symbol or a look-out tower, or all of these at once, it's not now. In a fabulous display of 'late style', Mousa Broch has reinvented itself for a new twenty-first century career.

People have settled down. Some are lying on damp turf banks around the broch that may conceal other smaller buildings. The broch itself, centre of this attention, seems very tall and mysterious now, smooth-walled and shivery with lichen, with its slight inward lean. It is rimmed with light, and as I watch from a seat of turf, it seems to loom near, then fade, to darken then glow, but it's just the twilight playing tricks. A few yards away waves wash at the shore. People speak softly. There is a sense of expectancy, as in a theatre.

Then, at the darkest and most overcast hour, it begins. With a sound. Yes, from here and there in its dour walls, the broch is beginning to send sounds out into the night. Up there it begins to churr and purr; down here, to purr and hiccough. It's midnight, and slightly, discreetly at first, the Iron Age building is coming alive.

Very soon, summoned by the churring calls, a shape darts overhead, then vanishes. Then comes another, and then more, until in 20 minutes or so the broch is completely woven with dark darting birds. They are storm petrels. Hundreds of them secrete their nests in Mousa's ancient stonework and now they are coming in off the sea. They are arriving quickly, called in by their partners, and the broch thrums with their tiny magic-engine sound. You see a dip of wings, almost bat-like, glimpse a white rump as they appear, creep up the wall to their own door then vanish between its stones. As one bird arrives, another leaves to take its turn at sea; the broch is wreathed with them. They move quickly up from the waves to avoid predators. It is a great changing of the guard, as one partner arrives to liberate the other and take custody of their single egg. We can smell them: a musky oily sea-tang, the hidden scent in the stairway inside.

Folk stand and watch, or lie on the damp turf. No camera flash, because it hurts their tiny eyes. The lichen and the birds' jinky movement soften the outline of the broch until the building becomes almost humorous, like a stern uncle who can delight children with conjuring tricks. Or not an uncle, or even an aunt, but as the 'Song of the Broch' had it, a 'Great stone mother of the headland' with her children. She is calling her chicks out of the night air with this ridiculous purring and hiccoughing.

At least for the short midsummer breeding season, the broch is anything but defensive. It may be dour and stony-faced, but the broch makes everyone smile. What mattered, we thought, were the stones. Stone on ancient stone, architecture in stone, craft of stone, defence through stone – serious human stuff. But the birds know otherwise: what matters to them is the present, and the tiny spaces between. To the storm petrels, Mousa Broch is not a forbidding cylinder, but an artful collection of gaps: neighbourly apartments, each just big enough to admit a small bird and an egg.

If the Iron Age architect or builders could return right now, and take their places among the party of admirers, they'd recognise their own expert handiwork – an Iron Age flowering of stone. They'd see the broch tower much as they meant it to be, but heaven knows what they'd think of us. You'd want to shake those craftsmen by the hand, because it couldn't be done nowadays, we no longer have the skills. But the builders are lost in time and we don't know who they were. In fact, broch-making is so skilled, some people believe there were itinerant teams of specialists, who went about the country. *Build you a broch, Sir? Ma'am? You know you'd like one. All the best families have a broch. The neighbours have got one – right across the water there. Good defence against raiders, too, because you just never know … It'll cost, oh yes, but it will stand for thousands of years.*

And then, when the people, for all their status, are gone to dust, it'll become a huge multi-storey nest box. They couldn't have designed one better.

No-one knows quite when the storm petrels colonised Mousa broch – another enigma, but since they have, the twenty-first century has turned and people have become anxious about the wild world and needy for natural encounters, and now it offers an experience with nature, a short midsummer night's dream in the north.

It's soon over, though. By August the adult petrels and newly fledged young are all gone to sea, not to touch land again for another year. Brochs belong in Scotland, but you can fancy that the birds carry a little of it away with them. They winter down in the south Atlantic. Each bird born in the secret darknesses of Mousa, at exactly 60 degrees north, will wander the southern oceans with a memory, an instinct to return exactly here, as though Mousa were a magnet made of stone. An unmoving ancient structure on a small northern island, its influence spreads half across the globe.

By 1am, it's lightening. The birds have done the needful and it's time to go. Everyone is making their way back across bog toward the boat. Some things don't change: such are the short summer nights Iron Age people would have known and relished too. Looking back at the broch from a half mile away, as it greets yet another dawn, it has settled back into stolidity and mystery. You'd never know it was alive. It keeps its secrets well.

5

They Came in a Small Boat
Alexander McCall Smith

Iona Abbey, AD 563

People have always made pilgrimages, and millions still do – to Lourdes, to Rome, or to the banks of the River Ganges; in smaller numbers to the birthplaces or homes of those they admire, to important battlefields, to places where something significant has happened. The pilgrim is a universal figure: the traveller with a purpose who sets out to find something that can only be found in some special place.

Iona, that small Hebridean island off the coast of Mull, is a place of pilgrimage – undoubtedly the most important such place in Scotland. There are other islands off the west coast of Scotland that are every bit as beautiful, there are other islands that have well-known historical and cultural associations – the island of Staffa, with Fingal's Cave, is only a few nautical miles away – but it is to Iona that people flock. Some of them may have only the vaguest idea of where Iona is and come because it is on an itinerary planned for them by a tour company; others may be interested in the island's early Christian associations; some at least come because they believe they will be moved by the spirituality of a holy place. You can see this modern pilgrimage taking place. There are the tour buses crossing that winding road across Mull; there are the full car parks on the Mull side; there are the crowds on the small ferry plying its way across that shallow channel of green water that is the Sound of Iona, a sound that appears again and again in those familiar paintings of Peploe and Cadell.

It may surprise us that so many pilgrims still make the journey to Iona. In our secular societies, especially in those of Protestant background, we feel vaguely uncomfortable at the notion of the spiritual quest, and even more uncomfortable than that at the idea of the journey in search of a miracle. And yet these things have not faded away entirely; they still linger, surviving the scepticism of Voltaire and Hume, surviving the triumph of science in the nineteenth and twentieth centuries.

A year or two ago, when I was in Australia, I was invited to an event in a house on the Sydney waterfront. The event was in aid of a charity, and the house was a very luxurious one. Expensive works of art were everywhere and the small group of people there – mostly women, and mostly elegantly dressed – were clearly well-off and, in some cases, I imagined, rather influential.

A woman came up to me after the talk, when the guests were milling around having coffee. She introduced herself as a lawyer, and went on to tell me that she had recently been in Scotland. 'I was not at all well,' she said. 'In fact, I was hopelessly ill with cancer. I had been given a short time to live; nothing could be done for me. And then ...' She paused. Those who have something to say that they know others will not believe often will look into your eyes to prepare themselves for mockery. She did this, and then continued, 'And then I visited Iona. While I was there, I felt an extraordinary jolt. It was just like that – a jolt.'

I listened.

'And then I came home and I was completely cured. The doctors could not believe what they saw. I was cured.'

This was not somebody from a Mediterranean culture of saints and miracles: this was a lawyer speaking under the rational sky of contemporary Sydney. She was convinced that what she experienced on Iona had been a miraculous cure. For my part, it seemed quite remarkable that we were having this conversation about a place of pilgrimage in Scotland, so distant, so different, so utterly unlike those Australian surroundings.

I find that I cannot believe in miracles. I suspect that behind every apparently miraculous event, there is a rational explanation compatible with the laws that science tells us govern our universe. But in my meeting with that woman I could not say to her that I simply did not believe her. I am sure that she was telling me the truth as she saw it; this had happened to her, and it had happened to her for reasons that might be difficult to explain. In her view, her visit to Iona somehow saved her life. Even if she simply experienced a spontaneous remission of her cancer that had nothing to do with where she was at the time, the fact remains that for that particular woman, her pilgrimage to Iona was the reason she was still there to tell me about it. So it is, perhaps, that the reputation of places of pilgrimage is perpetuated: those who are affected by them speak of their experience to others, and slowly a place becomes invested with special standing. And perhaps it is the fact that so many believe that a piece of ground is hallowed that ultimately makes it such. Holy places are made holy by men and women. Years of human hope and human striving seem to linger in such places. Chants, songs, prayers, tears – all these form the weather there. The buildings of a holy place, a place of pilgrimage, will often express all these hopes, all this faith, all this human yearning.

In the sixth century AD, Scotland was inhabited by Picts, Britons, Anglo-Saxons and people referred to variously as Scots or Gaels. Much of modern Argyll formed part of the Kingdom of Dalriada, which included not only that region of Scotland but also part of north-eastern Ireland. The people of Dalriada were closely linked with one another, and movement between what is now Ireland what is now Scotland was common. The missionary Saint Columba, the founder of the monastery on Iona, was, in fact, born in Donegal, the son of a high-born descendant of an Irish royal line. We would not normally know a great deal about somebody born, as Columba was, round about 521, but in Columba's case a biographer, the abbot known as Adomnán, wrote an extensive life of the saint not much more than a century after his death. That is a short enough period for the *Life of St Columba* to be reasonably fresh, even if parts of it are clearly fanciful. There are other sources, too, that address Columba's life, including poems and various mentions in Church documents and ecclesiastical histories. Unlike many earlier saints, Columba was not apocryphal: there was certainly such a man and he founded the monastic community on Iona that was to be the reason for the construction of very much later buildings in that spot, including the Abbey church that survives, in rebuilt form, to this day.

Iona is important today because of Columba and the choice he made in siting his monastery there, on that small island, on the very edge of Europe. That presupposes that he made a choice; Iona might, in fact, have been chosen for him, as a gift from the High King of Dalriada, Conall mac Comgaill. Whatever the reason for his going there, it was said that Columba landed on the island at what is now known as St Columba's Bay, in a currach, or hide boat, accompanied – as legend has it – by twelve companions. There may have been more; Columba's boat could have been over sixty feet in length and rowed by eighteen men. An early Irish brooch, dating back to the first century, survives to show us the construction of such boats, as does a carving on a stone pillar in County Cork. Such boats were robust enough for a sea journey and sufficiently capacious to carry the requisites for the starting of a monastic settlement.

Columba is popularly credited with the bringing of Christianity to Scotland. Current historical understanding, though, does not entirely support this as there were Irish Christians in what is now Scotland before his arrival. There are also the earlier saints who became conflated into and confused with the famous, but probably non-existent, St Ninian of Whithorn, whose activities preceded those of Columba. Yet even if Columba was not the first missionary to work in Scotland, it is widely accepted that he was active in seeking to extend the reach of Christianity among the Picts and that he travelled widely in doing this. Adomnán's *Life* contains colourful accounts of the saint's journeys, perhaps the most vivid being the story of how, having made his way up the Great Glen, he heard that a sea creature – none other than the Loch Ness Monster – had killed a local man. Columba ordered one of his monks into the water to entice it out of hiding, a real test of monastic obedience, one would have thought. The monster obliged and made for the bait, only to be sternly ordered back to its quarters by the saint. To the relief of those witnessing this incident – and in particular, one imagines, to the relief of the monk in the water – the monster did not argue with the saint and complied.

The buildings of the early monastic community on Iona would have been very basic; none have survived. That does not mean, though, that we have no idea of what these earliest structures were like: not only are there documentary sources that convey some idea of what was here, but the evidence of archaeology has built a picture of the settlement in Columba's time and in the early medieval period. And even if buildings themselves disappear, the land itself may bear witness: photographs of Iona taken from the air reveal the shape of the monastic enclosure, as clearly as any plan might do. The land is like that: man's works persist in the form of mounds, humps and ridges, showing us where long-vanished structures once stood, where fields were laid out, where quarries and wells and animal enclosures sustained the economic life of people of whom all other trace has vanished. The historian William Dalrymple talks about this in his book *The Holy Mountain,* in which he describes seeing the boundaries of Palestinian farms, levelled for other use, stubbornly springing up from beneath the surface in the shape of lines of cactus-like hedgerow, resisting obliteration, a persistent reminder of where fields had once been.

One of the best accounts of the layout and construction of the monastic settlement on the island is to be found in Anna Ritchie's *Iona,* in which she sets out the layered history of the site from its earliest day to the extensive reconstruction of modern times. The ground around the modern Abbey of Iona is perhaps best viewed as a palimpsest, the earliest layer of which is the Columban settlement. Adomnán's account of the early monastery provides some information as to what was there, although there is no evidence to show exactly where each building was. There was a church with, according to Adomnán, a chapel to the side. Then there were the monks' sleeping quarters, which may have taken the form of individual huts or larger shared accommodation. There was an eating and living place and a house for guests. Columba himself was said to have two separate places for his own use: one where he slept, the other where he wrote.

Columba's writing hut, not surprisingly, has been the subject of enthusiastic speculation and learned argument. It is a vivid notion: the idea of the saint perched in an elevated hut, away from distraction, writing on wax tablets or on vellum, recording the affairs of his missionary undertaking. We like the romantic notion of the writing retreat – an idea that crops up in differing forms: Roald Dahl penning his stories in a gypsy caravan at the end of his garden; J K Rowling producing her saga in an Edinburgh cafe to which she retreated for warmth; St Columba in his hut looking out over the green sea to Mull. A likely spot for this retreat is the hillock Tòrr an Aba where, according to Adomnán, Columba had a raised wooden hut. Excavations have supported the presence of a small building there, complete with supports for a stone table of some sort.

Surrounding the monastic buildings was a major earthen rampart known as a vallum. The extent of this was considerable, and its remnants can still be seen from the air, a widely described protective arc around the cluster of buildings making up the settlement. This earthwork was supplemented by drainage ditches, the whole effect being to create an extensive infrastructure, the early equivalent of that which today underpins a modern town or city. Within the vallum all the business of life would have been conducted, including carpentry, the firing of pottery, the melting and outing of glass and metals. There would also have been housing for animals and ground for the cultivation of the various crops known to have been grown there. In short, there was everything that was required to sustain a community, with, at its centre, and as the focus of communal endeavour, a place of worship, the Abbey church.

The influence of Iona's Abbey continued to grow well after the death of Columba. By the eighth century, Iona was a kingpin in a widespread network of monasteries in Scotland and Ireland, the burial place of Irish royalty and of others of importance. This period of ascendancy was rudely interrupted by the arrival of the Vikings, whose depredations in the western highlands and islands included the sacking of the Abbey in 709 and again in 802 and 806. The attack of 806 was especially bloody, with over sixty people found at the monastic settlement being killed. Viking raids on Iona continued sporadically, the last recorded one being in 1209, although the extent of the damage done in this late raid is unknown.

Not all Scandinavian visitors to Iona were destructive. The

Heimskringla, an Icelandic saga written about the year 1230, tells the story of the visit of the Norwegian king Magnus Barelegs, who undertook an extensive pillaging trip of western Scotland and its islands in 1098. This is what the sage says of his visit to Iona:

> *King Magnus came with all his first to the only island, and gave*
> *there quarter and peace to all men, and to the household of all men.*
> *Men say this, that he wished to open the small church of Columcille;*
> *and the king did not go in, but closed the door again immediately,*
> *and immediately locked it, and said that none should be so daring as*
> *to go into the church; and thenceforward it has been so done*
>
> *Then King Magnus proceeded south to Islay, and plundered and*
> *burned there.*

It is round about the beginning of the thirteenth century that the building which became the modern Abbey was completed. The history of today's Abbey really begins at that point, even if that early building was on the site of the original Columban church. The Abbey was extended in the fourteenth century and was altered in the sixteenth and seventeenth centuries, prior to the later extensive restoration that was to bring it to its current form.

The Nunnery, alongside the Abbey, also dates from the early thirteenth century, and reflects the design of the Abbey church of the same period. The Nunnery's charming cloister was enlarged in the fifteenth century and is in a good state of preservation. The arches and columns of this building, along with its lovely stone carvings, instil a sense of peace and safety that only architecture on this relatively small scale can achieve. This is an architecture of low arches and contained spaces that does anything but intimidate or instil awe. Christopher Alexander, the exponent of humane architecture through books such as *A Pattern Language,* talks about the significance of cloisters and courtyards and of the feelings they engender in those who inhabit them. Alexander is a persuasive critic of those forms of modernist architecture that insist on flat surfaces giving no visual or physical shelter. He advocated niches and nooks – places where we can retreat, where we can look upon shared space that is protected by courtyard walls. His arguments are beautifully put; I give his book to friends with the same enthusiasm, perhaps, as Columba's monks preached their gospel. Architectural ugliness, architectural brutality, kill the human spirit. Small, peaceful places – places where you might reach up and easily touch the top of a column, places where a few steps will take you from one side to the other of a room or a chapel – these are strangely moving in a world in which large buildings, alienating in their immensity, crush and homogenise us. The Abbey and Nunnery on Iona are composed of spaces that do this healing work.

Monastic activity on Iona continued until the Scottish Reformation of 1560. It is thought that, although many monks moved to monasteries in Ireland, some may have remained, a few becoming parish ministers. Monasticism in Scotland, though, was effectively at an end, and the ownership and control of the Abbey shifted to local bishops, who survived in Presbyterian Scotland and indeed were encouraged in the reigns of James VI and Charles I. Eventually the Abbey became no more than a local church and even lost that role, leaving the island, once a great religious centre, without so much as its own minister to perform weddings and funerals. The ownership of the island passed into the hands of the dukes of Argyll and, with bishops abolished in the Church of Scotland and nobody taking much interest in the affairs of a small island off the coast of Mull, the Abbey church and its associated buildings fell into disrepair. Soon they were little more than roofless ruins. Hebridean islanders are great ones for making the good use they can of readily available building materials, and the stone and wood of the Abbey buildings would have been a tempting source for the building of croft houses, fanks and any other structures needed to make life bearable on a poor island far from the resources of the mainland.

The Abbey on Iona might have been forgotten about for a good time longer had it not been for the interest that was aroused by a series of visitors drawn to the island by its romantic reputation. Rosalind Marshall's *Columba's Iona: A New History* tells the story of these early tourists and their traipsing around the neglected but nonetheless romantic ruined Abbey and Nunnery. One early tourist, William Sacheverell, who visited the island in 1688, referred to Columba as 'Columbus' and took a distinctly jaundiced view of the religious traditions of the island, which he regarded as unduly austere. He liked the architecture, though.

Marshall relates how other visitors were receptive to stories of the severity of Columba and his followers, listening to stories of how the saint drowned those pagans who declined to convert, and how he put a curse on his own relatives who lived on the island, predicting their death as a means of limiting the island's population. In the late eighteenth century, Thomas Pennant, a naturalist, visited both Staffa and Iona and wrote an account of the Abbey that attracted widespread attention. He was not taken with the islanders, however, whom he described as stupid and lazy – an offensive calumny that has occasionally marked the attitudes of bigoted visitors to that part of Scotland over the years.

All that remained in order to secure the romantic reputation of Iona was a visit from Dr Johnson, who came with Boswell when they were staying on Coll, and from that *fons et origo* of nineteenth century Romanticism, Sir Walter Scott. Johnson, who had the good fortune to have Boswell to record his pearls of wisdom as he dropped them, said that there was nothing to be envied of a man's piety if it did not grow warmer on a visit to Iona's Abbey. Scott made two visits and was particularly interested in the carved stones and the graves. Poets followed, including William Wordsworth and John Keats. Wordsworth was moved to write lines slightly breathless in their effect, suffused with high-minded romanticism:

> *Homeward we turn. Isle of Columba's Cell,*
> *Where Christian piety's soul-cheering spark ...*

Numerous other poets have tried to capture the spell that the island seems to cast on people, many of them being included in the *Iona Anthology* published by the Iona Community. One of them, the versatile writer Marion Lochhead, whose career spanned the Scottish literary renaissance of the twentieth century, has a fine description of the island as a 'luminous gem of peace' and as 'dove island'. Sparse descriptions are worth screeds of more purple prose, or indeed poetry: Iona is exactly that – a luminous gem of peace. This description captures everything – the light of the Scottish islands, the scale and beauty of the place, and what it increasingly came to stand for after the formation of the Iona Community in the twentieth century. Iona is the polar opposite of a London Shard or a Trump golf course. It will also, I suspect, last longer.

The general literary and historical recognition of the significance of Iona saved the Abbey from even more ignominious ruin. Two later major restorations were to take place: one under the aegis of a remarkable Campbell, the 8th Duke of Argyll, a man who held a wide range of public offices in the second half of the nineteenth century and who took up all sorts of causes and enthusiasms, including theology, church matters – and Iona. The Duke wrote a book on Iona, a work that was much more than romantic rhapsodising, and in 1873 commissioned the Edinburgh architect Robert Anderson to assess and organise the restoration that would be necessary to prevent further damage to the Abbey and the other ecclesiastical buildings on the island, including St Oran's Chapel. Anderson encountered difficulties in getting local masons to do the necessary work but was able to bring over a number of skilled workmen from Edinburgh to begin the task of clearing rubble. A considerable amount of restoration work was completed over the following five years, and then a period of inactivity followed. Further work was done in 1897, when a temporary roof was put on the chancel and sacristy to allow for a day of celebratory services to mark the thirteen hundredth anniversary of Columba's death.

The Duke, his daughter and his third wife were clearly very attached to the Abbey at Iona and were aware of the responsibility their ownership of the island imposed on them. The Duke, however, saw little prospect of his son, the Marquess of Lorne, taking on this burden, and in 1899 he opted for the solution that was, many years later, to save the Abbey – ownership in the hands of the Church of Scotland. In this way, then, there came into existence the Iona Cathedral Trust. As is the case with many great projects in Scotland, bickering then ensued, with arguments as to which branch of the Christian Church the Iona heritage really belonged. Some Protestants did not like the thought of Catholics having access to the Abbey; some romantics wanted it to remain a ruin; the Duke himself said of his trust deed, in a letter quoted by Rosalind Marshall, 'My deed will be grief to the Roman Catholics, to the Anglicans, and to the Scottish Anglicans. All pretty nearly equally disliked by me.' That's the spirit that still lingers in our national psyche: there are a lot of people we feel the need to dislike.

The Duke gave the Abbey to the Church of Scotland but it did not come with an endowment. Today the National Trust for Scotland is aware of that sort of problem and is wary of taking on buildings that do not come with a personal trust fund. The ducal family had been sanguine about this: the people of Scotland would come up with the funds, they hoped. The people of Scotland, however, were slow to respond. An appeal leaflet sent out by the Trustees resulted in a grand total of twelve responses. The following year, however, loans were pledged and in 1902 work was started on the church's roof and windows. By 1905 enough had been done to allow a proper service to be held, conducted under cover, after a gap of three and a half centuries. The First World War interrupted the restoration, but it picked up again in the 1920s and by 1931 the church was once again a sound and working ecclesiastical building, complete with a single great bell from Taylor & Co of Loughborough. Work was still to be done on the remaining buildings, including the chapter house; for this an injection of new enthusiasm and vision was to come from one of Scotland's most charismatic and influential figures of the twentieth century, George MacLeod.

I remember going as a student in the late 1960s to hear George MacLeod speak in St Giles' Cathedral. Of the lectures and talks I attended as a student in Edinburgh I remember rather little, but I vividly recall MacLeod in the pulpit talking about world poverty and our indifference to the hunger and suffering of others. One of his phrases particularly impressed me: with the authentic indignation of a real Christian socialist, MacLeod spoke of how he had recently seen a newspaper headline proclaiming *Threat of a wheat surplus.* 'Threat?' he thundered. 'Threat? In a world in which, even as I speak, there are many dying of starvation!' These were powerful words.

There had been others holding retreats on Iona before this, but George MacLeod took the idea further. He had served as a minister in Govan, in Glasgow, where he had witnessed demeaning poverty and deprivation; he wanted to establish a community that would respond to the spiritual needs of the growing urban population. Retreats focusing on social justice issues and the mission of the Church of Scotland in that respect could be held on Iona, he thought, giving a focus to efforts to foster engagement with those living in the poorer reaches of Scotland's cities.

MacLeod was no armchair dreamer. He took workmen and craftsmen to Iona and continued to agitate for the reconstruction of the chapter house and other buildings. His relations with both government conservation authorities and the Trustees were often strained, but by the end of the Second World War the reconstruction of those three elements was complete. Later on, dormitory accommodation was finished, along with the restoration of the Abbot's House and the re-roofing of St Oran's Chapel. Today the island is in the care of the National Trust for Scotland, while the Abbey is the responsibility of Historic Environment Scotland. The buildings and the Abbey's artistic patrimony are in safe hands, with the Iona Community continuing to play an important part in keeping the Abbey a place of spiritual pilgrimage. Custodians estimate that one-third of those visiting the Abbey today come for spiritual reasons, even if those reasons are loosely defined. The remaining two-thirds come to look, but one imagines that at least some of them return from their visit better people. And that, surely, is a good thing for any collection of ancient buildings to achieve.

My first visit to Iona many years ago brought tears to my eyes; it must do that to many visitors, not just the over-sentimental or the sad. Today, when I pass it in my sailing boat, I feel the same way as I did then, and I remember W H Auden's echoing words in his bucolic 'Streams', a lambent paean to water – 'wishing … the least of men their figures of splendour, their holy places'. We are all the least of men, and no matter if we have no religious beliefs to speak of, we need our holy places. And both Columba and George MacLeod were, I think, figures of splendour.

6

The Masons' Marks
Kathleen Jamie

Glasgow Cathedral, AD 600s

A cart drawn by two wild bulls trundles out of the hills, and at length rounds into a narrow glen not far from the Clyde. A burn flows though the glen and by its banks the bulls stop. The cart, actually a hearse, is bearing the body of a holy man named Fergus, who will be buried here in 'the place that God ordained'. Here too the mourner who had followed will establish his church, at the 'dear green place'.

Every Glaswegian knows the story of St Kentigern, called Mungo, and his life and miracles, but as you walk along High Street and turn on- to Castle Street, it's hard to imagine the landscape Kentigern would have known. The craggy hill east of the burn became the Necropolis; and the burn itself has been banished underground. A *People's History of Glasgow* of 1899 delights to report that 'The Molendinar has been transformed in- to a common sewer, and a handsome roadway now takes its place.' The handsome roadway is Wishart Street, and as for the burn, a mere few yards of flowing water are visible above ground at Duke Street, fenced off and ignored.

Kentigern died in the depths of a seventh century winter, by then an old and feeble man. He was buried in or near his own church. A full 500 years passed before his biographies were written. They were commis- sioned to coincide with a great new project. It was the twelfth century, the reign of David I, and cathedrals were being raised all over Scotland, pinnacles pointing heavenwards. St Andrews, St Giles, Dunblane, Paisley Abbey, the Border Abbeys – buildings that spoke of power as well as wor- ship. Glasgow Cathedral was founded on the hill where Kentigern's early church is supposed to have stood. His relics still lie in the crypt.

Now the city swirls round the cathedral. It has its precinct, a bit of breathing space, enough to allow a visitor or pilgrim to stand back and appreciate the full scale of the work, but it takes its place among buildings taller, bigger, much newer: hospitals, universities, museums. It's a wonder it's still here at all, given 900 years of weather and wind, Reformation zeal and Victorian re-thinks, motorways and pollution. Soot and city smoke have darkened its honey-coloured sandstone, but the cathedral stands. Faith and love may keep it safe, but we must also thank its medieval builders. How are we to imagine them?

Maybe it's not so hard. Though the cathedral has an active Church of Scotland congregation, the building itself has long been in the care of the State and nowadays it has its own permanent team of conservators. One gloomy midwinter day I met Johnnie Clark, master stonemason and works manager. He and his team were working up on the roof of the Blacader Aisle, an addition which extended the transept southwards. In warm clothes and hard hat, Johnnie came nimbly down the scaffold to meet me. Though still young, he had already worked fourteen years at the cathedral, having served his own apprenticeship here. He had the hearty build of a man well used to climbing ladders and working stone.

Of the Blacader Aisle behind him Johnnie said, 'It's also known as the "Dripping Aisle". Originally they wanted to make it two storey, but it never happened. There was never a roof on it at one point, and we're still having problems with it leaking.' He shook his head. 'It's never been right. It's like a flat roof, and flat roofs in Scotland, specially in the West …'

This is a different attitude to a cathedral, a builder's attitude. Stone and mortar and getting it right.

Johnnie showed me round. We began by standing on a pavement of grave slabs, looking up at the east elevation, and the work of the original twelfth century stonemasons. Johnnie explained the modern policy of non-intervention unless necessary. It's an attitude different to the Victorians', who cheerfully demolished two towers at the cathedral's west side, intending to replace them with something grander which they never actually delivered. Now it's a much more softly-softly approach.

Craning up, I saw places high in the structure where, here and there, an original stone had been replaced. You could tell because the new stones shone pale yellow among the blackened originals.

'The ones we replaced were badly weathered. You don't like to intervene but you can see there we've had to. It was just the angle, a poor choice of stone. This new stone is from County Durham. The original stone would have been locally sourced.'

'Do you know where the quarry was?'

'I was told round about George Square! Hard to imagine now. Come and I'll show you the south side.'

We moved around the building and again we looked up.

This time Johnnie said, 'You can see there's a bit of twist here, a bit of settlement? But that keystone up there, that was one I had to cut. It's an honest repair.'

'What does that mean, an honest repair?'

'It's true to what it would have been, if the building hadn't moved. That's why it's so proud. See how it juts out? "Honest" means true to the way it would have been originally. It's following the proper line, it's the rest of the building that's twisted away.'

Because it was pointed out to me I could see that whole building was indeed skewed, stained glass windows and all, subtly but definitely awry, and slightly alarming.

'Is it still moving?'

'I think its settled now. It's not going to come down. It's moving because that's where the well is, down there. That well would probably have been the life source of the cathedral. I widnae drink from it, mind!'

We moved further around the building, still walking on a pavement of ancient grave slabs, and as might be expected, it was the south-west corner that was in most urgent need of repairs, being the corner that took the worst of the weather. High up on a pinnacle, a new finial had replaced an eroded original. There was even a new-fashioned gargoyle leaping out of the building, a ferocious one.

Johnnie paused, looking with an appraising eye at some feature high up.

'See the wee lancet windows? The arch stones are almost half a ton in weight. That's a Scots sandstone, Cullaloe from Burntisland. It's a different colour but the closest geological match to the original. We're eventually going to be working on the Rose Window as well, the west window.'

'You could spend your whole career here, then?'

'I could be here for another 40 years, aye. I don't mind, I love working here. It's a stonemason's dream to work on a cathedral like this. It's the best kind of cutting you're going to get, a bit of everything and it's always a challenge.'

It's not only the stones that need attention, it's the mortar between as well. The first conservation efforts, back in the nineteenth century, had seen the original lime mortar replaced with cement; that's now known to have been a mistake and these days conservators have reverted to the traditional lime, because lime mortar breathes.

'The sandstone's like a sponge, it takes in moisture and it needs to evaporate. Also, we have to remove vegetation and weeds. Brush it. But it's in pretty good nick.'

There was a question I was longing to ask, looking up at the steeple against the grey winter sky.

'Can you get up there?'

'We've actually worked up there, away up the steeple, because a bad storm did some damage. We repointed up there and replaced some stones. We had to get steeplejacks in to build us a cantilever scaffold. I got to cut the two stones at the very top. Aw, for me I was just … it was always my dream to go up there. We could see away, away for miles. Lovely view of the Necropolis as well. North Glasgow, south Glasgow, it's a great view. They'd have been brave back then. Building it. It would have been wooden scaffold. You can see the line of plug holes, that's where the scaffold would have been tied into the building. We use stainless steel tube, but it would have been impressive to see them working, the medieval stonemasons. A busy, busy site.'

Nowadays the masons' workshop is a covered yard with workbenches and a portacabin for an office, almost under the looming Royal Infirmary. There, Johnnie showed me a blackened and broken stone fleur-de-lis about a foot high that had been removed, and the new, honey-yellow replacement ready to take its place. Down on the workbench the stones are bigger and much heavier than you might imagine, but having the stone down from the dizzy heights and into the yard means the mason can take a template from it, and start to cut a new stone to exactly the same dimensions. The new stone arrives from the quarry as a long block, then to shape it, Johnnie said, 'It's just a series of checks and splays. The techniques have never changed. Same tools, same mason's mallet and chisels. The chisels we use are tungsten-tipped, they would have been fire-sharpened back then. This mallet's nylon, theirs would have been oak. But if a medieval mason came on site today, and if you had your tools set out, he could identify them right away. And the technology they had, the scaffolding and that. They would have had wooden things, maybe horse power to hoist the stones up. We're quite fortunate but, as I say, the technique has not changed.'

Johnnie took up the mason's mallet and chisel and began to work on a new stone. His tapping made a bright, hollow sound. 'It's all in the technique. It's just a smooth rhythm. To get that fleur-de-lis shape, its all straight lines.'

'It can't be that easy,' I said.

'Stick to the rules you'll not go wrong. That was a second-year apprentice did that one. It would take a couple of weeks.'

Having a permanent team of conservators on site allows Historic Environment Scotland to maintain another tradition, that of the apprentice. The old craft skills are passed on, in a four-year course, master to apprentice, much as they were 900 years ago. The apprentice then sits a skills test, and is then out in the world.

It must be a satisfying moment, I thought, for a young apprentice to see his own stonework hoisted up and placed high on a cathedral pinnacle. Or her work. At that moment a young woman walked by wearing a white hard hat, so there was one development in the long tradition.

'That's Lara. She's just done her skills test; she's very good. I don't tell her that too often!'

*

We must assume all the original medieval masons were men, and anonymous. The saints and bishops were named, but not the masons and carpenters, the actual builders of our great Scottish castles and cathedrals. However, recent and ongoing research may shed a little light.

After Johnnie had returned to his leaking roof, I opened the heavy door and entered the vast and silent cathedral. There were few people around, some Japanese tourists, a volunteer guide in a blue surplus, and a man with a clipboard and a pocket torch who was busy peering at the wall on the north side of the nave. This was Glasgow University research student Iain Ross Wallace, known as Ross, who has devised a project concerning masons' marks.

Twelfth century masons may have been pre-literate, may not have been able to write their own names, but each had his own unique mark. A mason's mark is a small, sometimes strange device the mason would cut into his finished stones, or suite of stones, as a sort of signature. These masons' marks probably served to identify one man's work from another's, so that they could be paid appropriately, and also as advertising. By his unique mark, a skilled mason could be noted, so that he could attract further business.

Ross already had a full career behind him before taking a late degree in archaeology; the masons' marks are a new and consuming enthusiasm. With the help of the torch, played slantwise across the dark stones, Ross illuminated several different masons' marks on the walls and pillars, all but forgotten over the centuries.

'Look here,' he said. 'And on this pillar. There are carvings everywhere. Some are positioning marks, arrows to show what way up a piece was to go. But see this bow-tie shape? Or this double-v?'

The more I looked, moving along the walls and around the soaring pillars, the more I saw: marks like semaphore flags, and complex little aerials.

As part of his research, Ross is compiling a catalogue of these marks – it now runs to some 700 different ones in Glasgow Cathedral alone. We could see only the low ones, but he assured me there are many others way high up in the clearstory, 60 foot up, where young and nimble undergraduates had gone looking. More are doubtless obscured by brass plaques and memorials mounted on the cathedral walls.

'700 marks is not to say there were 700 masons on site at any one time, some of the marks are variations on a theme, but it does indicate the scale of the undertaking – many masons at many benches.'

Each with his apprentice and labourers. And the carpenters, and the gaffers and the carters and horses. The stone-tapping and sawing and shouting, the trundling and whinnying. As Johnnie said, a busy, busy site.

Some of the marks, Ross believes, continued down the family. A man's mark passed to his son, who added a line, then to the grandson, who added another, until a complex device evolved over generations. He has identified marks which suggest to him that three generations of the same family might have been employed on the build at once, that entire careers could have been spent here, then as now.

We walked around the nave, then down the steps into the gloomy lower crypt where St Kentigern's tomb is draped in a cloth, and his ancient well occupies a corner. There too, Ross illuminated more and more marks. It's as though the cathedral is murmuring a silent language, whispering names that we can't know.

Some masons may have spent their careers here, and equally, some may have been itinerant. Part of Ross's research project is to try to trace their movements across the country. If the same mark occurs in several different buildings, castles or cathedrals, across the country, it would strongly suggest its owner moved from job to job, or was perhaps retained by one particular grand family. By their marks, it might be possible to track these movements.

Ross said, 'I have an image, a mason with cart and horse, with his labourer, bench, some tools and templates, turning up at your castle door, asking if you want your windows replaced. Showing you the templates. You can have this, this, or this. It was the IKEA catalogue of the day.'

Intriguingly, Ross is developing a theory that masons' marks are descended from the Viking runic alphabet; they certainly look a bit runic. They might be evidence of Viking influence in Europe and, in turn, evidence of French or German influence in Scotland. It would appear that some master masons were brought from the continent to Scotland, teaching as they went, literally making their mark. Skilled workers from Europe are not a new phenomenon. As things stand, the only medieval master mason we know by name is John Morrow, a fourteenth century Parisian who worked at Melrose Abbey, Glasgow Cathedral, St Andrews, Paisley … But if a Madame Morrow came from Paris too, to make what she could of rural Scotland – that we'll probably never know.

*

It's said that Glasgow is the only mainland Scottish cathedral to have survived the Reformation relatively undamaged. St Andrews lies in ruins, abandoned and robbed out. Elgin likewise. Dunblane and Dunkeld have been partially restored. It was the sixteenth century, a great unbuilding: altars were ripped out, relics carted off, silver and lead sold for scrap as church hierarchies were dinged down and Presbyterianism established. The walls and pillars of Glasgow Cathedral are scarred and repaired, showing places where statues and sconces were ripped away. There's a story, perhaps fanciful, that it was the people of Glasgow who saved the cathedral from the zealots.

It is also said that of all the losses of the Reformation, early church music was the greatest. But on 12 January 2017, the eve of St Kentigern's day, a notable event was held in the cathedral. For the first time since the Reformation, vespers were sung for St Kentigern.

It was, of course, dusk, rush hour, and sleet was falling. The pews of the choir filled with a congregation happed in coats and scarves, and some in clerical attire: Church of Scotland, Roman Catholic, Greek Orthodox. In due course, seven cantors dressed in red surplices walked down the aisle, and for 45 minutes, as the winter night fell, and the stained glass darkened, their voices chanted and sang Latin versicles and antiphons and the five psalms of the day, and then special verses for the saint himself.

This 'First Vespers for St Kentigern' had been restored and edited from a thirteenth century manuscript, the Sprouston Breviary, which is in the care of the National Library of Scotland. The work of reconstruction had been done by Greta-Mary Hair and Betty I Knott, and the vespers were sung by the Cantors of the Holy Rood, with the support of the Minister and the Friends of Glasgow Cathedral. It was a coming together, in faith and art and architecture, and quite transporting. The slender arches of the choir were lit, showing their graceful stonework. The choir, though tall, seemed to become intimate, warming as the cantors' voices rose and fell. Perhaps the sound also made its way down to the crypt, where the bones of St Kentigern lie. Did the old bones stir, hearing their name sung once again, after more than 450 years?

Afterwards, there was no applause; we had heard an act of worship not a performance. When it was over the cantors filed out with hands clasped, but afterwards they appeared relaxed, waiting to receive the congregation in the great nave along with the minister of the cathedral and the musical experts who had made the vespers possible. It had been, as the organisers said, despite their modesty, a historic moment.

With the sung vespers still in my mind, I walked down the long nave, wondering what changes the cathedral would see in another 500 years' time. What reconciliations. Perhaps the poor Molendinar Burn could be uncovered and restored to nature, to flow by the cathedral, a dear green place.

If the cathedral still stood.

Of course it would still stand, if there were the will and the skill. At the back of the nave, under a pillar, I spotted three burly figures in black fleece jackets. They stood somewhat aside, not worshippers or clergy, not tourists, not cantors, kings or theologians, but stonemasons, all with their arms folded, satisfied.

7

Rock of Ages
Alistair Moffat

Edinburgh Castle, 1100s

I can't recall the precise date but it was a cold and frosty Saturday in November, 1975, when Edinburgh Castle turned out to be a witness to a radical change in my life's direction. Like many Scots in the mid seventies I had gone to London if not to seek my fortune then certainly in search of a job. I found one immediately, teaching in a South London comprehensive school for girls. It didn't go well. Many were noisy, feisty, bored kids counting down the days until they could stop being truants and leave school legally. Jean Baker was so keen to go that one morning she ran into my first floor classroom, shot past my desk and jumped out of the open window. Landing on the sloping grass below, she was miraculously unhurt. But, like Jean, I realised that I had to leave – quickly, and preferably by the front door.

My girlfriend at the time was also keen that I should depart since her flat in Kilburn didn't have a spare room, a problem after our hundredth argument. She was an actress able to articulate my shortcomings with theatrical clarity and matching volume, accompanied by sweeping hand gestures, some of them missing only by inches. But Clare did me a great service. In the trade paper *Stage and Television Today*, she spotted an advert, something that she was sure would suit me – and her. The job was based in Edinburgh, a very long way from Kilburn.

The Edinburgh Festival Fringe Society was looking for an Administrator, someone to run the vast diaspora of performances that clustered around the official Festival. In 1972 I had founded a successful arts festival in my home town of Kelso and that seemed to impress the Fringe board sufficiently to invite me up from London for an interview.

I arrived early, more than two hours early. As I walked up the Waverley Steps to Princes Street, I wondered how to kill time without fretting too much over what I might say to my interogators. The sun was shining.

Perhaps a walk would do it, but when I turned left at the top of the steps, I saw the drama of Edinburgh Castle dominating the cityscape and re-alised I had never visited it. As I walked up Castlehill, a loud bang boomed through the winter afternoon and a passer-by looked at his watch. I checked mine. My interview was at 3pm in the Royal Mile Centre in the High Street in exactly two hours' time.

Emerging from the canyons of the Old Town, the Esplanade seemed a sudden gust of openness with its immense panoramas to the north and south. I am not certain but I think the entrance to the castle was flanked by two guardsmen with rifles standing at ease in front of their sentry box-es. There were very few people around, only the occasional well-mufflered visitor, and admission was free in those far-off days before anyone cared about overheads or security. You could just wander in. I nodded to Bruce and Wallace and passed under the archway they were guarding. It was like entering another world. I felt I had the castle to myself.

As I made my way uphill into the shadows under the Argyle Tower and through the Castle Gates, it seemed as though they were closing silently behind me. The cobbled roadway wound around the rock, outcrops show-ing through the cobbles and cut stone, all appearing to fit snugly togeth-er, rubbed smooth by time. There were more soldiers at the barracks and the Governor's House, and one group climbed into a khaki Land Rover to drive downhill. This was a massive, well-defended castle and the presence of soldiers simply added to a sense of continuity, of time collapsing on itself.

I had no guidebook, map or plan and can't remember if there was anywhere to buy one. A shop probably wouldn't be open in November anyway. The roadway climbed higher around another outcrop of rock that looked as though the man-made masonry had failed to contain it and took me under what seemed an older gateway and into a citadel within a cita-del. I don't recall how I got there but I found myself in a square with the National War Memorial on one side. It seemed a building constructed en-tirely from names. Carved on the walls were battles: Loos, Waterloo, the Somme, Minden and many others. On long lecterns set below there were books of the names of the dead. A place for remembering set in the centre of Scotland's history.

Above the square stood what seemed to be the smallest building in the castle, perched on its highest point. St Margaret's Chapel is also the oldest, dating from the early twelfth century, and its simple sanctity seemed to reach across the centuries. I turned and looked out northwards across the Forth to Fife and, closer at hand, to Princes Street and the Georgian New Town behind it. It seemed a perfect scene, graphic and bright in the winter sun. At that point in my life, twenty-five years old, I was not well travelled but it occurred to me at that moment that Edinburgh was the most beautiful city I had ever seen. A good place to live and work. London was full of grand buildings but it was flat, dirty, crowded and hurried. And beyond the ceremonial streets around Buckingham Palace and along the riverbank, there were few vistas, certainly nothing like the panoramas from the old chapel and also from Edinburgh's other hills. Walking up through the great castle, its defences and gun batteries, the military buildings buffed smooth by the old winds, it seemed that I had made my way up through history's strata to look out over the present – and perhaps towards my own future.

It was half past two, time to walk quickly down the High Street to my interview. Which seemed to go well. The chairman of the Edinburgh Festival Fringe Society was Andrew Cruickshank, a wonderful, warm and clever man who had enjoyed great success as an actor, most famously as Dr Cameron in the series Dr Finlay's Casebook. When he commented on how glowing the reviews in the local paper for my festival in Kelso had been, I told him that I had written them myself. He dissolved in laughter and smiled very warmly at the end of the interview. I dared to hope I might get the job. And I did. It was a turning point in my life and the beginning of twenty-three happy years of living in what is indeed the most beautiful city in the world.

During my time there the Festival Fringe grew four-fold and sometimes, to find an hour out of the hurly-burly to think, I used to walk up to the castle for some peace and the long views. Admission was still free. And when I walked into work in the High Street in May and saw the scaffolding beginning to go up on the Esplanade for the Military Tattoo, I used to gulp at the thought of the Festival racing towards me. Even now I remember the feeling.

Forty years later I walked up Castlehill once more. Or, at least, I shuffled up the narrow street as part of what seemed like a very long queue. It was 19 July 2016, one of the busiest visitor days of the year as the sun beat down on the chattering crowds. A selfie-snapping conga funnelled its way into a narrow corridor of crowd control barriers under the Tattoo scaffolding and into the arena where marching bands would oompah up and down in August. As guided tours gathered I sidestepped and slipped through gaps in the throng as it made its way to the entrance. There were no soldiers guarding it, no rifles and no sentry boxes and the only uniforms were worn by Historic Environment Scotland staff attempting to manage the crowd. I had deliberately chosen one of the busiest days of the year. In

2015 Edinburgh Castle opened its gates to 1,568,508 visitors with 249,923 coming in July alone. On that sunny summer day in 2016, about 10,000 shuffled across the cobbled entrance. And it felt like it.

The queue for tickets was very long, doubling back on itself in the sort of serpentine arrangement of barrier tapes usually seen at airport security. I guesstimated 200 people waiting and in the half hour it took to reach the ticket window, I heard English spoken only once, and by Canadians. Most of the queue was made up by groups of East Asians and many of them were young women, selfie sticks at the ready. When I finally reached the window, a smiling, courteous young man relieved me of £16.50 and £5 for a guidebook. With annual revenue of around £20m from entrance fees alone and more to come from the tearooms, restaurant and gift shops, Edinburgh Castle is big business.

Having chosen to go on one of the most crowded days, I found several places to watch what visitors did and I queued with them to see the Scottish Crown Jewels, the Stone of Destiny, the Great Hall, St Margaret's Chapel and the other attractions. Aside from those who chose to cluster around the carrying voices of official guides, visitors generally seemed to pay little attention to where they were. As the queue for the Crown Jewels inched up the stairs and through an olive green door marked 'Chubb', a well known brand of locks and safes, groups of friends talked to each other, scarcely glancing at the sceptre, the sword of state or the crown sitting on its scarlet cushion before blinking back out into the sunshine. Some of them had kept their sunglasses on even in the darkened crown room. Others had barely lifted their heads from their phones or tablets as they texted and sent photos of an experience they had barely experienced. Perhaps views of the castle and their visit needed to be fixed on a screen rather than simply looked at. Or were they collecting something?

Selfies clicked at every corner and I had constantly to avoid getting between a camera and what it was about to photograph. What did catch attention was not so much the castle's treasures or buildings but the views from the battlements. Two or three deep, most visitors crowded at the Argyle Battery to look north over the New Town to the Forth and Fife while many had climbed the steps outside the National War Museum to look west over the battlements. At the other end of the castle, the Half Moon Battery was roped off, but in any case the Tattoo scaffolding would have obstructed views of the Old Town and east towards the sea.

Being a tourist is tiring, and the tearooms and cafes were full but quiet. And even though there is almost always a refreshing breeze blowing across the castle crag, it was very hot and humid on that July day. Finding a table at last in the Queen Anne Building I made the mistake of ordering soup, the cheapest item on the menu. It was excellent, but hot and I was grateful for the cooling fan set up by thoughtful members of staff.

I decided to take my own tour around the castle. And to understand something of how it grew, I tried to imagine the castle crag before the castle. Perhaps it looked like Traprain Law in East Lothian, bare-headed, massive and singular despite the bite taken out of one corner by quarrying. But what made the Edinburgh crag more attractive was surely geology, the way in which the glaciers had rumbled from the west at the end of the last ice age, been forced to divide by the stubborn obstruction of the hard volcanic plug and leave in its eastern lee the sloping tail of rock and debris that allowed access, and where the Old Town would come to be built. With steep, smooth, sometimes sheer cliffs on three sides, the crag was surely occupied and held by people of power from prehistoric times. In the millennia when the Nor Loch filled in the declivity that is now Princes Street Gardens, the crag will have looked even more formidable. It is sometimes claimed that Edinburgh Castle is the oldest continuously oc-cupied fortification in Britain and it surely must be. As I walked around, looking at its structures, dodging the drifts of visitors, I felt myself begin to think like a historian.

No-one needs another history of Edinburgh Castle, the gift shops were stuffed with brightly illustrated booklets, but the process of asking ques-tions about origins and practicalities did help me understand better what I was looking at. Clearly the castle is not a building but many structures with related roles, a military compound, built up over centuries. Although the nearest thing I saw to a soldier was a private security guard, the army is still present. Next to the entrance to the barracks, name plates announce the headquarters of the Royal Regiment of Scotland, the Scots Guards office, the Royal Scots Dragoon Guards office, the Headquarters of the Edinburgh Garrison and, oddly, the UK North Counter Intelligence Section.

All of these buildings are of course perched on top of the history of the castle as well as being part of it. An archaeological dig adjacent to the Redcoat Cafe, where the One o'Clock Gun is fired each day, revealed the gossamer traces of first millennium BC roundhouses, and the radio car-bon dating of organic material suggested that a community was living on the crag between 972 BC and 830 BC. This was the era of so-called hill-forts, high places where powerful men ruled and their retinues and fam-ilies clustered around them. Probably a little later than the carbon dates, two deep ditches were hacked out of the very hard volcanic rock near the

Gatehouse to make the spectacular site even more secure.

Such is the drama of the crag's setting that the prehistoric hillfort almost certainly had spiritual significance. The separation of secular and religious power is a very recent way of thinking about society, and the kings or chieftains who occupied the fortress were very likely to have had a priestly as well as a military or political role. The farming communities around the crag depended on the seasons and the weather to help them deliver the bounty of the harvest, and the emphasis on hillforts and high places suggests that prehistoric peoples of the first millennium turned their gaze to the sky and worshipped or attempted to propitiate sky gods. To paraphrase, the castle crag was also probably a sky temple where ceremonies were enacted at the turning points of the farming year. And the way in which St Margaret's Chapel, a small and simple structure amidst the chunky solidity of barracks and armouries, sits on the highest point may be seen as a pleasing continuity.

Watchers from the wooden stockade that encircled the early citadel will have seen something remarkable in the early summer of AD 81 or AD 82. Out in the Forth Roads the sails of a fleet of galleys appeared, making way up the firth, steering towards the southern shore. To the south, men on the ramparts saw the columns of a vast army snaking down off the higher ground at Liberton, perhaps 10,000 men, more than anyone had ever seen, marching towards them. The king on the crag was impressed but not anxious. He knew they were coming and knew what they wanted. The Empire was moving north and its soldiers needed food.

Led by the great general and governor of the province, Gnaeus Julius Agricola, and chronicled by his son-in-law, Tacitus, a Roman army had come to the north of Britannia to bring its native kindreds into the Roman Empire. Having arranged a rendezvous with the Classis Britannica, the British Fleet, on the shores of the Forth, Agricola had divided his three legions and their auxiliaries into two columns to encircle the warlike Selgovae of the Southern Uplands and protect his allies, the Votadini and their king on the castle rock.

All armies, and especially those on the scale of Agricola's, need supplies and from the harvests in their territories in the Lothians and the Borders, the Votadinian kings could supply what Roman quartermasters needed. Before the legionaries buckled on their armour to begin the long tramp northwards, envoys had probably agreed good terms for the grain of the farmers of the Votadini. And their king will have been plied with diplomatic gifts. A Roman brooch was found on the crag by archaeologists.

The name of the kindred the diplomats dealt with is hard to parse and

Votadini may simply derive from a personal name, Fothad, possibly a divine ancestor or name-father. It changed only a little in the centuries after Rome, and Y Gododdin was also the title of a great epic poem that was almost certainly composed and performed in the royal hall on the castle crag. It is one of the earliest surviving texts in Old Welsh, the Celtic language spoken across the Lothians and the Borders as well as much of Dark Ages Scotland and an ancient cousin to modern Welsh. The name of the bard who sang of the deeds of Y Gododdin was Aneirin, now part of the canon of Welsh Christian names.

The great epic tells the tale of a fateful raid in the south, the journey of the warband of Yrfai, Lord of Edinburgh. He was not the king on the crag but perhaps his general. He led the royal warband, a cavalry force, to Catterick in North Yorkshire in AD 600 to confront the warriors known as Y Gynt, the Gentiles, the Heathens. These were the Angles, ambitious and aggressive immigrants whose recent ancestors had sailed the North Sea to colonise what is now Yorkshire, Durham and Northumberland. Lord Yrfai's men knew themselves as Y Bedydd, the Baptised, the Christians. But their faith did not save them and on the banks of the River Swale, where it runs rapid near the old Roman fort, the warriors of the Gododdin were slaughtered. By AD c640 King Oswald of the Anglian realm of Bernicia had captured the castle crag and its fortress. Its Old Welsh name of Din Eidyn, the Fortress of Eidyn (another personal name), was changed to Edinburgh and for 300 years it formed part of the glittering kingdom of Northumbria.

All of that history, these tales of bravery and rivalry, are cast to the wind. Nothing now remains on the crag to remember this formative period when power, language and culture in eastern Scotland shifted decisively. There is no trace or hint of Yrfai's fortress or of the fortifications of Oswald's Anglian lords. Not until much later, in 1093, does the castle come back into focus, and then only vaguely. After the death of her husband, Malcolm III Canmore, and her eldest son on a raid into Northumberland, Queen Margaret is said to have turned her face to the wall and died of grief. The chroniclers wrote that she ended her exemplary life in Castra Puellarum, the Castle of the Maidens, a name that is used until the sixteenth century. It may have been a reference to a convent of nuns maintained by the saintly queen.

Her youngest son, David I, did not expect to become king of Scots but nevertheless he was a gifted, innovating ruler. Between 1139 and 1150 he held a parliament in the castle and commissioned the building of a chapel in memory of his mother. It probably formed part of a square stone keep like those that survive at Bamburgh and Carlisle and were built in the same period. On the highest point of the crag, the position of the keep will have been commanding, visible from a distance. After David, Scottish kings stayed often at Edinburgh Castle and it began to develop slowly into its modern form.

Its castle shaped Edinburgh profoundly as the early medieval buildings of the Old Town huddled in its protective shadow to the east. It was a landmark and a seamark, clearly visible from the firth and the destination to which all roads and tracks led. Now the castle defines Edinburgh, it is the quintessential image of the city, unlike any other. There are Georgian terraces in Bath, medieval streets and closes in York and Chester but no city in the world has a vast fortress at its centre with the operatic drama of Edinburgh. There was no need for the most romantic of the landscape painters of the nineteenth century to embellish any aspect. All that the likes of William Blake, Caspar David Friedrich or Eugene Delacroix needed to do was paint what they saw.

And that is all that anyone who wants a sense of Edinburgh Castle's power need do – simply look at it from the city's streets and suburbs. If the texters, the selfie-takers, the footsore and the plain bored prove distracting, all that needs to be understood of the enduring, breathtaking magic of the castle are the views of it and from it. They are eloquent, and in one sense timeless. From the stockades, from the batteries, watchers could see what sailed the Forth or what approached on the landward roads. On bright, sharp, sunlit winter days, the Lomond Hills of Fife seem close with the grey outline of the Highland line beyond, to the south and east the rampart of the Moorfoots and Lammermuirs rolls gently down to the fields of East Lothian and the North Sea, and from the western battery the arrow-straight line of the railway to Glasgow vanishes into the distance. As I looked out from those vantage points, the crowds melted away into silence and slow-motion, the years rolled back and Scotland lay before me.

8

Cool Scotia
James Crawford

The Great Hall, Stirling Castle, 1503

I was standing right at the centre of Stirling Castle's Great Hall, looking up. Above me was a huge wooden ribcage, the exposed timber-framing of the Hall's massive hammer-beam roof. It reminded me at first of a ship's hull, like I was peering into the superstructure of some hulking old galleon. Footsteps on the pristine, slate-grey flagstones echoed around me, accompanied by the familiar tourist hum of voices and the incessant – and artificial – shutter release clicks of smart-phone cameras. I looked for longer than was comfortable, neck straining, eyes moving back and forth along the cross-hatchings of beams. Spotlights were directed upwards too, warming the texture of the wood, but also casting shadows, adding more lines to the arrangement, more complexity.

It was undeniably beautiful – if slightly dizzying – and a remarkable feat of engineering. The hammer-beams are a type of truss: a series of triangles set at intervals along the supporting walls. The 'hammer' is the name given to the horizontal at the top of each triangle, which projects out to support the open rafters. An English invention – they were used originally in the roof of the Palace of Westminster in 1397 – they migrated north a century later as a key design feature of the Great Hall. You can lose yourself in the interplay of struts and beams, the intricacy of the medieval craftsmanship. Look up and you are looking back half a millennium.

Well, not quite.

The roof above me wasn't five hundred years old. It's not even fifty years old. I'm older than the roof. In fact, the roof is still a teenager, a structural adolescent, completed in 1999. It was built out of 100 cubic metres of oak – which amounts to some 350 trees. The wood was extracted from a designated site of special interest just north of Aberfoyle. Selected felling and deer fencing were used to encourage re-growth and, because mechanical equipment is not allowed within protected forests, Clydesdale horses had to be brought in to get the trees to the access roads. In the sawmill they were converted into 'box hearts' – their sides cut away so that each beam was formed out of the 'heart' of its original tree. This makes them stronger, less likely to warp or twist. The off-cuts became panelling beneath the roof slates. The construction of the roof was put out to tender, and much of the creation of the initial frame was carried out in a workshop near Chippenham, with the trusses and joints assembled in the traditional way on a flat floor. This kind of attention to detail was a hallmark of the project.

In order to give the Great Hall its new – old – roof, the whole structure had to be encased on-site in an 'envelope', a mixture of weatherproofing, steel and scaffolding that was 70 feet long and 85 feet high. For much of the 1990s, the Hall was hidden behind this great grey tent, like a patient behind a surgeon's screen. And it wasn't just the roof that was being worked on. It was also the stonework, parapets and chimneys; the harling and stained-glass glazing; ironmongery for doors, handrails and candelabra; loom-woven wall hangings in chenille and gold thread. Only half of the original sandstone floor remained, and it was in too poor a condition for actual use. Instead it was preserved in place, with a new floor constructed on top, supplemented by underfloor heating to remove the need for radiators.

When the envelope was opened on 24 February 1999, it came with a surprise. The exterior of the Great Hall had been reharled using the original lime-wash finish. Archaeologists and experts from the Scottish Lime Centre had carried out detailed investigations to find original traces – discovering one large section which, not long after its original application, had been obscured and protected from the elements by contemporary building work. The finish was called 'Royal Gold' – a bright, creamy yellow that turns pinkish when the sun is low: a startling burst of colour, in particular when set against the aged greyness of the rest of the castle. Almost inevitably, it was the harling that received much of the initial media attention, sparking vociferous debate over the perceived rights and wrongs. The science couldn't really be faulted – the accuracy of the reharl was confirmed by hard evidence (more so, indeed, than with the hammer-beam roof, which was extrapolated from a single eighteenth century survey drawing, alongside the remains of a similar but far from identical roof in the Great Hall of Edinburgh Castle). But it wasn't really about the science. And it wasn't really about the colour either. It goes deeper than that.

When it comes to buildings, 'restoration' is a loaded word. It provokes. It asks questions – and often gives answers that we may not like or want to hear. It pulls at the threads of our history, culture, politics, community and identity. It is, in the broadest sense, unsettling. And it is also, fundamentally, about that most personal, elusive – and often exclusive – of concepts: taste.

*

In the late eighteenth century, it was the diminished state of the castle that was provoking anger. Looking out from his lodgings while passing through Stirling in 1787, Robert Burns was so incensed by the sight of it – and the *absence* of a roof – that he diamond-cut the following lines in the window glass of his room:

> *Here Stewarts once in triumph reign'd,*
> *And laws for Scotland's weal ordaine'd;*
> *But now unroof'd their Palace stands,*
> *Their sceptre's fall'n to other hands;*
> *Fallen indeed, and to the earth,*
> *Whence groveling reptiles take their birth –*
> *The injur'd Stewart-line are gone,*
> *A Race outlandish fill their throne;*
> *An idiot race, to honour lost;*
> *Who knows them best despise them most*

This poem wasn't really about architecture of course: it was about politics. For Burns, Stirling Castle had become a grey symbol of the extinguished vibrancy of a royal dynasty he admired and whose passing, on some level, he still mourned. 'It is singular enough that the Scottish Muses are all Jacobites', he wrote. 'Surely the gallant but unfortunate house of Stewart, the kings of our fathers for so many heroic ages, is much more interesting than an obscure, beef-witted insolent race of foreigners whom a conjuncture of circumstance kickt up into power and consequence.'

It was *life* that Burns felt had left the castle. The buildings were still the same: diminished not by ruination but by context. As Burns knew, there had been a time when this place had been all about colour. During the reigns of the Stewart Kings James IV and James V, Stirling was characterised by ostentatious showmanship and conspicuous consumption. Nothing was held back. James IV injected the Renaissance passionately into Scottish culture, transforming his court into a great theatre of art, learning and ideas. The famous Dutch scholar Desiderius Erasmus – who acted as tutor to the king's illegitimate son Alexander – was glowing in his admiration of James: 'he had wonderful powers of mind, an astonishing knowledge of everything, unconquerable magnanimity and the most abundant generosity'. The Spanish ambassador Pedro de Ayala described him 'as handsome in complexion as a man can be' and praised his fluency in Latin, French, German, Flemish, Italian and Spanish. The sixteenth century playwright Sir David Lindsay concluded that he was 'the glory of princely governing': vigorous, outward-looking and cosmopolitan.

One of the few people to have any words of criticism for James was his favourite court poet William Dunbar. On the one hand Dunbar felt the royal generosity was exploited by a swarm of sycophants and charlatans – and on the other he nursed the grievance that the king didn't pay him enough. In his poem 'Schir, Ye have Mony Servitours', he listed a bewildering array of court attendants: officials, 'kirkmen', craftsmen, doctors of law and of medicine, philosophers, astrologists, artists, orators, knights, minstrels, 'hurlers and flingers', shipbuilders, stonemasons, carpenters, glaziers, goldsmiths, jewellers and apothecaries. Dunbar's nemesis was the Italian John Damian – an 'alchemist' whom James funded indiscriminately for at least a decade in his attempts to discover the elixir of life. This was the same Damian who, in September 1507, built himself giant wings out of bird-feathers and attempted to fly from Stirling's ramparts all the way to France. To Dunbar's glee – of course captured for posterity in verse – the flight ended with the Italian landing in a dung heap at the base of the castle rock and breaking his leg. 'In a myre up to the ene / amang the glar did gyld', as Dunbar put it. Several hundred years later, another great Scottish poet, Edwin Morgan, was similarly inspired by the incident. Morgan, writing as James, is philosophical about the possibilities offered by Damian's experiment. Given the King's incorporation of the College of Surgeons in Edinburgh the previous year, he reckons the royal coin well spent whatever the outcome:

> Oh for Christ's sake gie the signor his siller.
> Alchemist my erse, but he's hermless, is he no?
> He'll never blaw us up in oor beds, I tak it.
> If makkin wings is his new-fanglt ploy
> It'll no cost the earth – a wheen o skins,
> Or silk if he can get it, wid for the struts
> ...
> And noo for the warst-case scenario:
> The bird-man whuds doon splat, doon tae his daith.
> Oh what a bonus: we'll hae ane public dissection.
> My Charter will hae wings, it'll tak aff,

Whit can we no dae gif we set oor minds tae it?
Tell Signor Damiano, be he limpin or be he a corp,
The College o Surgeons stauns honed and skeely and eident.

Unsurprisingly architecture was central to the transformation of the Scottish Court. The Stewarts had unashamed international ambitions. They wanted recognition and respect across Europe, and they bought and built with an enthusiasm that belied the relatively meagre size of their royal coffers. It was James IV who commissioned the construction of the Great Hall – with its 'gold' exterior – at the end of the fifteenth century. This was just one part of a massive project of palace improvements that also took in Edinburgh, Holyrood, Linlithgow, Falkland and Dunfermline, and which was continued by James V throughout the first half of the sixteenth century. These two Scottish kings, father and son, staged an unprecedented overhaul of the old fabric of royal residences. James V brought perhaps even more brio to Stirling Castle than his father. Influenced in no small part by a desire to impress his second wife, the French noblewoman Mary of Guise, he constructed an entirely new palace block. This building remains perhaps the greatest single symbol of Scottish Renaissance architecture – a structure that set the tone for the design of noble houses for centuries to come. On the outside its battlemented facades alternate big windows with cusped arches holding life-size statues. There are over two hundred stone sculptures adorning its walls – more than just about any other building in Britain at that time. Figures range from soldiers and child-like cherubs known as *putti*, to James himself (being crowned by a lion), Roman gods, and even a luridly grotesque Devil, with large breasts, a mask covering its crotch and cloven hooves.

No expense was spared on fitting out the interiors either – reams of silk and velvet in reds and purples for the chambers of the king and queen; Florentine embroiderers employed to work with ball after ball of golden thread; four-poster beds draped with curtains of violet damask. In the palace of James V, the walls sported a series of massive, intricately detailed tapestries, including a sequence depicting the royal 'Hunt of the Unicorn'; while the ceiling of the inner-hall was decorated with forty-odd solid oak carvings. These sculptural portraits, known as the 'Stirling Heads', mixed likenesses of the Stewart family with great figures from history and mythology including Julius Caesar and Hercules. They were hand-painted with shockingly bright pigments – in particular blues, reds and greens. All of this would have made for an explosion of colour. And in style and execution the palace was said to be at the leading edge of contemporary art and fashion. How else, the Stewarts thought, would you draw attention to a kingdom set at the top of an island at the north-westernmost fringe of Europe? They treated the courtiers of the continent like magpies and resolved to draw their eyes to the shiniest bauble. *Come join the cult of the Stewarts, the family with the divine right to rule.* This was a deliberate re-branding of Scotland and Scottish royalty. *Cool Scotia.*

You suspect Burns – despite his egalitarian principles – would have loved all of this: the humanist sensibilities, the intrigue, the constant procession of extravagantly weird hangers-on, the profusion of court ladies (James IV in particular had an unerring eye for his mistresses), the music, the plays, the songs – and patrons who paid good money for good poetry. All the same, it was still a Stewart – James VI – who walked out and shut the doors of Stirling Castle behind him for the last time. James had been baptised and crowned in the buildings constructed by his grandfather and great grandfather. But he had also been kept in the castle as a virtual prisoner for much of the first thirteen years of his life. You wonder how much – or rather how little – affection he had for the place.

After inheriting the throne from Elizabeth I in 1603, London became his new home. The palace at Stirling, which had already been replaced in preference by Edinburgh, was essentially emptied of people and purpose. In December 1616, James wrote to the Scottish Privy Council that, 'we have had these many years a great and natural longing to see our native soil and place of our birth and breeding, and this salmon-like instinct of ours has restlessly, both when we were awake, and many times in our sleep, so stirred up our thoughts and bended our desires to make a journey thither than we can never rest satisfied till it shall please God that we may accomplish it'. It was a sentimentality tour, a chance to visit places that, to James, were already part of history. He came to the palace for a brief stay in July 1617, and then never returned to his first home, or to Scotland, again.

The castle Burns looked out on in 1787 had, for over a century and a half, been reduced to a tired and somewhat squalid military outpost and prison (and three years later its Great Hall would be turned into a barracks, a role it would continue to perform all the way up to 1964). It had even acted as a stubborn government bulwark against the forces of the final, tragic figure in the Stewart line – Charles Edward, the 'Bonnie Prince'. The rebels laid siege to it unsuccessfully in 1746, then ran to the hills for their last, disastrous stand at Culloden. 'A poor friendless wand'rer may well claim a sigh', Burns wrote of the Prince, contemplating his flight into the wilderness, 'Still more, if that wand'rer were royal'. He romanticised the end of the Rebellion, but nonetheless, in an anonymous letter to an Edinburgh newspaper, concluded: 'that they failed, I bless my God most fervently'. Burns knew the stories of the Stewarts were both poignant and potent (David Daiches, the twentieth century Scottish literary critic, blamed him for ensuring that 'this absurd and anachronistic rebellion was transmuted into a source of legitimate emotion for all Scotsmen'). But he also knew that they were in and of the past. And, by this time, so too was Stirling Castle.

*

In 1903 a man called Alois Riegl, Professor of Art History at the University of Vienna, published a short essay titled 'The Modern Cult of Monuments'. It was a concise, philosophical musing on the problem of what to do with old buildings in the modern world. Today, over a century later, it is still considered one of the most important texts ever written on the subject.

Riegl's theory is that our attitudes towards preservation, conservation and restoration are determined by a series of discrete – and often mutually exclusive – values, which he also terms 'cults'. These cults can in turn be split into two categories: those that are about memory, and those that are about the present day. For Riegl, whether we know it or not, we all belong to at least one of them.

The first cult Riegl calls 'age value'. If you believe in age value, then your overriding attitude towards buildings is that they must be left alone: 'every work of man is perceived as a natural organism in whose development man may not interfere; the organism should live its life freely'. By this measure deterioration and decay are inevitable, and to intervene in any way is a kind of sacrilege. Indeed, it is the impact of time that is the whole point – you judge a building as beautiful or important *purely because it looks old*, not because of any historical or artistic relevance. Of course, the end point of all this is that every monument will eventually, one day or another, die. But then won't we all?

Next is the cult of historical value, which judges a building as important because it represents a precise and significant moment in time. As Riegl puts it, this cult 'aims for the best possible preservation of a monument in its present state – this requires man to restrain the course of natural development and, to the extent that he is able, to bring the normal progress of disintegration to a halt'. Historical value is all about pressing the stop button on time, keeping a building as close as possible to its original form: conserving it for good, but going neither forwards nor backwards. It represents a deliberate denial of the ageing process – but is similarly opposed to restoring things to how they once were.

Riegl then moves on to the 'present-day cults'. The first is 'use value', which takes a simple, pragmatic approach: 'an old building still in use must be maintained in good enough condition to accommodate people without endangering their lives or their health'. If anything disrupts this – a hole in the roof or a collapse of a wall – then it must be repaired immediately. At the same time, 'use value is basically indifferent to the kind of treatment a monument receives, as long as the monument's existence is not threatened'. So nature and 'age value' can do their worst, but only so far as they won't affect a building's capacity to remain in use.

And finally, there is the cult of 'newness'. This last cult stands absolutely opposed to imperfection. It is a cult of youth. It judges ageing as a disease, and natural processes as destroyers of art and beauty. It always wants to see things at the moment of their creation. Which means that, 'if a monument bearing signs of disintegration is to appeal … the traces of age must be removed first of all, and through restoration of its form and colour appear once again like a newly created work'. Newness is, of course, the sworn enemy of age value.

To add to the complexity, people shift between 'cults' dependent on their own personal knowledge and their preference towards any given monument. Two separate buildings could be treated in exactly the same way, but you love what was done to one, and hate what was done to the other. As Riegl acknowledges, there can be so many competing factors at play that consistency is almost impossible. Unless, he says, you subscribe solely to the first cult, to age value, which, 'is valid for everyone without exception. It claims not only to be above all religious differences, but also to be above differences between the uneducated, art experts and laymen … Even the most limited peasant will be able to distinguish between an old church tower and a new one'. Basically, if you want to avoid an argument, then let all structures live and die in peace …

Riegl knew how debates on conservation and restoration in the latter half of the nineteenth century had become increasingly polarised. Movements had grown up, counter-movements had emerged, rhetoric had escalated to such an extent that the treatment of buildings became a metaphor for the very nature of good and evil. Take the pre-eminent Victorian art critic John Ruskin on the process of restoration: 'it means the most total destruction which a building can suffer', he wrote in his 1849 book *Seven Lamps*. 'The thing is a Lie from beginning to end. You may make a model of a building as you may a corpse, and the model may have the shell of the old walls within it as your cast might have the skeleton … but the old building is destroyed, and that more totally and mercilessly than if it had sunk into a heap of dust, or melted into a mass of clay'.

Ruskin's nemesis at the time was the English architect Sir George Gilbert Scott, who was commissioned regularly to carry out what he called the 'faithful restoration of our ancient churches'. Scott increasingly found himself caught between two opposing camps and bearing the brunt of the invective. 'I am in this, as in other works, obliged to face right and left, to combat at once two enemies from either hand, one wanting me to do too much, and the other finding fault with me for doing anything at all'. The baiting of Scott continued even after his passing – in 1878, the designer William Morris, natural successor of Ruskin and leader of the newly formed pressure group the Society for the Protection of Ancient Buildings, referred to him as a 'happily dead dog'. This was strong stuff. In the end, Riegl concluded sadly, 'we seem to face a hopeless conflict'.

Which brings us back to Stirling. In 1845 (over half a century after Burns cut his poem into the window glass) the Reverend George Cupples, writing in *The New Statistical Account of Scotland*, lamented publicly the diminished state of the castle's Great Hall. He still praised its 'noble and magnificent fabric' but continued that it 'is now occupied by mess-rooms and other accommodation for the garrison, and although in good preservation, is much deteriorated, both in its external and internal appearance'. Included in this deterioration was the removal of the great hammer-beam roof – dismantled around 1790 to allow the addition of a new attic floor to the barracks (what, these days, we would call a loft conversion). Another half century on and King Edward VII complained that the military were 'irrevocably damaging' the castle and ordered its care transferred from the War Office to the Office of Works, who were, as of the passing of the 1882 Ancient Monuments Act, charged with looking after the nation's most important historical buildings. From the outset, however, the first Inspector of Ancient Monuments, Charles Peers, took a hard line against restoration. 'The work carried out upon the ancient buildings in the charge of the Board of Works is to be that of preservation only … restoration as commonly understood (viz. the insertion of new work into the old) will only be permitted … in those cases where the safety of the building absolutely demands such treatment'. And even where safety did demand it, Peers was explicit that 'no attempt should be made to give the appearance of other than modern origin'. This approach was very much in keeping with Riegl's pragmatic definition of 'use value'.

Move on to the mid-point of the twentieth century, however, and attitudes had shifted. The castle had remained in constant military use over this time – and in particular during the two World Wars. Yet in 1949, the Secretary of State for Scotland suddenly and unexpectedly invoked the 'R' word. Asked by parliamentary question what steps he intended to take for the future protection of the Great Hall, he replied 'my department has always had in mind as a long-term policy the desirability of restoring the historic buildings in Stirling Castle'. When the military withdrew in 1964, work began immediately and continued for the next three and a half decades. It is fascinating to think of the challenge this must have presented. Removing the massed debris and detritus of centuries of army occupation, peeling away the layers to find the castle that was once abandoned by a Stewart king. Time and again situations arose where, to paraphrase Charles Peers, the safety of the building demanded treatment. At the sharp end, in among the dust and rubble, there isn't much time for the philosophical musings of Riegl. To an 'age-valuer' all of this was deeply wrong however. Once you intervene, you can't stop. You are entering a realm of supposition and subjectivity. You are setting something new in motion. You are starting an argument that you can't win. But perhaps there is value in that too. Perhaps Riegl's conflict isn't always 'hopeless'? Perhaps it is simply inevitable.

When conservators came to work on the palace exterior at the start of the new millennium, they employed what they described as 'minimal and reversible intervention' so that the stonework was stabilised and deterioration halted as far as possible – removing moss and lichen with water and soft brushes; and filling fissures and pointing cracks with removable acrylic resins and mortars. The overriding principle was 'historical value'. But the interiors required much more substantial work. Here was the cult of 'newness' in action. Just like the Great Hall, many of the rooms had been left as bare shells – although some original features, such as stone fireplaces and wooden doorframes, remained from the early 1500s. Using techniques like tree-ring analysis – to identify the source of the original wood – researchers looked wherever possible to use the same materials throughout the work.

Two of the largest and most time-consuming aspects of the project involved the recreation of the palace tapestries and the 'Stirling Head' roof carvings. For thirteen years an eighteen-strong international team, based at both the West Dean Tapestry Studio in Sussex and a publicly accessible workshop on-site at the castle, designed, weaved and finished their new interpretation of the 'Hunt of the Unicorn'. While they drew inspiration from original sixteenth century tapestries held in New York's Metropolitan Museum of Art, the weavers were explicit that this was, nonetheless, a new work. The process was, according to Caron Penney, Director of the West Dean Studio, 'akin to walking in virgin snow with one track running through it. You set out not wanting to break into another path … eventually you find the confidence to break free and find your own route'.

The replica Stirling Heads were carved not by a team, but by one man, John Donaldson, from the same oak that was used for the originals – remarkably, traced back to a source in Poland. Samples of the new bare oak carvings are now on display in a permanent exhibition held in the upper floors of the restored palace buildings. Donaldson's craftsmanship and detailing are exquisite. So much so that it comes as something of a shock when you see the painted Heads back in place, looking down at you from their mounts on the palace ceiling. The colour-schemes – pieced together from forensic examinations of traces left on the surviving originals – are bright, lurid even, and frequently clashing. I found myself wishing they'd just been left as beautiful, polished, un-coloured oak. The restorations clearly aren't to my taste – but since when did taste have anything to do with historical accuracy?

It is, of course, the same story with some of the world's most famous carved sculptures: the Parthenon Marbles. Go to view them at the British Museum and you will see exactly what you want to see – the apogee of human artistic achievement all fashioned in clean, milky-white marble (made even whiter by being rubbed with wire wool in the 1930s to remove 'dirt'). Of course, what we now know is that, when first erected on the Acropolis some two and a half thousand years ago, they would have been painted in astonishingly bright colours. The 'dirt' that was scoured away included some of the last traces of this ancient pigment. So our vision of the pristine, minimalist and monochrome classical world is a fallacy. And the basis for one of the western world's absolute measures of good taste is a fiction. Had Ruskin – whose love of classical statuary left him famously ill-prepared for the reality of bodily hair – known this in the nineteenth century, you suspect he may have spontaneously combusted. Even when the scientific evidence tells us otherwise, we don't want to hear it. Our preconceptions about history are deep and ingrained. And often wrong. They are arguments waiting to happen.

This, however, is one of the things I love most about our old buildings. About the way we live with the fragments of the past among the present. Riegl's essay is so fascinating because it exposes a conundrum with no easy solution – and perhaps with so solution at all. Go to Stirling Castle and gaze up at that hammer-beam roof. Stare at a ceiling of technicolor oak portraits. Lose yourself in the intricacy of new tapestries inspired by medieval master-weavers. Peer at the 'gold-washing' on the outside of the Great Hall. Love them or hate them, but remember that you are looking at much more than just restored timber, paint, textiles and harling. You are looking at debate and conflict, at centuries of shifting views and disagreements: invective flying back and forth, personal friendships descending into irreparable animosities.

How we treat our heritage goes to the heart of who we are and what we believe. It is personal and emotional and endlessly antagonistic. It is about class, education, art, fashion, politics and, of course, taste. It is about being right and being wrong – sometimes at exactly the same time. Or to put it another way, it is about the essence of human drama mixed up in something as simple as the colour of a wall.

9

Never-Failing Springs in the Desert
James Robertson

Innerpeffray Library, 1600s

A library may be a small affair, or something quite the opposite.

When, in 1867, the young, Dunbar-born environmentalist John Muir set off on his thousand-mile ramble from Indiana to the Gulf of Mexico, he took three books for company: *The New Testament*, John Milton's *Paradise Lost* and Robert Burns's *Poems*. He felt, presumably, that these contained ample brain sustenance for a two-month solitary walk.

Contrast this with the tenth century Grand Vizier of Persia, Abdul Kassam Ismael, who reputedly took his collection of 117,000 books with him wherever he went, on four hundred camels trained to march so that the books stayed in alphabetical order. He did this, so it is said, in order to feel at home.

Perhaps this was also why John Muir opted for three books he already knew intimately, rather than three he had not read. When you set off into the new, the strange, the possibly dangerous, your instinct may be to take something familiar and reassuring, rather than risk being in the company of an author who – you discover too late – bores you, or with whom you have no empathy. Those driven from home by war or famine, or simply in search of a better life, carry the words of their poets and songwriters with them, on paper or in their memories. But once they arrive somewhere else, find a foothold – however tenuous – then the desire to expand thought and knowledge, to meditate on new things, comes again. Libraries spring up in Syrian refugee camps; illegal Mexican immigrants in American cities set up *salas de lectura*, reading-rooms where ideas can be discussed. To open a book is to open your mind to possibilities.

The kings of ancient Egypt established libraries in their farthest-flung territories, and had the words 'Clinic of the Soul' inscribed over the entrances. There is no such grand announcement on the approach to Innerpeffray Library, which is set on a drumlin – a small hill sculpted by glacial ice – above a gentle bend of the River Earn. You are guided there by discreet signage on a country road between Auchterarder and Crieff, down a farm lane to a car park beside the nineteenth century schoolhouse (now the residence of the Keeper of Books). From the car park there is a short walk along a spongey grass path. Huge trees tower overhead. This is deepest Perthshire, still and peaceful. Not a lot appears to have changed in many years. The idea that a building full of possibilities awaits you at the end of the path is scarcely more believable than that the birdsong might suddenly cease, leaving you in some other, unworldly world. You pass weathered gravestones, ancient yews and a long, low building roofed with flagstones – the chapel of the Drummond family – and only then, just keeking over the west gable of the chapel, does the library come into view.

It is a fine, two-storey edifice, white-washed, harled and slated, elegant and unfussy. Constructed between 1757 and 1762, it was described by a later visitor as having the appearance of a Scottish Presbyterian church from that era, but it was custom-built for secular, not religious purposes. In fact it can be seen as a monument to that eighteenth century reconfiguration when, as the American writer John Dos Passos put it, the professor was taking the place of the clergyman as the venerated figure in Scottish society.

Books, too, were venerated: they were keys to better lives – lives more prosperous as well as better-lived. The Bible gave individuals access to God and encouraged self-knowledge: other books gave them access to the world and hence to self-improvement and communal advancement. The Innerpeffray librarian had his lodgings on the ground floor: the books he looked after have theirs in a grander space, a 35ft by 24ft room on the floor above, protected from damp and illuminated by a south-facing triple window as well as single windows to west and east.

Long before the books came, this was a place of learning and re-flection. A chapel associated with the Augustinian abbey at Inchaffray stood on this spot from at least 1283. The present chapel, now barren and cold within (except when used for literary talks and other events associated with the library), was re-founded as a chantry by the then Lord Drummond in 1508, and four chaplains were maintained to say prayers for the souls of his family and that of his king, James IV. But in 1560 the Reformation led by John Knox swept away such practices, the chapel's interior furnishings were removed or destroyed, and it was never again used – at least, not publicly – as a place of worship.

Another century passed, and another Drummond – David, the third

Lord Madertie – was caught up in the wars of the 1640s. He fought as a Royalist alongside the Marquis of Montrose, went into exile after Montrose's final defeat and execution, but returned in the mid-1650s to marry his childhood sweetheart, Beatrix Graham, Montrose's sister. In 1679, civil and religious violence erupted again as Charles II's government sought to crush its Covenanter opponents. Beatrix recorded in her diary that David, by then in his sixties, 'would not be held from riding out … to disperse the unlawfull Assemblies of disaffected folk'. This does not sound like a man much inclined to relax with a book. Yet, the following year, he drew up a will in which he left 3,000 merks (£165 sterling) to maintain his library of some four hundred volumes, which seems already to have been housed, in part, in the west end of the chapel. The will also made provision for the purchase of new books, the employment of a librarian and the building of a schoolhouse. Crucially, the books were to be made available, at no cost, to all inhabitants of the surrounding area who wished to consult them. After Beatrix's death in 1691, Lord Madertie increased the endowment to 5,000 merks (£277). He himself survived until around 1694: we know this because the last time he signed his name in one of the library's books was in that year.

From one of the darkest periods of Scottish history, a man who had wielded his sword in political and religious conflict chose to invest money and hope in a future that might give priority to the printed word, to reflection, to study and to learning. 1680, therefore, marks a kind of turning-point, in intention if not immediately in reality. At Innerpeffray in that year was founded the first, free, public lending library independent of any other institution, in the British Isles.

Madertie's title and property passed to a nephew, William Drummond, 2nd Viscount Strathallan, who carried out his uncle's wishes and established a trust, the Innerpeffray Mortification, which exists to this day, to administer the endowment. To 'mortify' in Scots law is to assign or bequeath in perpetuity land, property or money to an institution, usually for religious, educational or charitable purposes. Several decades passed when there is scant evidence that the books, still housed in the loft of the chapel, were being widely accessed, although librarian succeeded librarian and at one point the trustees had to fight off a takeover bid from the Presbytery of Auchterarder, which suggests that the books, at least, were coveted. All changed, however, when Robert Hay Drummond inherited Innerpeffray in 1739, at the age of twenty-seven.

Destined for a high-flying career in the Church of England, Hay Drummond nevertheless took his responsibilities as a Scottish laird seriously. His first act was to examine the library catalogue and his second to decide that it needed new accommodation. After various false starts and delays, building work commenced in 1757 and the new library was ready for its books five years later. By this time Hay Drummond, a staunch Hanoverian and model citizen of the now United Kingdom of Great Britain, was Archbishop of York, a position he held until his death in 1776.

As beautifully located and as delightful a building as it is, Innerpeffray Library does not reveal its true significance through its setting or physical appearance. The first question likely to occur to a visitor, noting that the nearest settlements of any size are several miles away, is, 'Why here?' The answer lies in the fact that the library was founded in a pre-industrial and largely pre-urban age, when the countryside was more evenly and densely populated than it is today. People were used to travelling long distances, mostly on foot: Innerpeffray, far from being remote or isolated, was the meeting-place of several roads. Until Kinkell Bridge was built in 1760 it was also where a main north–south route crossed the River Earn: there may once have been a Roman bridge, for centuries there was a ford (Robert Hay Drummond's grandson Francis, who inherited the estate in 1804, drowned trying to cross it when the river was in spate in 1810), and as late as 1900 there was a rope or chain ferry.

It has been estimated that during the period 1700–1900 approximately one thousand people lived within a twelve-mile radius of Innerpeffray. There were, therefore, many potential book borrowers in the surrounding area. The Scottish Reformers placed enormous value on people being able to read the Bible for themselves, and both Kirk and, before the Union of 1707, Parliament insisted on education being available to as much of the population, girls as well as boys, as possible. The national mythology is that, while Scotland's people may have been poor compared with the English, a higher percentage of them, throughout the seventeenth and eighteenth centuries, were literate. Travellers often commented on how eager Scots of all classes were to enter into debate on almost any subject from religion to farming methods.

Not that this in itself proves a high level of literacy, although it might indicate a national liking for disputatiousness. Very few families could afford to dispense with the labour of their children beyond the age of nine or ten and, even if they could, their schooling was likely to be seasonal or sporadic. Nevertheless, in the eighteenth century more and more journals and books were being published and distributed, and their contents could be shared through readings at private and public gatherings. The King

James Bible remained the central text of family and community life and was intimately known, as Robert Burns's 'Cotter's Saturday Night' shows, not just in the image of the sire reading to his kin after supper, but in the detail of what passage he might choose:

> *The priest-like father reads the sacred page,*
> *How Abram was the friend of God on high;*
> *Or, Moses bade eternal warfare wage*
> *With Amalek's ungracious progeny;*
> *Or, how the royal Bard did groaning lie*
> *Beneath the stroke of Heaven's avenging ire;*
> *Or Job's pathetic plaint, and wailing cry;*
> *Or rapt Isaiah's wild, seraphic fire;*
> *Or other holy Seers that tune the sacred lyre.*

But the very nature of Presbyterianism – with its inbuilt tensions between authority and democracy, conformity and challenge, obedience and curiosity – meant that the desire for knowledge stimulated *by* Scripture could not be confined *to* Scripture. Once you had opened the Bible and read it for yourself, or heard it read, you had effectively opened yourself to every other book under the sun. Thus Scottish popular culture learned to respect and value the printed word, and this was in part a reflection of the intellectual flowering, centred on Edinburgh but with outgrowths across the land, which we now call the Scottish Enlightenment. And thus, in 1840, even as the bloom of that age was fading, Thomas Carlyle could proclaim the Man of Letters as a modern hero, and write: 'No magic *Rune* is stranger than a Book. All that Mankind has done, thought, gained or been: it is lying as in magic preservation in the pages of Books.'

One of Innerpeffray's special assets is its register of borrowers. Apart from the period between 1927 and 1950, when the keepers appear to have been negligent in their duties, the register records every loan made from 5 June 1747 – a James Sharp took out *The Life and Death of the Twelve Apostles*, promising to return it in three months 'under the penaltie of ten shillings' – to 27 May 1968, when Agnes Torbet borrowed five books, including *Lives of the Primitive Fathers*, published in 1640. After the Second World War borrowings were infrequent, and once Agnes had returned her books lending ceased. But between those two dates the register tells us much about who was using the library, and what they were reading.

From 1747 to 1800, 1,483 loans were recorded, mainly of religious volumes although William Robertson's *History of the Reign of Charles V* was the most heavily borrowed. Ministers, schoolmasters and others whom one might expect to be bookish appear in the register, but other users' occupations include barber, cooper, dyer, farmer, gardener, glover, mason, merchant, miller, quarrier, smith, surgeon, watchmaker, weaver and wright. Apprentices and servants also took out books, as did a small number of women (but other women may have read the books borrowed in the names of their menfolk).

All this does support the view that the literati of Edinburgh were operating in neither an intellectual nor a geographical bubble. Burns, despite being hailed by one of those literati, Henry Mackenzie, as 'this Heaven-taught ploughman', went to school for three years and was a wide-ranging reader even while labouring on his father's farm. When he and his friends established the Bachelors' Club at Tarbolton, they did so because they wanted to debate the ideas and events of the day. What was going on in Ayrshire was undoubtedly also going on in Perthshire, perhaps in part stimulated by the contents of Innerpeffray Library.

Over the next fifty years there were 4,533 loans, with religious books giving ground to history, philosophy, natural history and science. In the second half of the nineteenth century the novels of Sir Walter Scott became the most popular items, and usage again increased – but then, so too did literacy levels. In 1897, a particularly busy year, 866 books were borrowed. If the library's usage declined thereafter, this was mainly because of the arrival of a golden age of free access to books and information elsewhere.

The Public Library Acts of the 1850s had given local burghs the right to raise taxes in order to establish libraries. The problem was, the relatively small number of ratepayers tended to be very reluctant to see their taxes rise for the dubious benefit of giving the working classes free access to knowledge. Who knew where that might lead? From the 1880s, however, this move towards a universal public library system was massively boosted by the philanthropy of Andrew Carnegie: local government authorities could apply to Carnegie's charitable foundation for funds to build libraries. What resulted was a network of working monuments dedicated to the printed word. They varied enormously in size and style, yet the tiny reading room added on to the village hall at Tarves, in Aberdeenshire, and the mighty edifice that is Dumbarton Library grew from the same seed – a recognition of the transformational power of books. In the end, well over 2,500 Carnegie libraries were built worldwide, 660 of them in the British Isles, at least seventy of these in Scotland.

The first of them all, the Central Library in Carnegie's home town of Dunfermline, opened in 1883. From the French Beaux-Arts-influenced libraries of James R Rhind in many districts of Glasgow, to the equally splendid libraries in a range of architectural styles from Dumfries to Wick and from Dundee to Stornoway, the Carnegie libraries became places of self-education, sanctuary, peace and discovery for hundreds of thousands of people, many of whom lived in circumstances that closed down opportunities to change their lives for the better. As William McIlvanney put it in his poem, 'In the Library':

> *In the library the first time*
> *I stood in a pool of awe.*
> *Wonder for taking, acres of promises.*

The experience of Dundee, the city nearest to where I now live, was not untypical. In the early years of the twentieth century Carnegie funded five libraries there – more than anywhere else in Scotland apart from Glasgow – but these were not Dundee's first. A free public library had opened within the Albert Memorial Institute in 1869: subscribers who paid an annual fee had immediate access to new books, while those who could not afford to subscribe had to wait a year before they could borrow them. Then, in 1895, a library and public baths, paid for by a legacy from the mill owner Thomas Cox, opened at Lochee, but the popular demand for access to books continued to outstrip supply and the city corporation turned to Carnegie for help. The city architect, James Thomson, designed all five Carnegie-funded buildings, including Coldside, a single-storey beauty with a neo-classical curved frontage, and the imposingly pillared Blackness Library in the west of the city. Both are still in operation today. These are places that proudly announce through their architecture, 'We value books, and we value the people who want to read them.' When the Dundee songwriter Michael Marra composed his song 'Hermless' he impertinently (his own word) suggested it as an alternative, non-aggressive national anthem for Scotland. I like to imagine the meek, self-effacing hero of that song collecting his reading matter from one of these fine places:

> *Hermless, hermless*
> *There's never nae bather fae me*
> *I ging to the lehbry, I tak oot a book*
> *And then I go hame for ma tea*

Andrew Carnegie visited Dundee, for the third time, in 1911, to open St Roque's Library in the Blackscroft are. On this occasion he commented that he thought future generations would say, 'Well, well, there were men and there were cities in that day that did pretty well.' That building is now a music venue which acknowledges its heritage by using the name etched in stone over the entrance, Reading Rooms. Its website carries the cheeky strapline 'Authorised by the Dùn Dèagh Department of Counter Culture' and notes that

> *the site was laid out as a landscaped garden in the Italian style, in an attempt to upgrade what was described at the time as a 'sordid district'. Many Edwardians held the belief that by improving a district you could improve the people who lived there – they may even have been right!*

Between Innerpeffray's David Drummond and Andrew Carnegie there have been many other benefactors who left libraries to the Scottish people. Walter Stirling, a Glasgow merchant, left his own book collection as the basis for a free reference library in 1791: it occupied his former home in Miller Street, and was moved to other locations before settling in the Royal Exchange building, as one of the city's branch libraries, in the 1950s. Stephen Mitchell, one of a dynasty of tobacco merchants, left a substantial bequest in 1874 which, with additional funds from others including Carnegie (who laid the foundation stone), enabled the construction in 1911 of Glasgow's great Mitchell Library, designed by W B Whitie. James Dick, who with his brother Robert founded an enormously successful business making shoes and other items from gutta-percha, provided the funds for Kilmarnock's Dick Institute, a museum, art gallery and library which was opened in 1901 and remains a vital cultural asset for East Ayrshire to this day. On the other side of the country, the publishing firm of Thomas Nelson funded most of Edinburgh's branch libraries – but the capital's cathedral-like Central Library on George IV Bridge is one of Carnegie's. When it was finished in 1890, he sent a telegram to be read out at the opening ceremony: 'We trust that this library is to grow in usefulness year after year, and prove one of the most potent agencies for the good of the people for all time to come.' Over the entrance was carved Carnegie's favoured motto, 'Let There Be Light'. Ironically, a recent decision by the city council to permit a new hotel at the Cowgatehead will have the effect, if the development goes ahead, of cutting out much of the light that the Central Library's reading rooms have enjoyed for 130 years.

Of all the Scottish Carnegie libraries, two are linked in my mind by personal associations. One is Stirling's turreted and many-windowed Central Library. I retain fond memories of it because it was there that my mother took me to be issued with my own first borrower's tickets. There, too, aged about eleven and having exhausted my interest in the contents of the children's shelves, I was granted access to the adult department through heavy, glass-panelled swing doors. Pushing open those doors required a little effort but, in the exhilaration of stepping into a new world, I hardly noticed.

Far to the north, just a few miles from Andrew Carnegie's Highland home at Skibo, is the much smaller and simpler red sandstone library of Dornoch. It was there, more than half a century later, that I had to return my mother's last borrowed book after her death.

*

Innerpeffray may be Scotland's earliest public lending library, but it is not the oldest building in the country specifically designed *as* a library. That honour goes to Bishop Leighton's Library, built in the 1680s in the precincts of Dunblane Cathedral, only twenty miles from Innerpeffray. I first came across Robert Leighton in the 1990s while researching for my novel *The Fanatic*, which is partly set in the 1670s when the third Lord Madertie was charging round the countryside breaking up Covenanters' conventicles. Leighton, the son of a staunchly Presbyterian minister, reluctantly endorsed the return of Episcopacy following the Restoration of Charles II in 1660, and was made Bishop of Dunblane (Scotland's poorest diocese) the following year, when he was fifty. He has always seemed to me like a man born about a century too early, who would have been far happier in Enlightenment Scotland. In a sermon preached before the Scottish Parliament he argued that it was more godly to be calmly and meekly wrong than to be 'stormy and furiously orthodox'. If he had a voice like a trumpet, he said, 'I would sound a retreat from our unnatural contentions and irreligious strivings for religion. Oh, what are the things we fight for compared to the great things of God!'

As things transpired he was whistling in the wind rather than trumpeting. In 1670, he was appointed Archbishop of Glasgow at the personal request of Charles II, but failed to bring about any reconciliation between the Covenanters and the Government. He thought religious persecution was like 'scaling heaven with ladders fetched out of hell', while radical Presbyterians thought him guilty of 'holy wobbling', which makes him sound like a hopelessly reasonable man in an unreasonable age. In 1674 he retired, presumably with a huge sigh of relief, to Sussex. He died in London in 1684, leaving £100 in his will towards the cost of building a home for his collection of 1,363 books and 149 pamphlets. In fact, the final bill came to £162 2s 6d, the difference being made up by his friend the 1st Viscount Strathallan, whose son set up the Innerpeffray Mortification a few years later. There are definite similarities between the two libraries, which suggests that when Innerpeffray was designed eighty years later the Bibliotheca Leightoniana was a useful model.

Leighton's Library is on two storeys: the ground storey (now used for storage) has a barrel-vaulted ceiling and the upper storey, where the books are kept, is accessed by an external stair. The upper room is lined with presses which hold some 4,500 books. The library was established for the benefit of local clergy – Leighton was a considerable scholar, and his own books, which formed the nucleus of the collection, were mainly theological – but in the mid-eighteenth century it opened its doors to a wider circle of subscribers. This enabled more books to be purchased: there are significant works of philosophy and history from the Enlightenment and a large collection of pamphlets related to the Disruption of 1843. In 1988, three centuries after the library's establishment, a funding appeal was launched which led to it being refurbished and re-opened to the public in 1990. It is now run by a trust in collaboration with the library of the University of Stirling.

I grew up three miles from Dunblane yet was ignorant of Leighton's Library until many years later. No doubt my life has not been directly affected by its quiet existence. No doubt, too, Scotland would remain Scotland if this wee cultural gem were not at its heart. Of course, we could also all get by without Innerpeffray Library. If the world's first library for working-class people, the miners' library established at Leadhills, Lanarkshire in 1741, did not still exist, at this late day nobody would think to invent it. Without the Glasgow Women's Library, established in 1991 and now, after several flits, securely housed in the former Carnegie library in Bridgeton, Scottish women would survive. The library in the Royal Botanical Gardens in Edinburgh is the national repository for specialist botanical and horticultural books and other resources, but gardeners and growers would keep gardening and growing if it ceased to be. Poets would be no poorer, in financial terms at least, without the riches contained in the Scottish Poetry Library, in Edinburgh's Old Town. None of these places has the presence, the budget or the assets of, say, the National Library of Scotland or the libraries of our universities, such as the astonishing 2012 glass tower that is the Sir Duncan Rice Library at the University of Aberdeen. But that is not the point. The point is that these – and other curated collections of books in buildings across the country – are part of a complex set of narratives that tell us who we are and where we have been, and also suggest to us future directions of travel. This is why it matters that they came into being, and that they survive.

There is, as I have tried to show, a close historical link between access to books and Scottish aspirations to self-improvement, egalitarianism and liberty, but at root this is no tale of Scottish exceptionalism. People the world over respect books and libraries because they represent freedom of thought. To read a book in a library, or to borrow one and take it away to read somewhere else, is to set up a private relationship between you and the book – its author, its ideas, its characters, its complete otherness. No other activity can create quite such a relationship: that really is exceptional. It is why oppressors and suppressors of all kinds, secular or religious, ban books or burn them. And, as Michael Marra wrote in another of his songs, 'Houseroom', it is why in some places people risk death or indeed are killed trying to have that experience:

If you ever hear me grumbling
Give me the old heave ho
If it's I want my MTV
My prick shaped pool
And my interactive video

Don't give me houseroom
But a scornful look
As some soul makes a midnight sprint
Through a sniper's sights
For a library book

Weighing all this up, we might conclude that there must be a consensus in this land that libraries are a Good Thing. We would be wrong. There is a view, not infrequently expressed, that libraries are of the past, expensive spaces providing unnecessary services in the digital age. I have heard this opinion voiced by local councillors and council executives, the very custodians of the library as a public amenity. Perhaps it should not be a surprise that, in the face of ever tighter budgets from which to deliver education, social care, waste disposal and recycling, the idea grows that 'culture and leisure' are dispensable. This leads rapidly to the idea that a library, any library, is just a lot of books on shelves and that if volunteers can be found to manage the lending and returning of them then the books will look after themselves. It's an even shorter step from there to saying that a library is just a free bookshop, and why should everybody pay taxes for a free bookshop when those who really want books can go and buy them themselves, in 'real' bookshops? That is, if you can find such a place – there are some local authority areas in twenty-first century Scotland which contain not a single shop dedicated to selling new books. Yet, go into almost any public library and you will find it being used by children, students, pensioners, visitors and homeless people – for all of whom it is still, as it was in the nineteenth century, a vital place of information, investigation, refuge, hope and renewal.

In the libraries of our cities, it is often difficult to find a free desk, so great is the demand for a place to sit and read. A city that does not have a great library is something less than a city – it is not *really* civilised. Perhaps more tellingly, when a socially deprived neighbourhood loses its local library – sometimes the last remaining community space after the closure of factories, shops, pubs and schools – it feels to the residents like an act of officially sanctioned vandalism. That's because that's what it is. Andrew Carnegie wrote: 'There is not such a cradle of democracy upon the earth as the Free Public Library; this republic of letters, where neither rank, office nor wealth receives the slightest consideration. A library outranks any other one thing a community can do to benefit its people. It is a never-failing spring in the desert.'

One can argue with other aspects of Carnegie's career as an industrialist and capitalist, but that is a noble statement of principle, one that he backed up with vast amounts of his own money. It is a principle that needs to be loudly restated and proudly upheld a century after his death.

10

The Lost Estate
James Crawford

Mavisbank House, 1723

The path was barely half a metre wide, a muddy furrow that descended into a thicket of laurel trees. I passed through, turned a sharp corner, and for the first time I could see the valley. The ground fell away in wide humps covered in wildgrass. Somewhere below me was the north tributary of the River Esk. On the other side of the valley, just visible, a line of houses hugged the top of the rise. Ahead there were more trees: birch, yew and elm. Everything was overgrown, but the line of the path endured – an invitation to keep going.

I was alone and hadn't seen another person since starting out. It was a cold afternoon, almost preternaturally still. For long stretches there was no sound but my steps, although every now and then I heard skitterings in the undergrowth. The wildlife, at least, knew that I was there. As I approached one clump of ferns a fat ring-necked pheasant rose up in an explosive thrum of wingbeats and hurtled fast and low down the valley. Then all was quiet again. The land levelled out, the path widened, and through the trees I could make out glimpses of a wide meadow of tussocky grass. Crows started to call back and forth, as if they were passing a message down the line – *here comes a stranger.*

I caught sight of the house. It was just a glimpse, the dark triangle of a pediment in a gap between a distant holly tree and a row of almost leafless silver birch. The path twisted, the view was obscured, but with the next turn the house was there again. Soon I could just make out the sculpted stonework inside the pediment, an unresolved squiggle of bluey grey. Next there were a couple of large windows, two murky shapes topped with a triangle and semi-circle. Then they were gone.

The way became lost underneath a mass of fallen leaves. In some places the frost had not lifted and the leaves squeaked and crunched underfoot. In others they lay stacked and wet and I sank into them up to my ankles.

When I finally emerged from the trees the path widened. It was recognisable now for what it had been three centuries ago: one of the original driveways. It skirted the edge of the large meadow, then curved back towards the house, which was still obscured by its own bank of trees. Ahead, on the other side of a metal gate and a wooden stile, a bright blue shipping container sat squat and self-conscious. A mass of globe thistles – blue-black from the winter cold – fringed the final curve of the drive. Some reared up high over my head, their tattered lower leaves shrouding their stems. They accompanied me on this last stretch with their seed heads bowed, like a procession of mourners.

There was a shocking suddenness to arriving in front of the house. The landscape had mostly shielded it until then. Now it glared down at me – at first startled, then affronted. It was like walking in on an elderly relative in a state of undress. I didn't know quite where to look. A steel gate – at least twice my height – stood between us, covered in bright 'danger' and 'no unauthorized access' signs. The house loomed. It couldn't help it. Six of the nine windows facing me were bricked or boarded up. The other three were barred with struts of scaffolding. The once dignified steps leading to the front door were cracked, uneven, and covered in a welcome carpet of thick moss. In the late-afternoon light, the stonework was a shade of pale grey-blue – but always outlined in green. Weeds sprouted from every flat surface of the facade. Grass covered the eaves, cornices and lintels and ran up and down the slopes of the pediment – neo-classical architecture clad in a humble turf roof. If someone told you that this building had spent the last hundred years or so underwater, you wouldn't doubt them.

The house regained its composure quickly though. Its embarrassment at my arrival was replaced by haughtiness and studied indifference. Now it wasn't so much looking at me as through me, towards something distant. Who could blame it, in its current parlous state, for indulging in reveries of better times? Perhaps it was gazing all the way back to its birth – and to the man who, with unashamed boldness, had once conceived it as the embodiment, in stone, of a brand new Scotland.

*

On 24 October 1694, John Clerk, the eighteen-year-old son of the first baronet of the Midlothian estate of Penicuik, cast off from South Queensferry bound for the Dutch port of Rotterdam. His father wept at their parting, but the younger Clerk was too excited by the prospect of adventure to feel any distress. He was on his way to Leiden, one of Europe's most prestigious universities, and his ship, *The Dragon*, sailed as part of a large merchant fleet guarded by two forty-gun Dutch frigates. The frigates were a necessary defence: French privateers hunted the waters of the North Sea for cargo to seize for their Crown. Clerk's journey would take him through a war zone.

The fleet toiled for eight days in rough weather. They were within fifty leagues of the Dutch coast when, in the dark hours of a Sabbath morning, the attack came – five French Men of War approaching under full sail. Four coal ships were caught and set ablaze. Clerk watched them burn on the horizon as the fleet made a dash for the nearest port. In the chaos, a Dutch flyboat rammed *The Dragon*, damaging its mast and rigging, and threatening to break the whole ship to pieces. It was, Clerk later wrote, 'a dismal scene'. At that moment, with his youthful enthusiasm rather dimmed by abject terror, he wished only to return to the comforts of his country house at Penicuik. Daylight came, however, revealing that they had eluded the French and had made it to the coast. Within a week Clerk was ensconced in his lodgings at Leiden, just twenty miles north of Rotterdam.

His studies ranged across mathematics, philosophy, history, divinity and – prompted by the continual urgings of his father – civil law. He became an accomplished musician, skilled in both theory and practice, and was instructed in art and drawing by Willem van Mieris, son of Frans van Mieris, the renowned portraitist of the Dutch Golden Age. His closest friend at Leiden was Herman Boerhaave, the pioneering physician, botanist and chemist, with whom he maintained a lifelong correspondence. Clerk took the greatest pleasure from the opportunity to read the Classics with one of Europe's leading scholars of antiquity, Jacob Gronovius. 'I may truly say' Clerk wrote, 'that I was never so happy as when learning something out of a book'. In his early days at Leiden he recalled being so caught up in his studies that he would discover he had 'been a whole month without going out of the house or putting on my clothes'.

In the summer of 1697, against his father's wishes, Clerk left Leiden for Rome. 'Nothing in life had ever made me happy if I had denied myself this great pleasure and satisfaction' he wrote in his memoirs. Once in the Italian capital, he resumed his studies in law, and became the music pupil of the composer Bernardo Pasquini and the violin virtuoso Arcangelo Corelli. All the while he walked the streets of the city, consumed with admiration for the fragments of architecture the ancient Romans had left behind.

To the great relief of his father, Clerk finally made plans to return to Scotland. He travelled via Naples and Paris, but his heart remained in Rome. Of the French capital, he had little positive to say about its buildings. 'Everything I saw seemed only to be a copy of some great original ... Houses, palaces, villas, gardens, statues, pictures, were all mean in comparison with what I had observed in Italy.' By the winter of 1699 – five years after he had left – he was back at the family home of Penicuik House.

Few gentlemen could boast as eclectic and cosmopolitan an education – Clerk was one of Scotland's earliest and most conscientious Grand Tourists. On his immediate return, however, he had to put aside his cultural passions and find a job. In 1700 he was admitted to the Faculty of Advocates. Two years later he was elected to the Scottish Parliament as a member for the burgh of Whithorn. This sidestep into politics was, more than anything, an accident of marriage. His first wife, Lady Margaret Stuart, was the cousin of the Duke of Queensbury, the Lord High Commissioner to the Scottish Parliament. When Margaret died in childbirth, and Clerk sank into illness and depression, Queensbury sought to revive the young widower by ushering him towards the distractions of public office. The Duke was also, rather less charitably, looking to muster his forces for the battles to come.

Clerk was stepping into a political maelstrom. In his first parliamentary session of 1703 he was appointed to an inquiry into the public accounts and national debt of Scotland: assessing the dire state of the country's finances after the infamous Darien scheme, the catastrophic attempt at establishing a trading colony on Panama. Standing out as diligent and highly accomplished, he was recruited again in 1705 to a second inquiry, this time considering the difficulties in the nation's trade and commerce. Then came the big one – an invitation to the constitutional stramash to end all constitutional stramashes. He was nominated by Queen Anne as one of thirty-one commissioners to negotiate a Treaty of Union between Scotland and England. He was still just thirty years old.

Clerk's first reaction was reluctance. 'This choice, however honourable to me,' he wrote, 'was very far from giving me the least pleasure or satisfaction, for I had observed a great backwardness in the Parliament of Scotland for a Union with England of any kind whatsoever.' Queensbury was furious, and threatened to 'withdraw all friendship' – not least because, while it was the Queen who had made the official selection of commissioners, it was really the Duke, a keen advocate of Union, who had compiled her list. Clerk was being swept up in the relentless momentum of history: 'I suffered myself to be prevailed upon', as he put it. In April 1706, he travelled to London to begin the negotiations. Some ten weeks later he and his fellow commissioners returned to Edinburgh with a treaty of twenty-five articles – a treaty that asked the Scottish Parliament to vote itself out of existence.

The public response was angry and vociferous. Demonstrations were widespread; rioting isolated yet enthusiastic. The Kirk, fearing for its continued autonomy, filled its Sunday services with warnings of ruin and social collapse. God, it seemed, was firmly anti-Union. 'In a corner of the street', wrote Clerk, 'you may see a Presbyterian minister, a Popish priest, and an Episcopal prelate, all agreeing their discourse against the Union, but upon quite different views and contradictory reasons.' By this stage, he estimated that 'not even one percent approved' of what was being proposed. But he could see no alternative. 'Some are regretting the extreme poverty of the nation and scarcity of money; yet, notwithstanding, they exclaim against the Union as a thing that will ruin us; not considering how any condition of life we can fall into, can render us more miserable and poor than we are.'

The Scottish Parliament's 'Great Debate' lasted from 3 October 1706 to 16 January 1707. It was, as Clerk described it, 'a wrestling-ring where members came forward like prize-fighters ready to exchange blows rather than thoughts'. After many bouts, and against the overwhelming weight of popular opinion, it ratified its own dissolution by 110 votes to 67. The Treaty and Act of Union came into force on 1 May 1707, and by 23 October the first ever parliament of Great Britain was convened at Westminster. Clerk was one of its members. Just a year later he left politics and was appointed – thanks to Queensbury again – as one of five judges at Edinburgh's new Scottish Court of the Exchequer.

After the better part of a decade operating amid a constitutional earthquake, Clerk was free once again (as a judge he sat for only three months of the year) to devote himself to literature, art, antiquities and the classics: as he wrote at the time, in an echo of his student days, 'all my leisure hours are spent in books'. Yet a sense of ambivalence over the Treaty of Union – and his role in its adoption – never left him. In 1714 the Jacobite politician George Lockhart of Carnwarth wrote *Memoirs Concerning the Affairs of Scotland,* which set out the accusation that English bribery of Scottish parliamentarians had swung the vote. It was a slur that stuck and nearly 80 years later was sealed in the popular consciousness by Robert Burns:

> *O would, ere I had seen the day*
> *That Treason thus could sell us,*
> *My auld grey head had lien in clay,*
> *Wi' Bruce and loyal Wallace!*

But pith and power, till my last hour,
I'll mak this declaration;
We're bought and sold for English gold
Such a parcel of rogues in a nation!

Clerk dismissed Lockhart's account as 'silly' and set about writing a response to the claims that the Union had been 'brought about by compulsion and corruption'. Whatever heat he felt at the questioning of his own political conduct did not thaw the glacial speed of his work, however. His *History of the Union of Scotland and England* was some forty years in the making – eighteen of which involved him reading every classical history he could find to improve his style. The result of this massive undertaking was 360,000 words over six books tracing 'Union' as an idea which moved from 'the days of Julius Caesar down to the accomplishment of this great work in 1707'. His task was complicated further by his decision to write it in Latin – a self-conscious and ultimately clumsy attempt to place himself alongside his Roman heroes. As the years passed he held on tight to his ever-growing piles of draft manuscripts, unsure he would ever make them public. Finally in 1751, four years before his death, he submitted them to an Edinburgh bookseller with a cursory note saying they could be published 'if you think them worth your trouble'. The end result was sweeping, ambitious, muddled and defensive, and driven by the deeply problematic thesis of the Union as manifest political destiny. Yet for all its flaws, it shows us much about Clerk the man.

In particular there is a telling passage from the early part of his *History* outlining the Roman failure to conquer Scotland – or, as Clerk had it, unite them in 'a single well-grafted society'.

> *The Caledonians, either through love of liberty or from a deep-seated hatred of the Romans, continually rejected the society offered as though it were intolerable slavery. Nor ever after could they be induced to submit to a foreign king or a foreign people for longer than it took them to collect their strength and set themselves free. So the Romans could scarcely acquire Caledonia, much less keep it, a fact due in part to the bravery of its people and in part to its rugged terrain.*

You can sense Clerk's chest swelling in the writing. He follows this instantly, however, with a rebuke – to the reader and, you suspect, to himself as well: 'But the descendants of those Caledonians today should take care not to boast of their resistance too much, for to be proud of their refusal of Roman rule means admitting that one's ancestors were barbarians with no claim to civilisation whatever.'

I was standing in front of what was left of Clerk's personal claim to civilisation: the lonely shell of Mavisbank House. All buildings must, to a greater or lesser extent, absorb and exhibit some of the character of their creators. Few structures, though, can be quite so singular in their expression of one individual life. Mavisbank was Clerk. And Clerk was Mavisbank.

He embarked on its construction in 1723, a year after his father's death and his inheritance of the baronetcy of Penicuik. It was typical of Clerk that its design was both informed by and commemorated in a 1,500-line poem – 'The Country Seat' – which he composed in parallel. Styled after the most famous of Roman poets, Virgil (although sharing little of the literary merit), the poem was, in effect, an exhaustive guide to estate planning, covering everything from how to choose and landscape a site to advising on building materials, floorplans, heating, fire-proofing and even interior decoration. This was an instruction manual dressed up as a poem, a guide to taste, refinement and what Clerk called – and, indeed, claimed to possess – 'Fine Genius'. *'Choose not a Seat too lofty nor too low'* he advised:

> *But on a River's Bank or downy Plain*
> *That gently slopes to the meridian Sun.*
> *Let many lofty Trees with Spreading Tops*
> *Defend you from the Cold of Northern Blasts.*
> *Let here and there be seen some little Hills*
> *Fit pasture for your harmless bleating Flocks*
> *Let all the Fields in view be chequered round*
> *With flowry meadows Groves and plenteous Springs,*
> *Or Rivulets descending from the higher Grounds*

This description – which notably adapts classical principles to the vagaries of the Scottish climate – is well matched with the setting of Mavisbank. The house nestles part-way down the south bank of the River North Esk, sheltered by tall trees and protected by slopes to its immediate north and north-west. It would be hard to fault Clerk's location. Stillness and peace seem to define this little valley. And now, of course, absence too.

'The Country Seat' also advised on the form of the perfect house – going further than you would reasonably expect of poetry to list exact dimensions for breadth, width and height (all rooms on the upper 'chief' floor, for instance, were to be between 16 and 20 feet broad …). Indeed, Clerk argued that one dwelling was not enough for a truly refined laird. Four were required, each for a different purpose: the 'Royal Palace', the 'House of State', the 'Usefull House', and the 'Villa'. While Mavisbank perhaps falls somewhere between these last two, its role was clear. It was to be a site of retreat and contemplation. A refuge from the urban world where the pursuit of art and culture were paramount. A place where Clerk could forever lose himself in books. A place where he could live out his fantasies of antiquity. A place where he could be a true Roman.

Clerk was assisted in his design for Mavisbank by another keen devotee of the classical world – an up-and-coming architect by the name of William Adam. Today the Adam name is recognised as perhaps the most significant in Scottish architecture: thanks to the work of William himself, and also to his three architect sons John, James and, above all, Robert. At Mavisbank, however, it was Clerk who dominated. Adam prepared designs to his client's specifications, largely along the lines of the principles laid out in 'The Country Seat'. Wherever they deviated, Clerk requested revisions. In a letter accompanying his initial draft, Adam referred to the house as 'a very small box, and Genteell too' and suggested adding an extra storey. 'If I had complied' wrote Clerk, 'the fabric would have looked like a Tower, and been quite spoiled'. He did concede, however, that there was something rather too squat and dense about the house on its own – perhaps the reference to a 'small box' stung. So they made the addition of two pavilions linked to the main building by tall quadrant walls. The result, as Clerk put it in his poem, is of the building appearing to reach out to visitors in a 'Kind Embrace'.

I followed the line of the protective fence around the side of the house, a steel and razor wire perimeter that the 'The Country Seat' neither recommended nor anticipated. Certainly, it rather lessened the kindness of the intended embrace. All the same, even in its current dilapidated and hollowed-out state, the elegance of its design persisted. What I found more surprising, however, was that so too did a spark of life. I didn't feel – as Clerk once said disparagingly of Blenheim Palace – that it was 'more a monument for the Dead than a House for the Living'. Perhaps this was because the scale of the place was manageable. I could still see Clerk here with his second wife and young family, lost in his books and his manuscripts. If I squinted a little – ok, a lot – the weeds fell away and the cracks healed. What he called his 'summer pavilion' returned, and, just like an eighteenth century visitor once remarked, I could picture myself 'in a valley near Tivoli' on the outskirts of Rome.

I made my way up the steep hill at the back of the house. Once, this ascent was managed by a winding path of planted hedgerows, opening up at the summit to a wide plateau. Clerk – unsurprisingly an enthusiastic and committed antiquarian – believed he had built alongside what he called a 'Roman Station' and was delighted to have established a continuum between his own villa and an ancient imperial outpost. In reality this rise was what remained of an Iron Age hill fort – Clerk was closer to his 'barbarian' ancestors than to what he perceived as his intellectual forebears. There was no hedge now. Indeed, there was hardly anything at all. I was walking over a slope of exposed and denuded tree roots poking through an indeterminate mossy black mulch littered with tiny twigs and wood chips. At some point, heavy machinery had stripped this slope of all of its vegetation. The accompanying noise must have made for a short, shocking rift in the silence of the valley. I could, however, spot signs of new life in the exposed soil. When I looked up I saw two young deer watching me from the trees on the other side of the rise. We all stood still for a moment, and then, as I raised my foot to take another step, they were gone, their white tails flashing into the undergrowth.

Clerk had particular ideas about the role of nature in the ideal estate. 'Tis a beauty to see things natural' he wrote, and he counselled against too much intervention: 'Nature requires the Gardiners helping hand', he advised in 'The Country Seat', 'Yet never force her with unkindly art'. He favoured subtle curation, the adaptation of a site's given features – woods, trees, streams and rivers – that was unshowy, proportionate and seamless. From the top of the hill I could look north-east past the house and down the Esk valley. You could still just about discern the lines of planting, accentuated in the late autumn by the mix of evergeen and deciduous trees, the latter standing out in haphazard rows of vibrant orange. Clerk had certainly succeeded in creating an idyll, an estate that placed landscape and architecture in an elegant, beautiful balance. Beyond the most distant trees I could see the brown ridges of ploughed fields. And in the other direction, just over the hill to the north-west – although never visible from the house – was the village of Loanhead.

There is no mention of Loanhead in 'The Country Seat'. The closest Clerk comes to admitting the outside world to his rural retreat is to allow the option of a faraway view of a 'great Metropolis or Town', its 'gilded spires' gleaming in the sun – a useful reminder that the time must always come to leave behind what he called the intoxicating and 'powerful draughts' of the countryside and return to work. For some, however, there was no opportunity to ever *escape* from work. It was the nameless residents of the then twenty-odd houses of Loanhead – the colliers who hacked away at the extensive coal-seams beneath Clerk's Midlothian lands, the bearers who carried the lumps up to the surface – who helped to build Mavisbank.

There can be few environments further removed from 'The Country Seat' than the pitch-dark, multi-level, subterranean warrens of the 'room and stoop' mines, where it was only the 'pillars' of unexcavated coal that stopped the low roofs from collapsing. Paradise was built upon Purgatory, and it is one of the ironies of the current plight of Mavisbank that its structural integrity is compromised by subsidence caused by the removal of such large amounts from the earth beneath it. Coal was one of the main sources of the Clerk fortune. Indeed, a key reason for picking the location of Mavisbank was to allow closer management of the adjacent colliery. At that time, everyone in Loanhead – as in mining communities across the country – was bound to the coal they worked. They had no rights to leave or to find other employment. Runaways were pursued, returned, publicly punished and then sent straight back down the mines. 'Freedom' came from exhausting the seam, from extracting all the coal there was.

This, for Clerk, was very much as it should have been. He believed that his colliers could only elevate themselves through hard work. He once referred to them as 'a society of thieves', and it was written into his coal grieve's terms of service that severe fines were to be applied for any instances of immorality, indolence or drunkenness. Yet the residents of Loanhead were not alone in being judged – and found wanting – by Clerk. He regarded his landed contemporaries with a similar mixture of frustration and condescension. Admonishing them for living in crude, 'cold, unwholsome' old tower houses, he urged them to rebuild and rediscover the ancient standards – and in so doing, embrace the modern world. With Mavisbank, Clerk was creating a template. His house was about more than simply demonstrating personal taste and status. It was about redefining Scotland too. As he said at the time of the Act of Union, nothing 'can render us more miserable and poor than we are'. He looked around at his country, and wanted it to be so much better. He wanted it to be more like him.

Clerk's story, in its most basic terms, is a staple of family dramas down the ages. It is about someone who leaves the narrow confines of their domestic environment to discover a wider world through travel, education and experience. And when they finally return home – to a home they have enshrined in absent sentimentality – they are ashamed by what they find: the paucity of circumstance, ambition, taste or imagination. It is in this tension between the person they were, the person they have become, and the home and family they now see with new eyes, that the drama plays out. Of course, wrapped up in all this is an innate subjectivity. Improvement is, invariably, in the eye of the improver. Who, in the end, is better off? Everyone? No-one?

Clerk had embarked on his Grand Tour at a pivotal time in Scottish, European – even world – history. Society, economics, industry, art and culture: all were on the cusp of modernity. He had glimpsed the future, the radical change that was on the way, and he returned to Scotland as the most passionate of improvers. Mavisbank was his statement in thought and deed, a symbol of modernising zeal expressed through the simple perfection of antiquity. It was situated on the hinge between old and new Scotland. It was a Roman villa built to oversee a rapacious coal mining operation. It was the home of a former arts student, turned politician, turned judge, turned taste-maker, turned industrialist, turned patron of poets, painters, musicians and architects. Clerk wanted to leave behind what he saw as the noble barbarism of his nation's past and reach for the highest rung of civilisation. He was a Scotsman in Rome who became a Roman in Scotland. In his conflicted view of the Treaty of Union, he placed romanticism to one side as a childish thing, and turned instead towards secular economic pragmatism. All of this he poured into Mavisbank. Might this 'small box', this 'Usefull house', this compact (now crumbling and supercilious) relic just be the ambiguous foundation stone – and site of pilgrimage – for the whole Scottish Enlightenment?

I made my way back down the slope and past the south side of the house. It was in a more diminished state than the rest, with one part of the quadrant collapsed completely, and the rest smothered in ivy. Trees and bushes had colonised this second pavilion and its stonework buckled and gaped. The ground fell away and through the trees I caught a glimpse of the old walled garden on the valley floor – unlike Mavisbank, now restored and maintained handsomely as the backdrop to a modern private residence. I went for a last look at the front of the house, and as I walked back up the old drive I heard voices. In the stillness of the afternoon they were so loud that they made me start. After a few minutes two women came up behind me. They stopped alongside the security fence, we said hello, and then the three of us stared in silence.

I thought about asking them why they had come. As gawpers? As pilgrims? Just because, despite it all, Mavisbank was still there? Did they know the story of what had happened to Clerk's house since its heyday? How it had left the family ownership in the nineteenth century, been turned into an asylum and then, another 70 years on, was closed and bought by its last medical superintendent? Or had they seen the infamous picture of old cars and scrap metal strewn across the forecourt, and heard about the owner who ended up living in a caravan outside the shell of the house after it was gutted by a fire in the 1970s? I could have told them about the one corroded hubcap I had spotted lying in the long grass to the rear of the house, turned the same burnt orange colour as the fallen leaves, a solitary relic of that time. Were they aware how close the building had come to demolition in the late 1980s? That the National Coal Board had continued the work of mining beneath Mavisbank, causing the structure to deteriorate to the extent that Midlothian Council resolved that the only safe option was to pull it down? Maybe they knew personally some of the members of the volunteer watch who had guarded the house round the clock for eighteen days until a security fence could be erected? Maybe they had even donated money to the trust that is now working to secure the building's future?

But I didn't have the chance to ask about any of this. They turned quickly away, we all smiled at each other, one of the women raised her eyebrows in the direction of the house, and they walked off. I had hesitated and missed my opportunity. I followed not long after, breaking the house's gaze and turning my back. The sound came suddenly of two dogs barking. As I came out from behind the bushes I saw a Labrador playing with a Border Collie out on the wide expanse of the meadow. First the two women, now these two dogs and their owners, had broken the spell in the valley. The light was fading quickly. It was time to go.

I decided to make my way back across the meadow this time, following a worn indentation in the grass towards a massive chestnut tree that sat alongside Clerk's ornamental lake. I walked around the lake, its surface frozen. The silence had returned and was so absolute that it was like a presence. It was amazing how quickly the atmosphere shifted once again. From the lake, the house was not hidden, but framed between banks of trees either side. I felt compelled – almost every few steps – to glance over my shoulder towards it. I looked back at Mavisbank and Mavisbank looked back at me. I wasn't quite sure what I felt. Pity? Sadness? I didn't think so. In part, I experienced a sense of contentment, almost joy, that places like this still existed. Just as Clerk had warned in 'The Country Seat', I found the tranquility of the valley intoxicating.

All the same, what does the ruinous state of Mavisbank say about the survival of Clerk's vision? The building may have been a political and cultural statement, but not all physical symbols endure – nor are they meant

to. Ideas, however, can be much more persistent. I wondered if the affection I felt for Mavisbank was – perhaps perversely – related to the enduring conflicts I could sense permeating its fractured stones: conflicts between new and old, between modernity and heritage, between local and global, between the cosmopolitan and the traditional, between the elite and the majority. This was a deeply human building – proud and self-conscious and riven with contradictions; flawed and arrogant and earnest and admirable all at the same time.

It was almost dark now. The lights had come on in the houses on the other side of the valley. I had one last look at Mavisbank. A fine, cold mist was settling over the meadow, softening the house, blurring and obscuring its cracks and crevices. Its lights would not come on. I suspected that the irony would not be lost on the improving lairds that, a few hundred years later, their enlightened estates would have no practical place in our modern world. Country houses have been anachronisms since at least the early part of the twentieth century, and many have disappeared. What might Clerk or his contemporaries have done if faced with the plight of somewhere like Mavisbank today? Preserved it and venerated it as a cultural icon? Or knocked it down and built a spa hotel and golf course? I suspected they might have gone for the latter. Their brand of improvement had little truck with nostalgia. We allow ourselves more sentimentality these days. Maybe we have learned the lesson that, barbarian or sophisticate, you can't forget where you came from, or what made you, or what you made.

11

Kirks Without People
James Robertson

Auld Alloway Kirk, 1791

This is about four churches – three in ruins and one, though preserved, a monument to ruination. It is also about a historical episode in which my forebears played a shameful role.

*

The Auld Kirk at Alloway dates from 1516. Built on or near the site of a much older church, it was a ruin by the time Robert Burns was born a few hundred yards away, in 1759. 'To try to imagine Alloway without Burns is as difficult as trying to imagine the Sahara without sands – and quite as futile', was the opinion of the travel writer Theo Lang in 1953. Likewise, Scottish literature is unimaginable without the glimmering, bleezing presence of Kirk-Alloway, 'whare ghaists and houlets nightly cry', the main setting for Burns's great narrative poem 'Tam O' Shanter'. How young was he when he first passed this spot alone and in the dark? Was he afraid? It would seem so, and the effect never wholly left him. In his late twenties, he admitted that the supernatural tales with which a cousin, Betty Davidson, had filled his head as a boy had had 'so strong an effect on my imagination, that to this hour, in my nocturnal rambles, I sometimes keep a sharp look-out in suspicious places; and though nobody can be more sceptical in these matters than I, yet it often takes an effort of Philosophy to shake off these idle terrors'.

Today, busloads of tourists and schoolchildren descend on Alloway to visit the National Trust for Scotland's Robert Burns Birthplace Museum, the Burns Cottage, the Burns Monument, the Auld Kirk and the Brig o' Doon. The last was Tam's escape route from the witches who pursue him when he disturbs their revelries – 'a running stream they dare na cross!'

It's hard to picture this crowded Rabbieland as a lonely, eerie location, the haunt of 'rigwoodie hags' and Auld Nick in the form of a shaggy, black dog – even when you know the tale of 'Tam O' Shanter'. But at thirty-one, when he wrote the poem, Burns was at the peak of his powers, and knew how to mix the comic with the macabre, the dramatic with the ludicrous. A true product of the Enlightenment, his rationalism persuaded him that belief in witchcraft was superstitious, cruel nonsense, but he also under-stood the power of folk and fairy tales, and how directly they speak to the human psyche, drawing from the well of our wildest guesses and deepest fears. Burns's father, William, is buried in the kirkyard. William had died six years before Robert wrote 'Tam O' Shanter'. Did the poet envisage his own sire as one of the corpses propped upright and utilised by the witches as candle-holders?

> *Coffins stood round, like open presses,*
> *That shaw'd the dead in their last dresses;*
> *And, by some devilish cantraip sleight,*
> *Each in its cauld hand held a light ...*

The walls and gable ends of the Auld Kirk survive, but the roof is long gone. Apart from a pair of mortsafes – iron shields that would be locked in place over graves until the recently deceased had decayed sufficiently to be of no value to bodysnatchers – there is not much of interest within. The kirk is *special* because of Burns, and because of 'Tam O' Shanter'. I learned that poem by heart in my twenties, reading at the side of New Zealand roads while waiting for lifts. I had been away from Scotland for more than a year, working and travelling, and had picked up a second-hand selec-tion of Burns's verse that seemed to speak very insistently of 'home' to me. Although I knew nothing then of Alloway, the locations that are essential to the poem, and were essential to Burns, somehow made sense when I recited them on the way to Wanaka: to each place its story, to every story its place. You don't have to actually *know* the ford 'where in the snaw the chapman smoor'd', the meikle stane 'where drunken Charlie brak's neck-bane' or the thorn aboon the well 'where Mungo's mither hang'd hersel'. You don't even have to know if these are real or imagined places. You just have to believe that they are true points on Tam's mad, heroic journey. Once you have crossed that line, anything is possible

The kirkyard, on the other hand, with its many worn and leaning stones, has the fascination and sombre beauty of all ancient burial grounds. There are richly carved pictorial stones that tell of the lives they commemorate – the farmer, the blacksmith, the miller – and there are simpler markers with names and dates, recording lives that were all too often cut short. When you walk in graveyards, you walk among the people from whom we are made. Here lieth Scotland, in thousands and tens of thousands.

*

Is there any country in Europe that contains, per head of population, more churches, former churches and ruined churches than Scotland? It helps, in accruing the numbers, if your history includes the repeated destruction by invading armies of abbeys and monasteries in the borderlands; if your kingdom undergoes a comprehensive Protestant Reformation which destroys some, but takes over most, existing places of worship; if this is followed, over centuries, by neglect and abandonment of ancient sites tainted by association with the 'old' religion; if there are then numerous secessions and dissensions from, and split after theological split within, the now dominant Presbyterian strain; if a once suppressed Episcopalian minority survives to worship publicly once again in its own buildings; if, in the industrial era, the influx of large numbers of Roman Catholics from Ireland and elsewhere leads to the construction of new chapels and cathedrals to satisfy *their* spiritual needs; and if other variations on the broad Christian theme also arrive – Pentecostal, Quaker, Baptist, Methodist, Brethren, Jehovah's Witnesses and so on – and establish themselves in particular communities. The residual outcome of all this – and especially of the divisions within the Church of Scotland – is a prolific quantity of churches of all kinds.

The greatest surge in church-building occurred following the Disruption of 1843, when 474 ministers from a total of 1200 walked out of the Church of Scotland (the Kirk) to establish the Free Church. The cause of the split was disagreement over the Kirk's relationship with the secular authorities, and one of the most contentious issues was whether a congregation should have the right to choose its own minister rather than have one imposed upon it by the local laird. The 474 were known as Non-Intrusionists, and the election of ministers by congregations was a founding principle of the new Free Church. In upholding that principle these men lost their livings, their manses and their churches. When they left they were followed by the bulk of their congregations: the first need, therefore, was to borrow or build places in which to meet and worship. These new Free Church congregations had to raise funds for new kirks, and did so with astonishing speed and success. Consequently, in the second half of the nineteenth century, almost every town in Scotland, as well as many villages and rural communities, came to have at least two rival churches selling almost exactly the same doctrinal brand. There were some differences, of course, as a popular rhyme of the day pithily illustrates:

The Free kirk, the wee kirk,
The kirk withoot the steeple;
The Auld kirk, the cauld kirk,
The kirk withoot the people.

As further schisms and occasional reconciliations took place, still more new churches were erected while existing ones became either too big or too small for their congregations. Bridge of Allan, for example, when I was growing up there in the 1960s, had two Church of Scotland kirks. One of them, Chalmers Church, which my family attended, had originally been built as a Free Church in 1854 but had come back into the Established fold in 1929: it closed in 2003 and has since been split into private flats. The other, Holy Trinity, built in 1860, still functions as the parish church; it boasts furnishings designed by Charles Rennie Mackintosh in 1904. Across the street from it stands the Episcopal Church of St Saviour's completed in 1857. But there had also been the United Presbyterian Church (built in 1848 and replaced with a bigger version in 1895, in turn demolished after the Second World War) at the foot of Well Road, which was widely known by locals as the U P Brae. Within walking distance to the north is Lecropt Kirk and, in the opposite direction, Logie Kirk. And all this in a place that started as a scattered hamlet of a few hundred souls, grew to a douce, well-to-do spa town of 2,000 in the Victorian period, and today has a population of about 7,000.

This history can be replicated – often in magnified form – in communities the length and breadth of the land. But in the last fifty years Scotland has changed from an ostensibly thoroughly religious society – the Kirk had 1.3 million members in 1961, and almost everything apart from churches was shut, chained up or locked down on Sundays – to a thoroughly secularised one. De-sanctified churches have become private dwellings, offices, pubs, restaurants, antiques emporia, concert halls and climbing centres. Yet the built environment of Scotland is unimaginable stripped of its Christian structures, even – perhaps especially – those that stand or lie in ruins. They are testimony both to continuity and to change.

About a mile and a half from the house in Bridge of Allan in which I grew up stand the ruins of Logie Old Kirk. I can't remember the first time I came across this particular stone remnant of the past but I was probably about nine or ten. A mile and a half was then well within the circumference of my circle of wandering, on foot or bicycle, and Logie had the added advantage of being reachable without having to negotiate any main roads. You took the old bridle path to Pathfoot, passed the lovely 1731 house of Blairlowan, crossed the narrow road that leads up Drumbrae to Sheriffmuir, and walked or pedalled the rough track that runs along the foot of the Wood of Airthrey and comes out at Logie. This track is apparently called Back o' Dykes but I never knew it as that: the other names, however, retain the familiarity of the intensely local even half a century later. On the track's north side, the wooded hill rises steeply: to the south, beyond a stone dyke which presumably gives the route its name, are the grounds of Stirling University. In the mid-to-late 1960s the campus was in the process of being constructed, a subtle transformation of the old Airthrey Castle estate into something that seemed ultra-modern. Sleek concrete and glass buildings slipped neatly into the leafy landscape and around the man-made loch, created at the behest of the Haldane family who owned Airthrey in the eighteenth century. Occasionally I would cycle onto the campus and watch the men putting up student halls of residence, but it was Airthrey Wood and the Mine Wood (the site of old copper and silver mines) that held greater attractions.

Criss-crossed with steep paths, full of birds, deer, foxes and other wild-life, these woods stretched behind Bridge of Allan like a knitted scarf that changed colours with the seasons, separating the houses from the great rolling expanse of Sheriffmuir. They were my playground, with or without friends or family. When I was a little older, I would take our dog for long walks through them, or along the Allan Water or up the Wharry Glen or across the golf course and on to Pendreich and the Cocksburn Reservoir. I came to know these routes well, but each time they yielded new secrets.

Built into a rocky outcrop in the trees at Airthrey, and accessible only by negotiating a seriously steep bank, was what we called 'the folly', built by Robert Haldane in an age when such constructions were fashionable. I once explored it with our two-year-old Labrador who took such fright at the crumbling incline that I had to carry her back to safety with her claws dug into my arms – a tricky undertaking. According to *Erskine's Guide to Bridge of Allan* (1912) the folly was

> *a grotto, in which [Haldane] endeavoured to realise the poet's idea of a hermitage: and even advertised for a hermit to occupy it. The conditions, however, were rather too stringent for even a professional hermit, although it is said he might have secured one had the terms been modified.*

A few hundred yards to the east, at Logie Old Kirk, there was a hermit of sorts some four hundred years ago. I did not know this as a boy, but its sixteenth century minister was one Alexander Hume, a poet. He had been a poet at the court of James VI but in 1598, suffering from poor health and tired of 'prophane sonnets and vaine ballads of love', he withdrew to Logie and became its minister. The following year, he produced a collection entitled *Hymnes or Sacred Songs wherein the Right Use of Poesie may be Espied*. This contained his long and delightful celebration of Midsummer's Day, 'Of the Day Estivall'. The following stanzas are a sample:

The time sa tranquill is and still,
That na where sall ye find –
Saif on ane high and barren hill –
Ane air of peeping wind.

All trees and simples [herbs] great and small,
That balmie leif do beir,
Nor thay were painted on a wall
Na mair they move or steir.

Sa silent is the cessile [yielding] air,
That every cry and call,
The hils, and dails, and forrest fair
Againe repeates tham all.

Hume had actually composed this poem while still at court, and so we cannot be sure that Logie directly inspired it, even if Hume had made previous visits, which is of course quite possible. It is, certainly, a tranquil and calm spot.

As at Alloway, a place of worship has existed on the site since the thirteenth century or earlier: the present ruins date from Hume's period. The west gable, with its empty bellcote, and part of the south wall are all that remain. They have been stabilised as part of a recent restoration project, and the kirkyard has been tidied. There is a watch-house, used in the eighteenth and early nineteenth centuries to guard graves from the predations of Resurrectionists. Many of the gravestones are very ancient. When I used to come here on my own as a teenager it was a wilder, more derelict place, and I found it far more suited to meditation and peaceful reflection than the 'living' church I no longer attended or believed in. Once, I disturbed a roe deer grazing among the stones.

Long before I knew 'Tam O' Shanter', this was my own Kirk-Alloway.

It too had its own stories of witches convening amid the ivy-clad ruins, as they were said to have done in about 1720. At the back of Logie, on the road to the Hillfoots towns, is a precipitous hill known as the Witches' or Carlins' Craig. According to local legend, women found guilty of witchcraft were thrown to their deaths from this spot. Another tale has it that an elder of the kirk came upon the Devil up there in his habitual guise of a ferocious black dog. The elder, being conveniently armed with a gun and silver piece – without which a shot at Auld Nick is wasted effort – fired at the creature and saw it pitch to the ground; but when the foot of the cliff was searched only the corpse of a goat was discovered. The goat belonged to an old woman of the district: it is not recorded whether she was suspected of collusion with the Deil.

*

A hundred and fifty miles to the north, near the village of Evanton on the north side of the Cromarty Firth, is yet another ruinous church. You leave the A9 and go down a single-track road to the burial ground of Kiltearn, right on the shoreline. There is a new cemetery here, but the one that interests me surrounds the now derelict old parish church. This structure dates from the late eighteenth century, and many of the nearby gravestones are of similar or older vintage. Like Alloway, like Logie, the site was previously occupied by older religious buildings, possibly including a medieval monastery. And history lingers here in other ways too. Kiltearn's most famous minister was Thomas Hog, a hero of the Covenant, who was vociferously opposed to the reintroduction of Episcopacy during the reign of Charles II. Hog preached at open-air conventicles, was imprisoned for his radical religious and political views half a dozen times – twice on the notorious Bass Rock, the Guantanamo Bay of that age – banished furth of Scotland, imprisoned again in London and finally exiled to Holland, from where he was restored to his ministry after the Revolution of 1688–9. A year after his return to Easter Ross, he died, aged sixty-four. The lettering on Hog's gravestone is worn away now, but a plaque erected in 1940 reproduces it, a warning from one dark period of history to another: 'This stone shall bear witness against the parishioners of Kiltearn if they bring ane ungodly minister in here.'

Kiltearn's proximity to the shore suggests that access by water may once have been as important as access by land, but after the Second World War its location became too inconvenient for the population of Evanton and it ceased to be used for worship. Photographs from the 1960s show it with its roof and windows still intact, but the slates and roof timbers were stripped soon afterwards and it is now in a very poor condition. Rabbit activity has undermined some of the old graveyard, and the retaining wall which protects it from the sea is also in need of attention. It remains, however, a remarkably beautiful and peaceful place. When you stand among the stones and tablets crowded at odd angles across the green turf, and look to the sea, you are caught between two ages, the pre-industrial and the post-industrial: oil rigs sit out on the water, anchored like some vast art installation or a herd of metallic monsters – all intestinal pipes, craning beaks and claws and rusted legs. The number of rigs changes all the time. They are brought in to the shelter of the Cromarty Firth for refitting or repair or, increasingly, just because they are no longer needed out in the North Sea.

To one side of the roofless kirk is a plot enclosed by a foot-high cast-iron fender. Centuries-old tablets lie half-submerged within this boundary. There is also an upright sandstone slab, eight foot high and ten foot wide, so weathered that most of the names and dates have disappeared and only a few words are still legible: BELOVED, DIED, TAKETH, TRUST – and ROBERTSON. This is one of the principal resting-places – the other is at Rosskeen, between Alness and Invergordon – of my once-wealthy ancestors, the Robertsons of Kindeace.

This northern branch of a clan whose heartland was in Highland Perthshire traces its lineage back to a merchant of Inverness, John Robertson, who flourished in the mid-fifteenth century. A William Robertson purchased land at Kindeace, twelve miles north of Kiltearn, in 1629. Successive generations acquired more land, farmed well, occasionally fought duels but by and large steered clear of disputes, whether personal or political. By the 1700s the lairds of Kindeace and their kin were prominent, prosperous, stoutly Presbyterian members of Ross-shire society: Jacobitism, even of a romantic, after-dinner kind, would not have been one of their indulgences.

Numerous children were produced by the wives of these lairds: of those that reached adulthood, the daughters either stayed at home to help run the household or were married off to neighbouring lairds, Edinburgh lawyers or London gentlemen, while the sons became ministers, lawyers, merchants, planters or – especially – soldiers. The family's deep engagement in the burgeoning British Empire brought considerable rewards but sometimes at a great cost. In the second half of the eighteenth century Charles Robertson, the 5th Laird, had nine sons who survived infancy: one inherited the estate, one had a career as an army officer and two went into business in London; the other five all died overseas, three of yellow fever, one in battle in India, and one 'of lockjaw, occasioned by the biting of a snake'.

The present Kindeace House – a sturdy construction of four storeys – was built in 1798 and redesigned and extended in the 1860s. You sense, looking at its crow-stepped gables and symmetrical frontage, that these Robertsons liked things plain and functional: it was how they lived their conventional and comfortable lives. The high point of the family's fortunes was the nineteenth century, but things went into steep decline after the death of the 8th Laird in 1902. A combination of poor financial management and heavy taxes after the sudden demise of the heir, Gilbert, led to the land and the house itself being sold, and its seven surviving daughters and sons dispersing to Glasgow, England, South Africa, New Zealand and Canada. Among them was my paternal grandfather (who was born in 1877 and died in 1959, a year after I was born) and his sister Helena, or 'Great Aunt Nella', born in 1869. She lived to be nearly ninety-nine and my parents once took my sister, brother and me to see her at her home in London: I was three or perhaps four and remember only an austere, papery old lady clad in long black clothes. I was quite frightened, although she gave us chocolate bars.

All this history is a mere two generations away from me, yet it seems remote and ancient, not least because I have always felt politically at odds with what these ancestors of mine represent. Standing before that big sandstone memorial to them at Kiltearn, from which wind and rain have stripped nearly all their names, is like standing before a classroom blackboard, trying to decipher the rubbed-out lessons of the previous day.

*

Here is one lesson: history may fade, but it takes a long time to disappear completely. If from the village of Ardgay, far up on the south shore of the Dornoch Firth, you take the narrow road ten miles westward to where it ends at Croick, you come upon a tiny church. It is one of the so-called 'Parliamentary kirks' built under the supervision of Thomas Telford, and it is unhappily connected to the Robertsons of Kindeace.

In 1824, Parliament passed a Bill making available funds for the building of new kirks in the Highlands and Islands, so that more people, especially in what were deemed to be remote communities, could regularly attend a place of worship. These were of course to be Church of Scotland kirks: this programme was partly motivated by a desire to counter Catholic and Dissenting expansion. The modest sum of £50,000 was provided for the entire project, with a maximum of £1,500 to be spent on any one site.

The selection of sites and the construction programme was entrusted to the Highland Roads and Bridges Commission, whose chief surveyor was Thomas Telford. Nearly a hundred applications were received. From these, sites were chosen for the erection of thirty-two kirks and forty-one manses (as there were some places where a kirk already existed, but no home for the minister). Telford worked closely with his surveyors to come up with a simple rectangular design, 'particularly calculated to resist a stormy climate'. Windows and doors were of a standard size so that they could be made in bulk and fitted on site; variations on the basic plan, such as galleries or lofts, could be added at the landowner's expense. Building work commenced in 1826 and all the Parliamentary kirks were completed by 1830. Although several are now demolished or derelict, fine examples still exist at Ullapool, Kinlochbervie and Plockton, and on Mull, Islay and Iona. The one at Croick, built under the direction of the surveyor James Smith, is in the classic, unadorned style, harled and slated. Kirk and manse together cost a grand total of £1,426 10s 11d. The kirk was built to serve a population of some 450 mainly inhabiting the straths running deep into the hills, in particular Glencalvie and Strathcarron. Ironically, within a generation, most of that population would be gone.

The 6th Laird of Kindeace, William Robertson, was sixty-five when the new kirk at Croick was completed. It stood on a plot granted by a neighbouring landowner, but Kindeace owned or leased much of the land roundabout, including Greenyards, in Strathcarron, and Glencalvie. As he aged, Kindeace increasingly preferred his London residence to the house in Easter Ross, and left the running of his Highland affairs to his factor, James Falconer Gillanders. The latter was a man whose character seems to have been marked by a strict adherence to efficient and economic land use, regardless of the human consequences. Towards the end of 1841, Kindeace authorised that both Greenyards and Glencalvie be advertised for let as sheep walks. The announcements were published in the *Inverness Chronicle* in February 1842.

By this period there was a well-established chronology associated with clearing people from the land to make way for sheep, and the inhabitants of Glencalvie anticipated the worst. There were eighty-eight of them – four tenants, their families, their subtenants and *their* dependants, living in nineteen cottages, all but one of these built of turf with heather roofs. The minister of Croick, a 28-year-old called Gustavus Aird who had been there for less than a year, was consulted. He wrote a letter to Gillanders on behalf of his parishioners, stating that he had been assured by the laird's son, Major Charles Robertson, that the people would not be turned out if they continued to pay their rent as, without fail, they had always done. Gillanders responded with a bland assurance, but in March had writs of removal served upon the people of Glencalvie.

Two attempts were made by sheriff officers to deliver these writs, but on both occasions the women of the glen set fire to the papers and a large crowd turned away the officers, who were not unsympathetic to the people's plight. There the matter rested for three years, but it was not over. In the interim, circumstances changed significantly.

In May 1843 came the Disruption of the Church of Scotland. Gustavus Aird followed his conscience and joined the Free Kirk, thus losing his manse and living at Croick, and all but a handful of the people of Glencalvie and Strathcarron went with him. He later became minister of a new kirk at Creich, but in the meantime conducted services in the open air to large congregations. And then, in April 1844, William Robertson died in London and was succeeded, as 7th Laird of Kindeace, by his son Charles.

Charles Robertson had been in the 78th Highlanders and as a very young man had been present at the capture of Java in the Napoleonic Wars. But now he was with the 96th Regiment of Foot in Australia, where the army's role was to police the convict settlements, and also to be on hand to quash any trouble from the indigenous population. He could have stayed at home and done much the same kind of work. Like his father, Major Robertson entrusted the management of his property to James Gillanders. Before 1844 was out, the four tenants of Glencalvie were lured to Tain, supposedly for a meeting with Gillanders, and new writs of removal were successfully served on them. This time they had no minister of the Established Church to fight their cause. Gustavus Aird did what he could, and indeed the Free Kirk became a strong advocate for land reform and protection of tenants throughout the Highlands, but time had run out for the inhabitants of Glencalvie. In May 1845, they were evicted en masse. They seem to have had no fight left in them, and went peaceably enough, but a reporter from *The Times* witnessed their departure and wrote an extensive, outraged article castigating 'this most heartless wholesale ejectment'. Although the article came too late for those people, it did draw public attention to the widespread injustices still being perpetrated on innocent and vulnerable Highlanders by absentee lairds and their unrelenting factors.

At the end of that hard May, the Glencalvie folk and others – some 250 all together – gathered for Sunday worship one last time on the open hillside – 'the women all neatly dressed in net caps and wearing scarlet or plaid shawls, the men wearing blue bonnets and with their shepherds' plaids wrapped about them', according to *The Times*. By contrast, in the little church nearby, the congregation was 'miserably thin – but ten persons besides the minister.' The homeless refugees, for such they had become, then moved to the churchyard and set up camp there, under tarpaulins, rugs and blankets. The walls provided a little shelter from the wind, but they would not enter the kirk itself, for it was no longer their place of worship. They stayed for two nights, and then departed. Some did settle in nearby communities. Others went to the coast, to the cities of the south, or overseas, even perhaps to Australia where their laird was serving the Empire.

On the glass of the east window of the kirk, Victorian scratchings record the event. Some say the people left these marks, but they were Gaelic speakers, and few of them would have been literate at all, let alone in English, the language of their persecutors. More likely, one of them, a shepherd called John Ross, returned years later to memorialise what had by then become infamous: 'Glencalvie people was in the church here May 24 1845 ... John Ross shepherd ... Amy Ross ... Glencalvie is a wilders below sheep.' Most poignant of all the graffiti is the one that reads, 'Glencalvie people the wicked generation Glencalvie.' Whether this is the people's judgement on themselves or something more ironic, it reads almost as if the threat on Thomas Hog's gravestone at Kiltearn had been carried out thirty miles inland.

These sad engravings remain. Telford and Smith's fine wee kirk remains, and services still take place there in the summer months. Mounds remain in Glencalvie, marking where once were turf houses. Kindeace House remains, but with all its many acres sold off, its four storeys and stables divided into several homes. But all the players in this story are gone: levelled by time, and some of them weighed in the balances and found wanting. For the brutality was not over. There would be another, more violent clearance at Greenyards in 1854, again initiated by James Gillanders, who by then was married to Margaret, second daughter of Major Robertson, my great great grandfather. When I was a boy and these stories came among us, vague excuses were sometimes wafted around like bad smells: William Robertson had been in London, Charles Robertson in Australia, they hadn't known what was happening, it was all the fault of that monstrous man Gillanders. But one of my forebears authorised the deed, and his heir married his daughter to the monster. They were neither ignorant nor innocent of what was done in their name. They were responsible, and there is no disguising it.

12

The Making of a Classical Gem
Alexander McCall Smith

Charlotte Square, Edinburgh, 1791–1820

For years I wanted to write about Edinburgh but somehow found it difficult to begin. I was keen to say something about the spirit of the city – its feel and atmosphere – but gradually came to the view that, as a setting for fiction, the city was curiously elusive. There is no shortage of literary references to Edinburgh: apart from earlier writers, including Stevenson and Scott, the city has been captured in modern times by writers of fiction as different from one another as Muriel Spark, Ian Rankin and Irvine Welsh. It has also inspired poets such as Sydney Goodsir Smith and Robert Garioch, as well as a poet who is no longer widely read but is a particular favourite of mine, Ruthven Todd, whose 'Personal History' and 'In Edinburgh' offer striking distillations of the Edinburgh of the 1930s. Edinburgh worked as a setting, but I happened to find it hard to grasp.

I decided that the source of the difficulty was that this was a shy city – a city that conceals itself behind a beautiful and often elegant facade. It is not a city that wears its heart on its sleeve; it does not have the immediately obvious warmth of Glasgow, the romantic invitation of Paris, or the heady challenge of New York. It is a city in which people lead their lives in a relatively restrained way; it is a city of which a significant part – the New Town – seems to embody rationality and order. The architecture of the city is therefore crucial to its understanding, and its depiction in fiction. The civic essence of Edinburgh lies in its structure and the way that this structure brings people together and, critically, influences the way they look at the world, the way they are. People relate to one another in a particular way in Edinburgh because many who live in the centre of the city live in tenements, which are all about community and sharing. They live on streets in which architectural harmony has been, and is still, important. They can often walk to one another's houses or the shops that sustain them. Their lives are not lived in open public spaces, which are too cold in

Scotland to be inhabitable for long. The light is clear. The city, the country, says 'North'. A long and complex history is all about you, and its voices are in the very stone. All of this makes a difference.

I chose the New Town as the setting for the *Scotland Street* novels because it offered a complete world in which the characters could lead their lives against the backdrop of a very particular urban landscape – one that had a strong civic sense to it. And that is certainly there in the New Town. The layout, the scale of the buildings, the underpinning aesthetic – all celebrate citizenship and something very important in the urban environment: courtesy. Some cities just do not do that: they lend themselves to the domination of the rich over the poor; they emphasise commerce at the cost of the human; they intimidate by their size and ruthlessness. The Edinburgh New Town is courteous in the sense that it does none of this: it does not seek to overpower; it is calm; it invites you to walk rather than to rush; it respects the past – after all, it started its very existence looking over its shoulder to a classical age that had long since disappeared. And right at the apex of this great architectural and philosophical statement is Charlotte Square at the head of the most important New Town thoroughfare, George Street.

Charlotte Square came into existence because the Old Town of Edinburgh, the rambling, malodorous, fire risk that ran down the spine of the city from the castle to Holyrood, was too smelly, unhealthy and crowded to cope with the demands of a country on the verge of growth and prosperity. The Old Town was an organic rabbit warren of towering tenements, narrow closes and dark corners. It had plenty of character, and characters too – think of the figures immortalised in John Kay's *Edinburgh Portraits* – and it was democratic in the proximity in which persons of high status lived with persons much lower on the social pecking order, but something had to give. And so the process began of creating on the other side of the Nor' Loch a whole new vision, a prolonged flourish of classical elegance, at the summit of which lay a wide airy square of large town houses, looking in upon a fine urban garden and presided over, on its west side, by a commanding church.

Charlotte Square is undoubtedly the principal architectural jewel of the New Town and indeed one of the finest squares in Europe. Yet there is something slightly reserved, perhaps distant, about it today. There are numerous New Town streets, crescents and squares that have less of a museum feel about them because people actually live there. Nobody – or next to nobody – lives in Charlotte Square today. It is all about people who *used* to live there. So this dignified square seems a slightly cold, even haughty, place in a city that, until recently, had a reputation for *froideur* and reserve.

But even if Charlotte Square seems formal, an impression perpetuated by its popularity in the past with rather grand legal firms and, more recently, with rarefied financial firms, its history is very much the history of the Edinburgh New Town, and the people who have lived and worked in it are warp and woof in the fabric of Edinburgh's history. If you are looking for a lived-in atmosphere in the here and now, look elsewhere. But if you want to understand Edinburgh as a city of aesthetic ambition and rigorous intellect, then Charlotte Square is an important piece in the jigsaw.

At the very beginning of the story is Gilbert Elliot's *Proposal for carrying on certain Public Works in the City of Edinburgh*. This pamphlet, published in 1752, is identified by A J Youngson in his *The Making of Classical Edinburgh* as an important statement of thinking at the time. The *Proposal* begins with an observation of what a capital city is all about:

> *Among the several causes to which the prosperity of a nation may be described, the situation, conveniency, and beauty of its capital, are surely not the least considerable. A capital where these circumstances happen fortunately to concur, should naturally become the centre of trade and commerce, of learning and the arts, politeness, and of refinement of every kind. No sooner will the advantages which these necessarily produce, be felt and experienced in the chief city, then they will diffuse themselves through the nation, and universally promote the same spirit of industry and improvement.*

The pamphleteer then waxes eloquent on the advantages of London and its situation, a city whose neatness, large parks and public walks he much admires. London, of course, had its slums, every bit as unpleasant and dangerous to health as those in the Old Town of Edinburgh, but this was not the angle from which it was being contemplated. He then turns to Edinburgh – a sorry story, he feels, that needs to be spelled out:

> *The healthfulness of its situation, and its neighbourhood to the Forth, must no doubt be admitted as very favourable circumstances. But how greatly are these overbalanced by other disadvantages almost without number? Based upon a ridge of a hill, it admits but of one good street, running from east to west; and even this is tolerably accessible only from one quarter. The narrow lanes leading to the north and south, by reason of their statements, narrowness, and dirtiness, can only be considered as so many unavoidable nuisances. Confined by the small compass of the walls, and the narrow limits*

of the royalty, which scarcely extends beyond the walls, the hous-es stand more crowded than in any other town in Europe, and are built to a height that is almost incredible. Hence necessarily follows a great want of free air, light, cleanliness, and every other comfort-able accommodation. Here also many families, sometimes no less than ten or a dozen, are obliged to live overhead of each other in the same building; where, to all the other inconveniences is added that of a common stair, which is no other in effect than an upright street, constantly dark and dirty ... No less observable is the great deficien-cy of public buildings. If the parliament-house, the churches, and a few hospitals, be excepted, what other have we to boast of? There is no exchange for our merchants; no safe repository for our public and private records; no place of meeting for our magistrates and town council; none for the convention of our boroughs, which is entrusted with the inspection of trade. To these and such other reasons it must be imputed, that so few people of rank reside in the city; that it is rarely visited by strangers; and that so many local prejudices, and narrow notions, inconsistent with polished manners and growing wealth, are still so obstinately retained ...

Whatever is the opposite of civic pride – civic shame, perhaps – lies at the heart of this wail, and the important thing about it was that the feelings it expressed were shared by people who were prepared to do something to remedy the situation. Most notably, George Drummond, the Lord Provost of Edinburgh, had the ability and vision to galvanise the city's merchants and local politicians into action. An early first step was the building of the bridge that would overcome the natural geographical division that pre-vented expansion to the north and link the two parts of the city. Then in 1766 the announcement of a competition started the public process. This called for plans for a New Town 'marking out streets of a proper breadth, and by-lanes, and the best situation for a reservoir ...' This competition was won by James Craig, a young man who had entered into an architec-tural apprenticeship in Edinburgh in 1759 and who was therefore quite inexperienced. His scheme was judged by the Council to be the best of the six submitted, although it was not until he had submitted changes to it that it was finally approved. The resultant plan drawn up by Craig was then made available to potential builders who wished to purchase a feu and begin construction.

Craig's plan at this stage did not include the designs of buildings: it was, rather, a street plan. Looking at it today it seems simple and straightforward: a grid system dominated by two squares at either end. As such, it has been called pedestrian, with none of the flair that characterised continental city planning of the age. Where were the circuses or the wide spaces that dignified continental cities? Instead there is a series of rectangles with two boxes at either end. The saving grace, though, of Craig's plan is the fact that two of the three main streets are single-sided: Queen Street has an unimpeded view north and Princes Street looks down on an improved set of gardens. It makes the most of the city's geography.

Craig's plan says nothing about the nature of the houses to be built along his streets: that was up to other architects. As building progressed from east to west, there were few architectural flourishes, with the result that there was criticism of the plain nature of the houses that came to be constructed. They may have been plain, but they were nonetheless regular in appearance, a regularity that, to a great extent if not totally, has been preserved in the New Town and that adds considerably to the charm of the place today. That regularity was mainly achieved by feuing conditions that discouraged idiosyncratic difference.

The shape of Craig's New Town was informed not only by geography but by land ownership. And the positioning of St Andrew's Square in turn was dictated by the fact that the town did not own the land to the east; that prevented the square being lined up against both the North Bridge to the south and George Street to the west. In the west, Craig's plan did not take into account an obvious ownership issue: the land was encumbered by a servitude in favour of the Earl of Moray and by the limitations on the town's ownership west of Castle Street. As result of this, any idea of building a square to match St Andrew's Square at the west end of George Street was for a time frustrated. Negotiations between the town and the Earl eventually allowed for St George's Square, as Charlotte Square was known until 1785, to be built, but its precise dimensions were affected by the realities of neighbourhood.

Aware of criticism over the ordinary appearance of the new buildings on George Street, the city fathers chose as designer for the new square Robert Adam, one of the most prestigious architects of the time. Robert was the son of the architect William Adam. He trained with his father and helped him in his work on Inverary Castle and Hopetoun House. On William's death, charge of his practice was assumed by Robert's older brother, John. The youngest brother, James, was also an architect and together the three Adams began to work together on a number of important commissions, including Dumfries House and Fort George.

The architectural influences that formed Robert Adam's style were classical. He had visited Italy and had immersed himself in the works of prominent continental architects and artists, including Piranesi. Although he did not share the Palladian enthusiasms of some other British architects, Adam was familiar with the architecture of classical antiquity and used this as the basis for the development of his own characteristic classical style. His theory of architecture stresses what he calls *movement*, a concept explained rather attractively in his *Works in Architecture* in these terms:

> *Movement is meant to express, the rise and fall, the advance and recess, with other diversity of form, in the different parts of the building, so as to add greatly to the picturesque of the composition. For the rising and falling, advancing and receding, with the convexity and concavity, and other forms of the great parts, have the same effect in architecture, that hill and dale, foreground and distance, swelling and sinking have in landscape: that is, they serve to produce an agreeable and diversified contour, that groups and contrasts like a picture and creates a variety of light and shade, which gives great spirit, beauty and effect to the composition.*

Adam was considered particularly skilful at bringing buildings together to create a sense of unity and wholeness. His design for Charlotte Square does this not only for the square as a whole, but also for the individual sides, where all the houses on each block are somehow drawn together to create a harmonious single entity. This is a singular achievement, and it meant that Adam avoided the monotonous effect that some critics saw in other New Town streets, including George Street. The south side of Charlotte Square mirrors the north, while the east and west sides are distinctive; on the west side there is, of course, a church. Each block on these sides – flanking the end of George Street in the east and the church in the west – is designed so as to look like a single palace. That particular design is a classical feature, used extensively in, for instance, great country houses. The trick is to avoid the monotony of a long facade, and this is achieved by creating a central pavilion that connects through a linking section to a pavilion at each end. The linking sections are recessed, although only very slightly, thus avoiding the impression of a single undifferentiated line.

The facades of Charlotte Square are not elaborately ornamented; that is not Adam's – nor Edinburgh's – style. Ornament is restricted to the central section and the pavilions at the end of each block. On the northern and southern sections, Corinthian pillars are the principal embellishment; otherwise, ornament tends to be limited to panels showing the foliage that so appealed to Adam. What really impresses is not any ornament, but the scale: the large windows, the substantial fanlight over the doors, the soaring feeling created by the pillars. Once one knows about Adam's theory of architectural movement, it all makes sense.

Stand in front of Bute House (No. 6, on the northern side). Look at the facade and catch your breath. Feel the reassurance of the vision: this is a perfectly balanced statement. Between the two central pillars is a great window, topped by a decorated arch. Along the front of the house, under the level of this window, is a balustrade. Two stone medallions are placed neatly above the windows on either side of the main window.

The house invites you in – if you have an invitation, of course – through a wide front door placed in the middle; elsewhere in the New Town, the front door is usually at the side, as it leads directly to the staircase. This house, though, as the central section of an Adam terrace, must have its main door in the middle to maintain regularity.

An insight into what lies behind the facade of such a grand town house can be gathered by stepping into next door (No. 7), the Georgian House, as it is called, where the National Trust for Scotland will show you just how the prosperous residents of Charlotte Square, and those who ministered to them, lived their lives. Bute House, though, is the jewel, and like so many older houses, the list of those who lived there is a history lesson in itself.

Because of the significance of the building, a great deal is known about the occupants of No. 6 over the years. In the case of lesser addresses, the history of a building can be put together by a bit of research into title deeds and also by the palimpsest that is the collection of doorbells. Names linger above old bell pulls, often for years – brass plates left *in situ* telling us who lived in what flat. In an intimate city, such as Edinburgh is, these names might be known or traceable; families live in the same place for a long time; certain names recur; memories last.

No. 6 has had some extremely distinguished, not to say stratospherically grand occupants. There must be few houses in Edinburgh that can claim to have been lived in by a king of France, but this is a boast that No. 6 can make. After the revolution of July 1830 in France, King Charles X went into exile and lived for a while in Holyroodhouse. During a temporary absence from Holyrood, the king lodged with a famous society hotelier, Mrs Grace Oman, his entourage booking up her premises in Charlotte Square. The next occupant of real note was the 4th Marquess of Bute, who bought No. 5 next door in 1903. Bute was vastly wealthy, the family fortune being based on coal, but included vast swathes of Cardiff. Bute had a feeling for property and, like his father, spent a great deal on restoration. He had already restored No. 5, removing inappropriate Victorian alterations and additions. In 1922 his company, Mountjoy Ltd, acquired No. 6, and Bute set about returning the Georgian feel to the building. He later acquired No. 7 and No. 8 and was therefore able to get rid of later additions, such as dormer windows in the roof, and also to return fanlights and astragals that had been removed by previous owners.

In the early twentieth century Charlotte Square had had a narrow escape. Commercial use had altered its original residential purpose and there had even been plans to knock one side down and build a concert hall. But the mood changed, and the realisation had dawned on people that Adam's great architectural treasure was worth preserving. Bute's influence helped a great deal, and in 1930 one of the Scotland's earliest conservation orders was issued: The Edinburgh Town Planning (Charlotte Square) Scheme Order. That might have been one of the first salvoes in the conservation battle that was waged in Edinburgh over the years – a battle that had some shocking episodes (the proposed motorway through Princes Street, for example). That battle, of course, rumbles on, with greedy and insensitive schemes being proposed regularly, irrespective of the impact they might have on the architectural unity and beauty of this world heritage city. Spitting in the face of one's aesthetic luck is something that Edinburgh has done on many occasions, and still does.

The 5th Marquess of Bute, who succeeded his father in 1947, made his Edinburgh home in No. 6 rather than No. 5. The immense fortune that he had inherited, however, was in the sights of the taxman and considerably reduced by death duties. On his father's death, the 6th Marquess was obliged to dispose of further property in order to meet the inheritance-tax bill; in negotiations with the tax authorities, No. 6 was ceded to the National Trust for Scotland, along with No. 5 and No. 7. The 6th Marquess, though, was keen that No. 6 should remain a home, and the National Trust decided that the best way to achieve this would be to lease it to the Government to be used as the official residence of the Secretary of State for Scotland. In 1999 No. 6 became the official residence of the First Minister – or *heid bummer*, to use the demotic – and has so far been occupied by five incumbents of that office. This arrangement keeps Charlotte Square from becoming the sort of complete urban desert that results from the withdrawal of human occupation and the colonisation of all city centre space by offices and shops.

In August each year Charlotte Square comes to life with the holding in the garden space of one of the world's great literary festivals, the Edinburgh International Book Festival. The garden sprouts marquees, and crowds flock to listen to authors and exchange ideas. This is what civic space can become – alive with conversation and laughter. Tucked away behind the main entrance tent each year is the Authors' Yurt, where writers, publishers and journalists sit on padded benches to all intents and purposes like chattering Mongolian tribes. The atmosphere is perfect; outside, Adam's Charlotte Square looks down on this colourful meeting – grey, impassive, classical.

Every contributor to this book will have been there on numerous occasions – will have sat and talked to other participants in the Book Festival, or to other friends – talked about books and people and ideas of various sorts. If I close my eyes I can hear Alistair Moffat talking to James Robertson, or Kathleen Jamie and James Crawford, or any of the others who meet there each year. I can hear the laughter. Elsewhere, and at other times, there will be places in the New Town where people converse in exactly the same way; in the coffee houses, or bistros, or bars, all grateful, I suspect, that this magnificent swathe of architecture has survived and has allowed this intimate civic life to exist in a world of increasing anonymity and shapelessness. Thank you James Craig and Robert Adam and William Playfair and all the others who gave us this.

13

The Fire of the Dram
Alistair Moffat

Glenlivet Distillery, 1800s

At the Pass of Leny it is most obvious and abrupt. Beyond Callandar, the road rises suddenly from the boggy flatlands around the meandering River Teith and plunges into the mountains. It is like geography drawn by children. Twisting and turning as the cliffs of the gorge close in, the road winds around the flanks of mighty Ben Ledi before the long northward vista of Loch Lubnaig opens. As the landscape empties and the marks of people fade, the Strathyre Forest carpets the mountainsides. A row of telegraph poles by the roadside seems somehow forlorn, holding a fragile thread that connects two Scotlands. Leny is probably the most dramatic place to cross the Highland Line, the geological and historic frontier between two cultures.

Long before the Jacobite wars, the Clearances and the Industrial Revolution, Lowlanders vastly outnumbered Highlanders. And yet the latter's cultural iconography has been defining: all over Scotland weddings are now bedecked with tartan, the kilt almost mandatory, bagpipes play at all sorts of occasions, and haggis is eaten to celebrate the life of our greatest poet, a Lowlander from Ayrshire. And our national drink has become whisky, a word derived from the Gaelic *uisge* for water, as in the water of life, *uisge beatha*. Despite its branding and all of the misty mythology swirling around as the names of bens and glens abound, the production of Scotch whisky is not a Highland invention. It is in fact unique, the only cultural phenomenon in Scotland that is a true marriage of Highland and Lowland, and not an appropriation.

Beyond Perth, the transition is more gradual. Only after Dunkeld does the A9 begin to penetrate the mountains and even there the broad straths of the Tay and the Tummel keep them at bay for a few miles. Having been up at 5am on a spring morning to avoid the chaos of the Edinburgh bypass and the endless roadworks on the approach to the Forth Bridge, I was driving north on a mission. I wanted to discover not only something of the origins of whisky making but also how this unusual marriage worked. The oldest legal distillery in Scotland is at Glenlivet, not far from the River Spey, a district full of distilleries and their traditions. And a very long way from my farmhouse in the Borders. Despite its alternating dual and single carriageways, I was enjoying the great road through the heart of the Grampian massif. The sun was mostly behind me, lighting the western flanks of the mountains and I made good time. By late morning, I turned off at Aviemore and drove north-east and then south on a B road to Glenlivet Distillery. It was not picturesque, more like a factory in the foothills of the mountains rather than anything particularly sympathetic to its surroundings, but it told a fascinating story.

For some reason, lost in the confusions of local authority bureaucracy, Islington Borough Council had a central role in defining what was Scotch Whisky and what was not. Officials from the North London borough had summonses served on two pub landlords for serving whisky 'not of the nature, quality and substance demanded'. This appears to suggest that what was being sold in at least two pubs and probably many more may have been labelled or advertised as Scotch Whisky, but it was not. Under the provisions of the Mercantile Marks Act, a hearing was held in the summer of 1906 and a judge upheld the complaints. In all senses, it was a defining moment.

This early example of Protected Geographical Status might have expected a joyful welcome in Scotland, but in fact there was uproar. The legal definition of Scotch Whisky was actually a definition of malt whisky, the sort produced by time honoured processes in a pot still, usually in the Highlands. And the vast majority of whisky made in Scotland was not made in the Highlands or in pot stills. In 1832 Aeneas Coffey had invented a new process that could function continuously and produce vast quantities of whisky made from grain of virtually any kind. And like vodka and gin, the raw whisky is clear and without colour. Twenty years later, Andrew Usher, an Edinburgh whisky merchant began to blend these new grain whiskies with small amounts of the malts made in the Highlands. This gave the spirit colour and character, and Usher made it affordable. But the popularity of whisky took off for quite other reasons.

Brandy and soda had been the customary tipple for Victorian gentlemen, but in 1858 a calamity changed these social habits radically. In order to improve their ancient rootstock, French winemakers imported vines from California and also unwittingly introduced devastation. The new grafts brought with them a plague of insects known as *Phylloxera vastatrix*.

Like locusts, they destroyed the vines in all of the great wine regions of France and by 1865 production had collapsed as winemakers realised that they would have to replant. And the brandy made from wine began to run out or became extremely expensive. Whisky and soda took over and sales rocketed. Having been formed in 1877, the Distillers Company increased production of famous brands like John Haig, Johnnie Walker, James Buchanan and Whyte & Mackay and new distilleries were built on Speyside.

Fashion lent a hand. After Queen Victoria and Prince Albert fell in love with Scotland and bought a grand house at Balmoral, all things Scottish became very popular. Herself was said to be fond of a dram, and in an age when society took its cues from royalty, many became fond of what they began to call Scotch. And as the British Empire reached all the way round the world, its rulers introduced whisky to many more countries and, by the end of the nineteenth century, the dram was firmly on the map.

The foundations for this success were laid earlier in the century at Glenlivet and that was why I parked my car outside what looked like a big factory. Which is exactly what it has become on the back of tremendous worldwide demand. I had with me an old copy of David Daiches' excellent *Scotch Whisky: Its Past and Present*, and had learned a good deal of the background. The first records of distilling in Scotland date to the end of the fifteenth century although it is certain that something like whisky was made long before then. It was probably made by Scottish monks in the Middle Ages, and Pluscarden Abbey, near Elgin, also had a reputation for making excellent beer. As Daiches wrote, '[It] made the hearts of all rejoice and filled the abbey with unutterable bliss, raising the devotions to the pitch that the surrounding hills echoed to their hallelujahs'.

After the Reformation, ancestral variants of whisky were made in and around the Highlands by crofters and farmers and, as it grew in popularity, it attracted the attention of governments. They wanted to impose a tax. Most domestic distillers ignored the duty imposed on whisky, and in the more remote glens, the excisemen, the gaugers, had an impossible task. There were thousands of illicit stills. On windless days, they often scanned the horizon for the tell-tale columns of peat reek that would give away the location of a still. Getting to it before it was dismantled and hidden was harder, and one ingenious crofter rigged the flue from the still so that the peat reek fed into the chimney in his cottage. As I looked around the quiet countryside of the valley of the Spey and its tributaries, it was somehow cheering to read that the production of illegal whisky in this area was on a semi-industrial scale. And that bottles of Glenlivet were highly prized as being of very high quality. When George IV came to Edinburgh on a royal visit in 1822, he would drink nothing but Glenlivet. Even though its production was illegal.

The distribution of whisky was well organised and Thomas Guthrie, the founder of the Ragged School network and one of the leaders of the Free Church of Scotland, remembered when the farmer-distillers came to Brechin. Riding shaggy garron ponies, they brought casks of whisky for sale and often disposed of it under the eyes of the gaugers. They were powerless to act because the whisky sellers tended to travel in large groups. 'Everybody, with a few exceptions, drank what was in reality illicit whisky – far superior to that made under the eye of the Excise – lords and lairds, members of Parliament and ministers of the Gospel, and everybody else', wrote Guthrie, himself a minister.

The owner of vast tracts of the north-east of Scotland, Alexander Gordon, the 4th Duke of Gordon, took a hand in history. He was a pillar of the Scottish nobility, Keeper of the Great Seal of Scotland, Lord Lieutenant, and a representative peer at Westminster. Gordon decided that the production of whisky had to be brought within the law; it may have irked him that his estates were at the centre of an illegal trade. The problem he had to solve was that the rates of duty and the costs of licensing an illegal distillery were far too high. In 1823 he promoted an act of parliament to bring this industry out of the twilight and make legal production attractive and affordable. His initiative would turn out to be determinant and lay the foundations of the modern success of Scotch Whisky.

Not everyone agreed. Gordon encouraged his tenants to licence their distilleries and he was active in supporting George Smith, a farmer in Glenlivet, and in essence the founder of the brand. His unlicensed neighbours were none too pleased with Smith and, for years, he never left Glenlivet without a pair of pistols to hand. In other parts of the Highlands, illicit distillers had burned down licensed premises because they saw them as commercial rivals. A troop of cavalry soldiers occupied Corgarff Castle and their role was to back the efforts of the gaugers with force. Lying in the shadow of the highest of the Cairngorms, above Glenlivet, and commanding the heads of the glens of west Aberdeenshire, the castle was well placed to enforce the law and, over three years, hundreds of illicit stills were found and shut down, leaving the tax-paying distilleries to prosper.

The tour around the modern distillery is fascinating. I had only vaguely understood how whisky was made and how the many different malts acquire their characteristics. Over the centuries, techniques have changed very little as volume has expanded enormously. George Smith made 50 gallons of whisky a week or 12,000 litres a year and now, the annual output is 10.5 million litres. As the monks at Pluscarden might attest, the process of making malt whisky is essentially brewing followed by distilling. Barley is soaked to encourage the ears to germinate and convert their starch into sugar. Before it becomes too advanced, the germination is halted by heating and, at that point, barley is said to be malted. Sometimes peat reek is allowed to suffuse the grain and add an intense taste. The barley is then ground into grist and boiled in large copper vessels so that all the sugars come out. This is known as wort and after it has cooled, it is poured into large tanks called washbacks where yeast is mixed in and fermentation begins.

After a time, this liquid, which to my nose smelt very like beer, is then transferred to a copper still. At Glenlivet there are fourteen of these onion-shaped vessels with long swan-necks. When the barley wort is heated, the alcohol begins to distil as its vapour condenses in the swan-neck. This process is repeated and then the raw whisky is poured into oak barrels. These give the malt much of its flavour because most of them have had a previous life, filled with sherry or bourbon whisky. And the barrels are then moved across the car park at Glenlivet and stored in the row of warehouses for at least three years. Much of the output of the distilleries is sold to the blenders and the malt retained at Glenlivet is bottled and sold when it is twelve years old. The distillery also produces older malts, which of course are more expensive. But to my untutored palate, the twelve year old is superb.

I walked up the hill behind the distillery to discover what made Glenlivet so good. Of course, opinions vary but such is the mixture of magisterial knowledge and joy in David Daiches' book that I am inclined to accept his view that 'water matters'. More specifically, 'soft water flowing through peat over granite'. Uphill from the distillery at Glenlivet is the source of their water, or at least most of it for most of the time. In a field there is a white wicket fence surrounding what looks like an old Second World War bunker and a sign that names it Josie's Well. Probably named after Charles Joseph Smith of the founding family, this modest-looking natural spring supplies the distillery with a staggering 3,500 gallons of water each day. It appears to fulfil David Daiches' prescription that it must be 'pure, clear and soft and available in reliable quantities'.

As a very early member of the Scotch Malt Whisky Society, I am of the view that all malt should be drunk with water. It seems to release the flavour. And certainly some of the highly alcoholic whiskies of the Society need to be cut with water so that the nip in the nip does not dominate.

Daiches agrees and adds that the water that made the malt should be drunk with it, if possible. Glen Grant used to keep samples near the distillery dam so that discerning customers could taste their drams with the perfect accompaniment. Perhaps Glenlivet are missing a marketing opportunity here, or perhaps they need all the water that comes out of Josie's Well.

After looking at the well, I kept on walking, climbing slowly into the mountains and was rewarded with wonderful views to the north and the Laigh of Moray. I did not find any granite-based streams but when I did come across fast-flowing little burns (I came up to Glenlivet in early April), the water seemed in contact with peat, although it ran clear. Where rain and snow seep through fissures and small fractures to collect underground, the water must become mineralised in different ways and therefore affect the character of the malt it makes at the distillery. And these balances must change over time. As I tramped along a B road above the glen, I wondered what effect climate change will have on the water.

These were not matters that concerned George Smith in 1824. When he set about establishing the first licensed still, he ran out of cash before the Duke of Gordon came to his rescue with a loan of £600. And by 1834, he was the only distiller in Scotland's most famous whisky glen. It was a monopoly that would not last. Particularly after the devastation of the French vineyards and the drying up of supplies of brandy, others set up in that part of Speyside and, because its reputation was already established, they too called their malts Glenlivet. George Smith's son, Col. J G Smith was forced to take legal action and in 1880 he petitioned the Court of Session in Edinburgh. He asserted, correctly, that rivals were passing off their whisky as being associated with his and that their argument that Glenlivet was a place-name belonging to no-one did not hold if it was printed on the label of a bottle. The judges of the Court of Session came to a compromise. Other distillers could continue to use the name but only if it was hyphenated with the distillery that actually made what was in the bottle. And there appeared Glenlossie-Glenlivet, Glenfarclas-Glenlivet and others in the same vein. However, what consoled J G Smith was that only one, that belonging to his family, could call itself *The* Glenlivet.

Since then, much of the marketing behind malt whisky has focused on its Highland origins with pictures of bens, glens, stags and other wearily familiar scraps of iconography. But what I realised on my walk above Glenlivet and on my journey to the coast of the Moray Firth was that everything needed to make great whisky lay near at hand. Pure water tumbled out of the mountains to feed reliable springs like Josie's Well and, across the Laigh of Moray, the ripe barley fields waved in the breezes of late summer. Only a short distance from the foothills and Glenlivet, lay the fertile fields of some of the richest farming country in Scotland. It is this propinquity of essential and distinctive ingredients that make malt whisky the child of a true marriage between Highland and Lowland.

Matters of definition hampered producers in the early nineteenth century. After the action brought by Islington Borough Council and its ruling against blended whisky, the Distillers Company and others persuaded the London landlords to appeal. Their lobbying also encouraged the government to set up a Royal Commission to deliberate on what might be called Scotch Whisky and what might not. In a bizarre exercise, government officials entered thirty-nine pubs in England and twenty-three in Scotland and ordered drams. But they did not drink them. Instead a bottle was produced from a coat pocket and the whisky poured into it so that it could be analysed.

When the Royal Commission reported in 1909, it began by stating the obvious, or at least something that was obvious to anyone who had drunk more than one brand of whisky. 'On reference to the analyses, it will be seen that there is a very wide variation between whiskies from different distilleries.' It then quickly moved on to the point, the earlier judgement that the use of the word whisky should be restricted only to what is made by the pot still process. The Commission did not agree. The term Scotch Whisky could be applied to whisky mass produced in patent stills – in Scotland. If it was made in Ireland, then it had to be labelled Irish Whiskey, with an e. Which is ironic since the first licence granted by a British government was in 1609, long before Glenlivet, and it went to the Bushmills Distillery in County Antrim. The protection of the brand has been a continuous process and in 2011 the courts ordered retailers who used the phrase 'Scottish Spirits' on labels to desist. This was not Scotch Whisky.

As I walked back to my car, I tried to remember the first time I had drunk whisky. It was certainly not in a pub in Kelso where I grew up, and certainly not when I was under age. Everybody in a small town knew exactly who you were and how old you were. At the end of my first term at university, in 1968, I broke my ankle playing rugby and went home for the Christmas and New Year holiday on crutches. First footing (with a huge cast) around the doors on Old Year's Night, I was handed a glass of whisky and lemonade. It was very sweet, and so were the next few glasses. When I left the hospitable house, I nearly ended up in hospital again as I tripped on the ice covered ground, crutches flying. The following morning, my Grannie ministered to me, as I paid a stomach-churning penalty for drinking whisky. I vowed never to touch the stuff again.

Many years later, Pip Hills, an accountant who helped out theatre companies and was interested in the arts, inveigled me into joining the Scotch Malt Whisky Society. No thanks, I said. But when he persuaded me that malt whisky was completely different and I should try just the one dram, I was converted. Glenlivet is excellent, reliable and affordable, but I once acquired two bottles of a 30-year-old Springbank. The whisky was almost black and it had the most intense, complex nose and a glorious finish. I have never tasted better and I could never afford to acquire another bottle since prices of old whiskies (most do not age all that well after late teens and maybe twenty years but Springbank sure does) has rocketed. And so have worldwide sales of malt, reaching almost £1 billion in 2015. Malt whisky is drunk all over the world, in the fast-developing economies of China and India, and treated with reverence in France, the largest export market. With the opportunity given by the collapse of brandy production in France, there is a historical irony there.

I had come to visit a shrine of sorts at Glenlivet and, while the buildings themselves are well set out and the distillery most interesting, I felt I should have been worshipping in the landscape – all the way down to the fields of the Moray coastlands. For it is the union of Highland and Lowland that makes malt whisky what it is. And why has it become so popular? Because it is authentic, uniquely of this place and beautifully made. The words of David Daiches are apt. Here is his elegant conclusion to *Scotch Whisky: Its Past and Present*: 'The proper drinking of Scotch whisky is more than indulgence: it is a toast to civilisation, a manifesto of man's determination to use the resources of nature to refresh mind and body and enjoy to the full the senses with which he has been endowed.' *Slàinte mhath*.

14

On This Rock
Alexander McCall Smith

Bell Rock Lighthouse, 1807

They may be in the most inaccessible places, high white towers with few windows and very little decoration. Yet many of them are lovely to look at; none of them, I think, is ugly. They are lonely buildings, stoic in their isolation. During the day they are asleep – mute sentinels against the movement of the sea – but when night falls they come into their own, reminding us of their presence with powerful bursts of projected light.

I used to have little interest in lighthouses. Like many, I was aware of the Stevensons, the dynasty of engineers responsible for the building of Scotland's lighthouses, but I knew little about how these extraordinary structures were made, about the lives of the men who did the work or who kept the lights going until automation took over. But then I started to spend more time in Argyll, and lighthouses suddenly became of much greater interest. Having taken up sailing, I have had to try to understand navigation at sea and the role that lighthouses play in that complex subject. I have become one of those who one day might be very glad of the presence of a lighthouse.

The first lighthouse I see on my journeys to Morvern, where I keep a boat, is the lighthouse at Ardgour, close to the point where the Corran Ferry crosses the narrow waist of Loch Linnhe. Then, heading out to sea from Loch Sunart, I see the lighthouse that marks the north-eastern point of Mull, just beyond Tobermory. Half an hour later, rounding the high cliffs of Ardnamurchan Head, one of the most majestic of Scotland's lighthouses comes into view. There can be few sites as beautiful for a lighthouse anywhere else in the world. Perched on the westernmost edge of mainland Scotland, the Ardnamurchan Lighthouse looks out onto the Hebridean Sea; to the north-west are the small isles; behind them, blue, brooding and magnificent, are the mountains of Skye. The lighthouse itself is in the Egyptian style, with high, pointed recesses at the top of the tower; beside it, a great horn points out towards the open sea across which, thousands of miles away, are the shores of Canada. It is an arresting sight.

There is something rather moving about these lighthouses. They are undeniably beautiful structures, but to me they also speak of loneliness and of a hard history. The sea is very much a part of Scotland's past, but the story of that engagement is one of hardship, danger and loss. Lighthouses stand for all that; they are an immediate and unmissable reminder of that long relationship. And of all of Scotland's lighthouses, the Bell Rock, on the other side of the country, in the North Sea, has one of the most interesting and dramatic tales to tell.

*

Navigating the coasts of Scotland was always a perilous business – and to some extent still is. Earlier charts, such as they were, were notoriously inaccurate, putting islands, let alone rocks, in the wrong place and leaving large chunks of seabed unsurveyed. Even today, mariners face a positive obstacle course of shoals and dangerous tidal races, some of these currents being strong enough to make certain passages impossible: the Corryvreckan Strait, north of Jura, may only be navigated at slack tide if one wishes to avoid being sucked into the maelstrom of its famous whirlpool. Elsewhere, outcrops of rock lurk just below the surface of what appears to be deep water, ready to bring the unwary sailor to a shuddering halt. Like many sailors of questionable ability, I have come into contact with these hidden rocks from time to time. The sound of a rock underneath a boat is heart-stopping, even if the contact is slight and at low speed.

Prior to the development of modern aids, the task of navigation depended to a great extent on simple pilotage – the observation of features on the land from which a navigator might deduce his position. But there are clear limitations to such techniques: visibility might be compromised by the weather; without clear landmarks on the shore, the coastline might appear confusingly featureless; and of course at night, even with a full moon, very little can be seen of anything. Of course, lights have always been used to guide sailors – a fire may be made on a headland to guide ships home – but the limitations of such arrangements are obvious. Primitive basket fires, mounted on some sort of structure, might work in perfectly calm conditions, but the rising of the wind may extinguish such fires – and it is precisely in those conditions that the warning is needed. Accessibility would also be an issue. Dangerous rocks are almost always in awkward places where makeshift arrangements simply will not survive the onslaught of sea and wind.

With a growing population and increased economic activity following the Union with England, the density of shipping around the coasts of Scotland grew considerably. This meant that the sea's toll of men and material would inevitably increase: at the end of the eighteenth century, shipwrecks on the British coast were an everyday affair – a fertile source of employment for the wreckers who preyed on them. The extent to which shipwrecks played a significant part in many local economies is surprising. In some parts of the Hebrides, the booty of timbers from wrecks was used for making houses and fences – manna, some islanders believed, to which they had some sort of divine entitlement. Compton Mackenzie's *Whisky Galore*, of course, continued in that tradition: a ship load of whisky being a particularly welcome windfall for the inhabitants of a small island.

As Bella Bathurst points out in her remarkable biography *The Lighthouse Stevensons*, sailors themselves tended to be fatalistic about this attrition, accepting the fact that their seagoing lives would be short. In such a culture, a man overboard might not be helped: ending up in the sea was simply a risk that all mariners accepted as more or less inevitable – a very different attitude from our modern safety-conscious approach.

Not everybody in those days, though, was fatalistic. Those who owned the ships or the cargoes they carried were far from happy with the scale of their loss, and these were the people who most vociferously called for action. The people to whom these pleas were principally directed were the Commissioners of the Northern Lighthouse Board, a body set up by parliament in the late eighteenth century to oversee the construction and running of lighthouses around the Scottish coast. This was not the most proactive of bodies, and over the years it had become adept at providing reasons why it could not do very much to limit the appalling loss of shipping through shipwreck. But eventually, in the case of the Bell Rock at least, the Commissioners bowed to pressure and agreed to build a lighthouse – a building that stands as solid as ever today, performing the task for which it was built over two hundred years ago.

It is the position of the Bell Rock that made it a special case. This is a sledge of rock off the east coast, about twelve miles from the nearest land. From the point of view of mariners, it is in a highly awkward place, being more or less in the middle of an important sea route into the Firths of Tay and Forth, and nearby ports. The rock is in fact a reef of roughly six hundred yards, exposed at low tide but covered at high tide by several feet of water. The reef was formerly known as the Inchcape Rock, but in the fifteenth century it had a warning bell attached to it and became known as the Bell Rock. Unfortunately, this was removed by a pirate who had little interest in saving shipping from disaster, but the name stuck.

Over the years the reef had claimed many victims, most notably a warship, the HMS *York*, that foundered on it in 1799 in the course of a storm that sunk scores of ships around the Scottish coast. This was a high profile disaster – the entire crew was lost – and it led to renewed and vocal calls for something to be done about this egregious danger to shipping. The Commissioners of the Northern Lighthouse Board were embarrassed by the outcry, but they steadfastly refused to do anything about the hazard on the grounds of expense and engineering difficulty: the Bell Rock was simply too remote and dangerous to be suitable for a permanent lighthouse. Their intransigence, though, did not silence the proponents of building a lighthouse on the rock, and one of these was Robert Stevenson, who happened to be the Commissioners' own engineer.

Stevenson was not the first member of his family to earn his living as an engineer. Although he was the son of a merchant, his stepfather – who later became his father-in-law – was Thomas Smith, an Edinburgh tinsmith who began to work on lamps and reflectors for lighthouses more or less at the same time that the Northern Lighthouse Board was set up in 1786. Smith was an enthusiast, and his designs appealed to the Board. Appointed their chief engineer, he proceeded to design and construct lighthouses across Scotland. He took Robert on as his apprentice and in 1808 Robert succeeded Smith in his official post with the Board.

Smith and Stevenson were innovators. Their qualifications as engineers were marginal, but lighthouse technology was still in its infancy in their time. Earlier lighthouses, such as they were, were lit by coal fires; Smith developed oil lamps placed before parabolic reflectors. These were capable of producing a light of 1,000 candlepower, an improvement on previous performance but still a tiny flicker when put beside a modern lighthouse's 690,000 candlepower capacity.

In his new role as engineer to the Board, Robert Stevenson turned his mind to the challenge presented by the Bell Rock. In spite of the public pressure for something to be done about the toll of human life and ships that the Bell Rock was taking, the Commissioners were reluctant to engage with the problem. Stevenson was undeterred; he was aware that the building of a lighthouse on a rock that was covered at high tide was not impossible – it had been done in England – and he felt that the Bell Rock could be tackled in a similar way. He had paid a visit to the Rock in 1794, but had been unable to land, because of sea conditions. He went again in

1800, this time managing to land and inspect possible sites. This visit confirmed his view of the feasibility of a lighthouse there, and he noted that not only was there a possible place to put the foundations but that the geology of the rock was suitable for such a structure. Previously he had thought that a structure on legs would be best, as that would allow the sea to pass through without hitting the solid base of a conventional lighthouse. Now he changed his mind, deciding that a suitably strong building would be able to withstand whatever the sea could throw at it.

Stevenson's report to the Commissioners set out his vision of a solid lighthouse that, he said, could be constructed for a sum of some £42,000. The Commissioners replied that this was far too expensive for them. They also pointed out that, even if they were to decide to go ahead with the construction of a lighthouse on the Bell Rock, the task of building it would not necessarily be given to Stevenson, even if he was their own (and only?) engineer. In her history of the family, Bella Bathurst suggests that the Commissioners probably resented Stevenson's harping on about his scheme. And yet they were at least being made to think again. This reconsideration of the issue led to the taking of outside opinion, initially, and not very successfully, from the great engineer Thomas Telford and then, more productively, from John Rennie.

Above the door into my study in Edinburgh I have a portrait of John Rennie. It is one of two by the same hand – the other being in the collection of the Scottish National Portrait Gallery. The artist is particularly adept at catching human warmth, and has done it conspicuously well in this portrait. Rennie was a much-admired figure who also happened to be something of a workaholic. In the portrait he looks benign; it is a sympathetic face – the face of one who knows what he is about – a practical man of strong character. I look at that portrait every day as I set about my work, but until I came to look into the story of the Bell Rock I was unaware of the tale of professional ambition that unfolded around the construction of this lighthouse. The essence of the matter is this: two men were involved in the design and construction of the Bell Rock Lighthouse; each believed that the credit for the design should go to him. One (Stevenson) wrote extensively about his role in this; the other (Rennie) did not. Inevitably the one who wrote his account has the advantage – not only of publication of his side of the story, but of the famous name.

Robert Stevenson's account of the construction of the Bell Rock Lighthouse was published anonymously in 1813 as an appendix to James Headrick's *General View of the Agriculture of Forfarshire*. That Stevenson was the author is confirmed in letters he wrote now held in the National

Library of Scotland. He refers to himself in the third person throughout – as Mr Robert Stevenson or Mr Stevenson – giving no indication of his own authorship. On the background to the scheme he wrote:

> *Several plans and models had been submitted to the consideration of the Commissioners; but those of their engineer, Mr Stevenson, were ultimately approved of. This gentleman, in the year 1800, made a particular survey of the Bell Rock ... But so various were the opinions of the public regarding even the practicability of the work, and still more concerning the construction of the building best adapted to the situation, that, where so large a sum of public money was necessarily to be expended, the Commissioners judged it proper to submit the subject to the opinion of Mr Rennie ... This eminent engineer coincided with Mr Stevenson in thinking that a building upon the principles of the Eddystone Lighthouse, was both practicable and advisable at the Bell Rock; and to these gentlemen was committed the execution of this great undertaking.*

What conclusion should the reader reach from that? You'd be forgiven for thinking that the Bell Rock Lighthouse was Stevenson's design; that Rennie endorsed Stevenson's ideas in their entirety; and that the actual construction of the lighthouse was a joint responsibility. Although Rennie might have been prickly, it would seem that Stevenson really did try his patience with what would today be described as 'pushiness'. Roland Paxton's book *Dynasty of Engineers: the Stevensons and the Bell Rock* contains the text of a letter written in 1814 to Matthew Boulton by Rennie. This letter was a response to a commercial enquiry by Boulton's firm into Stevenson's background. Stevenson wanted to send an employee to the firm to acquire knowledge on manufacturing techniques. The tone of the letter speaks for itself:

> *When the Bell Rock Lighthouse was erected, Stevenson was employed to superintend the whole, there being a regular mason under him and a carpenter. The original plans were made by me, and the work visited from time to time by me during its progress. When this work was completed Stevenson considered that he had acquired sufficient knowledge to start as a civil engineer and in that line he has been most indefatigable in looking after employment, by writing and applying wherever he thought there was a chance of success. But few weeks passed without a puff or two in the Edinburgh papers. He has taken the merit of applying coloured glass to light houses*

which he stole from Huddart and I have no doubt the whole merit of the Bell Rock Lighthouse will, if it has not already been, be assumed by him ... I have no doubt the principal if not the sole object of his sending a man to your manufactory, is to acquire information respecting them, and to entice away some of your principal workmen. You ought therefore to be particularly circumspect in your transactions with this man ...

The unseemly competition over credit for the Bell Rock Lighthouse should not overshadow the extraordinary achievement of its construction. And that, rather than the design, was the marvel – for which Stevenson, as the supervising site engineer, deserved full credit. How do you erect on a regularly submerged platform of stone, miles out in a notoriously cold and unfriendly sea, a gently tapering building made up of massive stone blocks? How do you ensure that the pieces fit together, that the whole thing does not topple over or is washed away in the first storm, and that in the process of doing all this you accommodate and protect those doing the work? Of course, it can be done – and has been – just as it has been possible in our own times to make great platforms, drag them out to sea, and connect them to oil wells that bore deep into the seabed: *homo faber*, it seems, is ingenious in his ways and undaunted by such challenges.

Stevenson himself told the story of the whole process in his *Account of the Bell Rock Lighthouse*, published in 1813. The first task, he wrote, was to set up a base at sea from which to operate:

The first object was to moor a vessel as near the Bell Rock as she could ride with any degree of safety, to answer the purpose of a floating-light, and a store-ship for lodging the workmen employed at the rock. This vessel measured 80 tons. She had three masts, on each of which a large lantern was suspended, with lights, which distinguished this light from the double and single lights on the coast. Under the deck, she was entirely fitted up for the accommodation of the seamen and artificers, with holds for provisions and necessaries. Thus furnished, she was moored about 2 miles from the rock, in a north-east direction, in 22 fathoms water, with a very heavy cast-iron anchor, resembling a mushroom, and a malleable iron chain, to which the ship was attached by a very strong cable. In this situation, the floating-light was moored in the month of July 1807, and remained during the whole time the house was building, and until the light was exhibited in February 1811 when she was removed.

From this base, the workmen then erected a temporary beacon tower on the rock itself. This was fifty feet high and secured to the rock by chains. Work was suspended for the winter; the following spring it resumed and the base of the lighthouse, a large circle, was excavated from the rock itself. One can imagine the difficulty of doing this: because the rock submerged, there were only a few hours at the bottom of each tide when it was possible to do anything. Men had to be transported from the moored ship to the rock by rowing boat, a hazardous business if there was any sea running at the time. Pumps then had to drain the base to allow for further cutting –a task that must have seemed at times like building sandcastles on the tide-line of a beach.

On Sunday 10 July 1808 the first stone was laid by Stevenson with the masonic blessing: 'May the Great Architect of the Universe complete and bless this building.' This stone, together with all the others used for the construction of the lower part of the outer casing, came from quarries in Aberdeenshire, while the stone used for the inside and the upper walls came from quarries near Dundee. A work yard was established at Arbroath, where Stevenson said the stones were 'wrought with great accuracy', numbered and marked according to position in the structure, and then shipped out to the site. Cranes were erected over the base, and a small railway, raised on legs bolted onto the rock, ran round the outer walls, allowing stone to be delivered on trollies to the right place. When work started again after the winter of 1808, the four courses of stone put into position the previous work season were, Stevenson wrote, 'found to be quite entire, not having sustained the smallest injury from the storms of winter'. By September 1809 the walls had reached a height of thirty feet, and the following September Stevenson laid the final stone. The light first shone out to sea at the very beginning of February 1811.

Stevenson basked in the glory that the completion of the Bell Rock Lighthouse brought him. Becoming something of a celebrity, he was feted for his contribution to maritime safety, even being awarded a medal by the King of the Netherlands for his services to mariners. The icing on the cake came with a visit to the Bell Rock by Sir Walter Scott, whose reputation as an enthusiast for all things Scottish was widespread throughout Europe. Stevenson was thrilled that the great writer should compose on the spot these lines to mark his visit:

> *Far in the bosom of the deep,*
> *O'er these wild shelves my watch I keep:*
> *A ruddy gem of changeful light,*

Bound on the dusky brow of night.
The seaman bids my lustre hail,
And scorns to strike his timorous sail.

Rennie smarted in the background. He had been well and truly eclipsed by Stevenson, and attempts by his family to amend the historical record were unsuccessful.

One of the remarkable things about the building of the Bell Rock Lighthouse is that it was achieved with very little loss of life – at least in accidents. Stevenson reported that only one life was lost on the rock itself, when a blacksmith fell from a rope-ladder in high seas. Another life was lost – that of a seaman – at the mooring buoy, when a boat capsized. Of course these figures do not tell the whole story: the less direct toll of human life that was exacted in the workplace of that time was considerable: the lack of protection for the lungs of quarrymen and masons must have taken many lives, as must general working conditions in every trade involved. Minor injuries were potentially fatal and would not necessarily have been counted; nor would the slow, insidious mortality caused by excessively long hours, poor living conditions and inadequate pay. The real human cost of something like the Bell Rock Lighthouse would have been much greater than that which Stevenson claims.

But that sounds grudging, and we must remind ourselves that the Bell Rock Lighthouse, like all the other lighthouses around Scotland's coast, saved innumerable lives. They may have been important for trade and passage, but the humanitarian impulse that lay behind their construction was important too. The Bell Rock Lighthouse is still there, automated now, but continuing to do the work that it started to do on that February night in 1811. There are some public works that carry on for centuries doing what they were built for – stone bridges being examples – but these are, perhaps, the exception. Most buildings change their purpose and mutate into something else – look at the Royal Infirmary of Edinburgh, a set of great public buildings that became flats and offices; look at the wash-houses that became restaurants and shops; in Tobermory, on Mull, there is a well-built old public toilet block that recently became a busy ice-cream parlour, just as the old ferry building further along the bay became a fish restaurant. Obviously, buildings are better put to some use rather than allowed to decay, but there might be a case for remembering the dignity of our often rather fine buildings and at least considering appropriate public use before handing them over – sometimes with indecent haste – to private developers; after all, they were built for public good and form part of the common patrimony.

Lighthouses stand as a symbol of collective action for collective safety: they tell a story that goes beyond their immediate function. When I sail past one in my boat I sometimes think of that, but not too often. A more immediate thought is this: am I getting too close?

*A History of the Nation in
Twenty-Five Buildings*

1 – 12

1 **Geldie Burn**

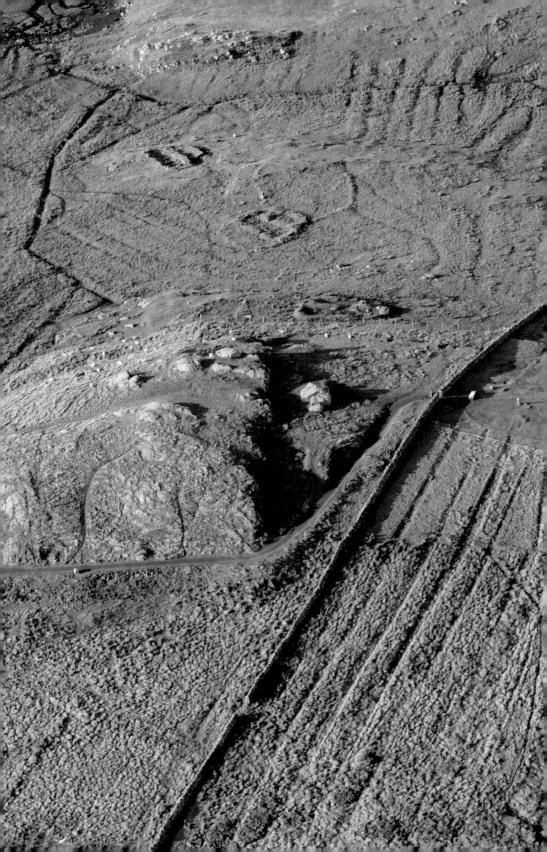

3 Calanais

4 **Mousa Broch**

5 **Iona Abbey**

6 Glasgow Cathedral

8 **Stirling Castle**

9 **Innerpeffray Library**

10 **Mavisbank House**

11 Auld Alloway Kirk

ABBOTSFORD. THE ENTRANCE HALL. 62.

15

Nothing Like My Ain House
James Robertson

Abbotsford, 1811

A place certainly well-suited to be displayed, to astonish, to stagger, and to sadden; but that it should ever have been lived in is the most astonishing, staggering, saddening thing of all.

So wrote Edwin Muir of Abbotsford after visiting there on a sunny July day in 1934. Muir, who would later target Sir Walter Scott and Robert Burns as 'sham bards of a sham nation' in his poem 'Scotland 1941', was bemused by what he found: if one stayed long enough, he wondered, might one uncover Abbotsford's secret life and understand the mania which drove Scott to create 'this pompous, crude, fantastic, unmanageable, heartless, insatiable, comfortless brute of a house'? Might one see why he sacrificed to it in turn 'his genius, his peace of mind, his health and his life'? But Muir did not linger. In fact, he could not get away fast enough from an atmosphere he found utterly oppressive.

It is not hard to share some of Muir's unease. In 1934 the world was still in the grip of the Depression. Huge numbers of people in Scotland lived in unrelenting poverty and squalid housing, and had little or no work – the unemployment rate was about 25%. So many were emigrating in hope of a better life that the population actually fell by 40,000 between the censuses of 1921 and 1931, the first time this had happened since the original census of 1801. (It would happen again in the 1970s and 1990s.) To Muir, Abbotsford and all it represented must have seemed strangely out of place and time; an edifice as contrived and irrelevant to the present as the role Scott had played there: 'a Border laird more convincing than nature' was Muir's verdict.

I came to Abbotsford, for I think the fourth time in my life, on a dreich November afternoon when all the world seemed to be hunkering down for winter. The house itself closes to visitors from December to the end of February, but the new visitor centre is a year-round enterprise. It has a gift shop awash with the kind of tartan-and-shortbread merchandise for which Scott is often held wholly blameworthy. There is also an audio-visual exhibition, which rightly assumes, in the second decade of the twenty-first century, no previous knowledge of a man once famous around the globe, but which is touchily defensive in its presentation of him: *honestly, he wasn't a toff, his books aren't boring, and he was quite go-ahead when it came to innovative technologies like gaslight.* But step beyond this weird manifestation of Caledonian dualism, and things become calmer. The house itself has been beautifully and lovingly restored, and despite what Edwin Muir wrote eighty years ago Abbotsford does reveal a great deal about its Author. As the critic Stuart Kelly has observed, it is something more than a house: it is a shrine and a source, a 3D Waverley Novel.

Even with most of the leaves gone from the trees in the richly wooded surroundings, you cannot see Abbotsford entire until you are almost upon it: the deliberate effect of planting, planning and wall-building begun by Scott two hundred years ago, when he was busily fitting his stone fantasy into a landscape he was also re-shaping. Writing to a friend in January 1814, the year he (anonymously) sent *Waverley* into the world, Scott tells how he spent the previous summer. By then he had been two years in possession of the old farmhouse of Cartleyhole – known locally as 'Clarty Hole', or *mucky hollow* – which he had renamed on the unproven theory that the monks of Melrose Abbey had had a river crossing there:

> We spent the summer at Abbotsford, which is far from being so pleasant as Ashestiel [his previous residence, a few miles further up the Tweed], all the planting being of my own making; but everybody (after abusing me for buying the ugliest place on Tweedside) begins now to come over to my side. I think it will be very pretty six or seven years hence, whoever may come to see and enjoy, for the sweep of the river is a very fine one of almost a mile in length, and the ground is very unequal and therefore well adapted for showing off trees.

For most of his life, Scott divided his legal career between his role as Principal Clerk to the Court of Session and that as Sheriff of Selkirkshire, and hence his time between Edinburgh and Tweedside. One senses that he squeezed the law in amongst all his other activities, rather than vice versa, and thought of both jobs, which were generally not too onerous, as duties – although their annual remunerations of £1,300 and £300 respectively were not to be sniffed at. It was a requirement of the position of Sheriff that he maintained a home within the bounds of his jurisdiction.

Not three years after sending the above letter, and with *Guy Mannering*, *The Antiquary*, *The Black Dwarf* and *Old Mortality* completed and published in the interim – a quite astonishing output – he writes to Joanna Baillie:

> *I have some thoughts of enlarging Abbotsford this year, and I have got a very pretty plan which may be executed at moderate expense, having the local advantage of plenty of stones on the property. I have always had a private dislike to a regular shape of a house, although no doubt it would be very wrong-headed to set about building an irregular one from the beginning; but when the cottage [the original farmhouse, eventually completely demolished] enlarges itself and grows out of circumstances, which is the case at Abbotsford, the outs and the ins without afford so much variety and depth of shade, and within give such an odd variety of snug accommodation that they far exceed in my estimation the cut-lugged band-box, with four rooms on a floor and two stories rising regularly above each other. From this you will be disposed to augur something rather whimsical, and you will be perfectly right.*

Scott's breenging, headlong dash to get stories out of his head and into print is mirrored in his drive to create this 'Flibbertigibbet of a home', which he also, tellingly, called a 'museum for living in'. He bought it with the money he had earned as a poet – his epic romances, usually in six cantos, such as *The Lay of the Last Minstrel* and *Marmion*, sold in their tens of thousands – but the Waverley Novels would prove even more successful, providing a vast reservoir from which to sluice money into the building of his 'romance in stone and lime'. Arguably, he took greater care over the narrative lines of Abbotsford than he did with some of his plots, but the same urgency, the same infatuation with history's whigmaleeries and relics, the same stuffing-in of detail – because he could not bear to leave it out – is evident.

The house had to occupy more than just its own space: it had to be in and of the land around it. He began with 110 acres and bought out his neighbours until he had £1,400. It wasn't enough to have a sweeping vista down to the Tweed: his improvements required altering the course of the river itself. He was forever planting trees, and in this at least he was not unique: re-timbering the often brutally denuded slopes of Scotland was an infatuation for many landowners. One of the best lines from any of his novels is when the dying Laird of Dumbiedikes, in *The Heart of Midlothian*, tells his dozy son, 'Jock, when ye hae naething else to do, ye may be aye sticking in a tree; it will be growing, Jock, when ye're sleeping.' We forget, sometimes, how much of our planned environment includes woods made by men who never saw them grow to their maturity.

When at the end of 1824 Abbotsford was finished (at least, insofar as Scott could stop himself from tinkering with it as a work-in-progress), an unusually large party of guests descended for the Christmas period. Among them was one Captain Basil Hall, who kept a journal of his stay. He recounts being taken for a five-mile walk by Scott over the estate, and that his host 'entertained us all the way with an endless string of anecdotes, more or less characteristic of the scenes we were passing through. Occasionally he repeated snatches of songs, sometimes a whole ballad, and at other times he planted his staff in the ground and related some tale to us, which, though not in verse, came like a stream of poetry from his lips.'

They reached a particular viewpoint, and Hall remarked that it must be interesting to engage in planting. 'Interesting!' Scott cried. 'You can have no idea of the exquisite delight of a planter – he is like a painter laying on his colours – at every moment he sees his effects coming out. There is no art or occupation comparable to this; it is full of past, present and future enjoyment ... Unlike building, or even painting, or indeed any other kind of pursuit, this has no end, and is never interrupted, but goes on from day to day, and from year to year, with a perpetually augmented interest.'

This has no end. Scott was painfully aware of the speed of the passage of time, and that there would never be enough of it for him to do all he wished to do or enjoy all that he longed to enjoy. A year goes by. By December 1825, with intimations of the financial disaster that would overtake him thickening fast, and having not long begun what would turn out to be his most moving work, his *Journal*, he writes of the pleasures he has had from being in company, even that of the most tiresome people. And yet –

> *from the earliest time I can remember, I preferred the pleasures of being alone to waiting for visitors, and have often taken a bannock and a bit of cheese to the wood or hill to avoid dining with company. As I grew from boyhood to manhood I saw this would not do and that to gain a place in men's esteem I must mix and bustle with them ... Still if the question was eternal company without the power of retiring within yourself, or solitary confinement for life, I should say, 'Turnkey, lock the cell.'*

Abbotsford would become that welcome yet lonely cell. The crash that left him owing £120,000 also isolated him emotionally and psychologically from the very society which lionised him and adored his books. Now, writing more and more of those books became the means of his redemption:

'My own right hand shall pay the debt.' Within a few months, his wife Charlotte was dead, but perhaps the loss he dreaded more was the one that did not materialise. 'To save Abbotsford I would attempt all that was possible,' he told his journal, a closer confidant than Charlotte ever was. 'My heart clings to the place I have created.' Whatever Edwin Muir felt, for Scott Abbotsford *was* a home, and a homely one at that.

And one, too, where physical objects (garden statuary, turrets, plaster ceilings disguised as ancient carved cedar) were not just extensions of his imagination but were paid for by it. Scott knew this and often wondered how long the spell could last. Wealth, property and position were all tangled up in the bursting fertility of his mind. How apt that the sound-proofed octagonal 'speak-a-bit' off his study, where he could have private conversations on legal and financial matters, was also where he kept his forestry tools. How 'in character' that the Wizard of the North should have a private stair down which, while the house still slept, he could creep to that study and write undisturbed for a couple of hours before masking himself at breakfast as the Laird of Abbotsford.

'My life has been a sort of dream,' he writes in one entry; and, in another, 'Life could not be endured were it seen in reality.' In Abbotsford, he made a place where dream and reality intertwined, and life *was* endurable.

A lawyer without history or literature, he believed, was 'a mere mechanic', and every nook and vacant space in Abbotsford is furnished with both. There are 9,500 volumes shelved in the library and study, many bound in Russian calfskin and bearing the motto *Clausus tutus ero* ('closed in I will be safe'), an anagram of his name in Latin, *Uualterus Scotus*. It was in the study that he laboured during the last six years of his life, churning out fiction, essays, a huge biography of Napoleon, histories of Scotland for adults and children – all to reduce his debts (which were cleared shortly after his death). When he turns from this, his 'task', it is to spend time with his intimate friend, the journal, into which he pours his soul. Anybody who thinks Scott is beyond their sympathy should also spend time with that book: it is the record of a shaggy, wounded beast, a great man brought low and facing his own mortality at every moment. And this makes the history with which he surrounded himself all the more overwhelming.

It is *everywhere*. The door and some of the stonework of Edinburgh's Tolbooth, the infamous Heart of Midlothian which gave him the title and primary location of one of his finest novels, are built into the exterior walls. A firebasket said to have belonged to Archbishop Sharp (*Old Mortality* is set in the immediate aftermath of Sharp's assassination by Covenanters) sits in the entrance hall's fireplace. There are locks of hair from the heads of Lord

Nelson and Bonnie Prince Charlie; Rob Roy's purse; Flora MacDonald's pocketbook; Lord Byron's mourning ring; Napoleon's blotter; a musketball and oatcake crumb from Culloden; war trophies picked up at Waterloo (Scott rushed to the battlefield as soon as he could, in August 1815). And everywhere, especially in the armoury, weapons: daggers, swords, pikes, maces, crossbows, guns, axes. Friends and admirers made gifts of some of these items to him; most, he collected himself. Montrose's sword, Claverhouse's pistol, Rob Roy's dirk are displayed alongside his own blunderbuss, and the sword he brandished while galloping around as a militiaman at Leith, preparing to repel French invasion. The armoury is a spikily disturbing room, but Scott loved it, calling it 'an unrivalled little retreat for convenience and delightful elegance'. Had childhood polio not left him permanently lame, he would have been a soldier – a profession compared with which he thought the writing of poems and stories essentially trivial. Or so he always *said*, but he was practised in the art of self-effacement (he did not publicly acknowledge that he was the 'Author of Waverley' until named as such at a dinner in Edinburgh in 1827) and so his stated opinions cannot always be taken at face value. Abbotsford, whatever else it is, is hardly an expression of modesty.

Scott may have had one foot firmly in the past, yet Abbotsford also presaged the future, not just because of its gas lighting but because the influence of Scott extended far beyond the entertainment value of his writings. His carefully constructed form of Scottish patriotism, a unionist-nationalist balancing-act *par excellence*, was the design template for Scots for the rest of the nineteenth century, enabling them to participate in the British Empire and yet retain their *special* national identity. Balmorality, Scots Baronial, Highlandism morphing into the Celtic Twilight and – thus – the Scotch kitsch of a thousand gift shops can all be said to flow from Scott's legacy, and Abbotsford is the architectural expression of that legacy. In that sense, Sir Walter really did lay the foundations of Victorian Scotland. But he did not act alone, nor could he have had such influence without the enthusiastic response and willing engagement of his nation. An earlier generation of Edinburgh literati – and European readers including Napoleon – had become infatuated with Gaelic and Highland culture through the cult of Ossian promoted by James Macpherson: Scott's romanticising of the Jacobite clans was a logical extension of that infatuation. In his stories and poems of Scotland he gave his compatriots – and the world – gifts which they found, when they unwrapped them, to be exactly what they wanted.

But it could not last. The bonds Scott made between valour and propriety, between heroism and honour, between tradition and the preservation of a society in which peasants, lawyers, merchants and lairds knew their places, or learned through experience to know them, or were killed or exiled because they would not, collapsed amid the slaughter and waste of the Great War and the rise of the democracy Scott so feared. There was no longer much that was heroic or honourable about dying for a lost cause, or killing on behalf of gluttonous empires; and little glory in fighting simply to survive. Scott's fall from grace – from being the Great Unknown, an author in whose works many a parent saw no moral danger to their children, to being the Great Unread, an author of no moral importance in an utterly changed world – was swift and almost fatal.

And yet Scott's own end *was* heroic – made mythically so by the efforts of his biographer (and son-in-law) John Gibson Lockhart, and by the shrine-like aura of Abbotsford. Physically broken by the work he set himself in those last six years, Scott had aged far beyond his sixty-one years when, after a voyage to the Mediterranean intended to restore his health, he was brought home to die. For much of the journey north from London he was barely conscious, but revived a little in familiar surroundings. Indeed, for a few days after returning to Abbotsford he rallied, and Lockhart and his factor Willie Laidlaw pushed him around the house and grounds in a bath-chair: 'I have seen much,' he kept repeating, 'but nothing like my ain house – give me one turn more!' He was like a child on a fairground ride, or one wanting another story before bedtime. There followed two invalid months in a bed set up for him in the dining room, and that was where he breathed his last, on a beautiful September day so warm that every window was open, and so still, as Lockhart put it, 'that the sound of all others most delicious to his ear, the gentle ripple of the Tweed over its pebbles, was distinctly audible …'

The last words he spoke to Lockhart implored him to be a good man: 'Nothing else will give you any comfort when you come to lie here.' You would have to have a very hard or a very cold heart to stand in that dining room and not be moved by the way Scott's light dimmed and finally went out.

*

To go from Abbotsford forty miles west to Brownsbank Cottage is to travel from the monumental dream palace of one writer to the inglorious refuge of another – two small rooms up a farm track, with a kitchen and bathroom extension tacked on at their rear – and yet they have some things in common. For Abbotsford too became a refuge from the world, and Brownsbank – as Hugh MacDiarmid, its occupant for the last thirty-seven years of his life, wryly put it – became 'a growing shrine to my vanity'.

MacDiarmid was born in 1892 as Christopher Murray Grieve and grew up in Langholm, seven miles from the border with England. He developed a lifelong antipathy to that country (mischievously listing 'Anglophobia' as a hobby in *Who's Who*) but reserved his real ire for those home-bred types he memorably dismissed as 'Scots Wha Ha'evers, village idiots, policemen, leaders of white-mouse factions … Commercial Calvinists, makers of "noises like a turnip"' and all the 'touts and toadies and lickspittles of the English Ascendancy'. MacDiarmid attacked Sir Walter Scott more ferociously than Edwin Muir ever did, but not as ferociously as he turned on his erstwhile ally Muir when they fell out over the future direction of Scottish literature and culture. Falling-out was something MacDiarmid was spectacularly good at. It was a habit Muir, a more placid man, neatly captured in his description of the band of Rose Street poets who were MacDiarmid's disciples as 'men of sorrows, and acquainted with Grieve'. In his 1936 book *Scott and Scotland*, Muir declared that 'the curse of Scottish literature is the lack of a whole language, which finally means the lack of a whole mind'. The solution, he concluded, was to write in English. MacDiarmid had just spent ten years almost singlehandedly generating a literary Renaissance based on the premise that the future lay with Scots and Gaelic. Not surprisingly, he was – to use a phrase coined by P G Wodehouse, a thoroughly English author whose work he nevertheless much enjoyed – far from gruntled.

MacDiarmid, a mountain of contradictory opinions who liked nothing more than to be 'whaur extremes meet', praised Walter Scott's preoccupation with 'the National Question' in, for example, his defence of Scottish paper currency in the *Letters of Malachi Malagrowther*, but condemned the Waverley Novels as 'the great source of the paralysing ideology of defeatism in Scotland, the spread of which is responsible at once for the acceptance of the Union and the low standard of nineteenth century Scots literature … '. Well, there may be truth in that, but the fact remains that Scotland, in the first half of the nineteenth century, desired, seized and embraced Scott's re-casting of its history, literature and culture. This was probably a necessary process, just as it became necessary, in the 1920s, for MacDiarmid to blast away some of the assumptions and complacencies with which that re-casting had become encrusted. It has taken far longer for MacDiarmid's magic to work than the Wizard of the North's ever did, and arguably its full effects have yet to be seen. Most Scots have never

heard of MacDiarmid, let alone read anything he wrote. Scotland never embraced *him*, in his lifetime or since. Had it tried to do so, he would probably have metaphorically nutted it before stamping off in high dudgeon.

I came to MacDiarmid's poetry and prose some years before I engaged with Scott's: in fact, had it not been for MacDiarmid bursting the padlock for me, I might never have opened the kist of riches that is Scottish literature and thus found myself studying Scott as a postgraduate student. I had hardly heard of MacDiarmid when he died in 1978, but a review of his posthumously published *Complete Poems* stirred my curiosity, and soon I was hooked. MacDiarmid revolutionised all my thinking on politics, culture, literature, language (Scots, especially) and Scotland. I was twenty years old, and had aspired to be a writer for as long as I could remember. MacDiarmid focused my attention on new ideas, broadened my perspective and sharpened my ambition, which I nurtured for the next fifteen years. It was therefore strangely fateful that, after all that time, I ended up living in his old home for two years, as the first holder of the Brownsbank Writing Fellowship.

In the autumn of 1950, not for the first time, Chris and Valda Grieve were about to become homeless. A publisher friend put them in touch with Mr Thomas Tweedie, who farmed at Candymill, three miles east of Biggar in Upper Clydesdale. Tweedie agreed to let them have Brownsbank, an empty but-and-ben on his property, rent-free. Perhaps he thought this would be a temporary arrangement, but in fact it lasted nearly forty years. It was a gesture of remarkable generosity: the Clydesdale farmer had no particular reason to empathise with a penniless Communist poet and his fiery-tempered wife. When Valda died in 1989, there was a danger that a little piece of Scotland's cultural history might fall into complete disrepair and be lost. Fortunately, the local museum was on hand to prevent that happening.

Biggar Museum Trust is an extraordinarily dynamic organisation which grew out of the magpie-like enthusiasm for collecting and preserving local history of Brian Lambie, the town's last provost, who lived from 1930 to 2014. The main museum now occupies a splendid new building on the High Street and is well worth visiting, but it was back in the 1960s that Lambie established the first of what eventually became six museums in or close to the town, and got MacDiarmid, the nearest celebrity to hand, to perform the official opening ceremony in 1968. (Lambie's great-great-great-great grandfather, incidentally, was the stonemason Robert Paterson, who devoted himself to repairing the graves of the Covenanter martyrs and was the inspiration for Scott's *Old Mortality*: such are the threads that create the web of a small country.) Brownsbank, bought from the Tweedie family, became the sixth of Biggar's museums. The cottage was badly in need of restoration: every single item in it was catalogued and removed, the structural repairs were done, and then all the contents put back exactly as they had been. I stayed there from 1993 to 1995. Even more than Abbotsford, it really was 'a museum for living in'. Those two years changed my life, enabling me to leave my employment as a bookseller in Glasgow and become a full-time writer. This book is concerned with the question of who built Scotland. I can say with certainty that MacDiarmid's influence, and then the tiny Lanarkshire cottage he and Valda lived in, played a big part in building me.

Living there did not come without challenges. I moved in in February, and found it a cold and primitive place. After the city, the nights were as black as pitch. I was kept awake by mice dancing reels in the roof space – whole squadrons of them, it seemed, although I probably overestimated the numbers, as later I found that the less tough among them tended to move out in winter, opting for kinder conditions in the surrounding countryside. Draughty, subject to power-cuts and often battered by foul weather, Brownsbank nevertheless offered me opportunities that far outweighed these inconveniences. Waking in the morning to multiple images of MacDiarmid staring at me from the walls, as if chiding me for not being up and working, I got up and worked. That, after all, was why I was there.

In any case, how much more challenging it had been for the Grieves in the 1950s. When Chris and Valda took up residence there was no electricity, an outside toilet, and their water supply came from a spigot in the garden. After a heavy snowfall followed by a rapid thaw they were faced with the problem of how to get sheep off the roof. Over time, Valda collected earth from molehills to create flowerbeds. She cooked curries and soups on a primus stove and the open fire, lit the house with oil-lamps and made curtains from odd scraps of material. The simple, stone-built, nineteenth century cottage was not well-insulated or fuel-efficient, but with a good fire going it could be made cosy. Compared with other places they had lived – Valda never forgot the hardships they endured in the 1930s on Whalsay in Shetland, where they survived on mackerel and potatoes given to them by their neighbours – it was almost luxurious, and made more so in the 1960s when volunteer students and members of the Young Communist League rallied round to build the front porch, kitchen and bathroom and install electricity, lighting, running hot and cold water and a flushing toilet. The world came to MacDiarmid at Brownsbank, and from Brownsbank he went out to the world. He was forever being invited to give talks and readings, often in Communist Eastern Europe, and Edinburgh, with its Rose Street pubs, was only an hour and a half away by bus. More than anything, Brownsbank was home, one from which, as it turned out, the Grieves would never be ejected.

When I lived there, one of my duties was to show the occasional visitor round. The tour didn't take long. When folk who had known Chris and Valda arrived, they usually approved of the restoration and the fact that it was again a place lived in by a writer, even if they missed the tobacco fug, the stacks of newspapers beside Chris's chair, and the pervasive smell of wet terrier. The wood-panelled walls were still hung with paintings, photographs and caricatures of MacDiarmid; the shelves still held his collection of pipes, Valda's wally dugs, the green Penguin crime novels they both devoured, the familiar bric-a-brac accumulated by Valda, whose taste was eclectically indiscriminate. I came with a few books and keepsakes of my own, an Amstrad word-processor, a record player and records – there was hardly room even for these – which I fitted in among the museum's artefacts as discreetly as possible. For two years I felt as if I were living in spaces left in other people's lives, even though those people were gone. It was not an unpleasant experience. In fact, it was quite comforting. I felt welcome, although never for a moment – and despite those stares from the ubiquitous portraits – did I think that their ghosts were watching over me.

Halfway through my time there, I wrote a long poem, 'The Blues at Brownsbank'. It's a while since I've looked at it – but then it's well over twenty years since I wrote it. As I reflect on that passage of time, one stanza in particular stands out:

What do I touch when I touch an object here? –
This lamp, this chair, this book with the note in his clear
Downsloping hand that says 'To Valda with all my love.
Where would I – or Scots poetry – have been without her?'
What do I feel when I feel nothing of their presence?
This place is better than haunted, it is real, inhabited;
Inanimate, it has not felt the passing lives of cottars,
Cottars' wives, folk of the land who sucked, shat, mated,
Fought, loved, died, age after age, after them a poet
And a poet's wife, a widow, now me, and through it
All we are nothing to the stones. Though we build a space
From them for our lives, our lives are nothing. This we must face.

I'm not so sure now – if I was sure then – that 'our lives are nothing'. But even if it is true that the buildings we inhabit remain immune to our cares, our passions, our lives, something of those lives is always detectable by other humans, if through no other medium than memory or through being told their stories. This is what makes Abbotsford and Brownsbank special places: they retain the stories of those who once lived in them. It is we who must decide if the stories mean anything.

Scott and MacDiarmid were prodigious workers who happened to be writers. Of course, they wrote – would have written – wherever they found themselves. They could not help it. MacDiarmid composed most of his best poetry and his liveliest prose long before he settled at Brownsbank: in Montrose, in London, in Shetland, he had things to say, and he said them. Scott's hands, according to Lockhart, never could rest still. There is a scene in Lockhart's *Life* when a man is distracted, night after night, by a hand writing page after page of manuscript in a window in Castle Street, Edinburgh. 'Some stupid, dogged, engrossing clerk, probably,' somebody suggests; but in fact it is the hand of Walter Scott, writing the bulk of *Waverley* over three weeks in July 1814.

Far from Abbotsford, far from Brownsbank, the words found their way out, had to be set down. But in these two writers' houses, so utterly different in size and status, the one world-famous and the other almost completely hidden from the world, I feel that somehow the words, like pigeons, have found their way home.

16

Surgery's Temple
Alexander McCall Smith

Surgeons' Hall, 1830s

As a student, I used to walk past this building every day of the week, on my way to the Old College, further down the road. I never paid much attention to it; I knew what it was, but it was also just one of the buildings that made that walk down Nicolson Street and onto South Bridge such a curious hotch-potch of architectural styles — and of purposes too. Cheek by jowl with the Royal College of Surgeons of Edinburgh was a cinema, the La Scala, a run-down, narrow establishment at which, during the performance, a member of the staff would walk down the aisles spraying the air with a strong-smelling disinfectant of some sort. A block or so further on was Drummond Street, with its bars and barbers, and the sprawling premises of James Thin, the bookseller. Every building looked as if it had been there for a long time, doing exactly the same thing that it had been doing years before. The stones were all darkened; on commercial premises there were ancient painted signs, the lettering still intelligible; at night the area had a feeling of mystery — on misty, mysterious evenings it seemed perfectly possible that Burke and Hare might still be prowling.

Everyone knew the building as Surgeons' Hall and understood that this was where prospective surgeons had their examinations. From time to time, groups of anxious-looking people could be seen milling about at the entrance — candidates facing the ordeal of the fellowship examinations. But in the days before doors-open schemes, which admit the public to buildings across the city, few people knew what lay within. I had only the vaguest idea, and it was not until I was invited to a Burns Supper in the College that I saw the interior. After that there was the occasional lecture and formal occasion that allowed me to see inside.

It is not surprising that among Scotland's great public buildings those places associated with the Scottish medical tradition should figure so prominently. Scotland has long been proud of its medicine and has helped train doctors for countries in all corners of the world. If exported Scottish medical talent is marginally less likely to be found in far-flung places than used to be the case, then it is still not at all unusual to find specialists trained by its medical colleges in virtually any country one cares to name. This was brought home to me some years ago when I had the misfortune to swallow a fish bone in Kuala Lumpur. The bone lodged in my throat and I required an operation the same day. To be whisked off the street into a hospital in a strange country is an unsettling experience, but how reassuring, as one lay on the table to be told, as I was, by the surgeon: *Don't worry – we're all Edinburgh people.* The surgeon was a Fellow of the Royal College of Surgeons of Edinburgh, the anaesthetist had also trained in Edinburgh, as had another of the doctors who looked after me in the hospital.

This medical tradition has deep roots. In the case of surgeons, the story goes back to the emergence of the craft of surgeons and barbers, and its incorporation at the beginning of the sixteenth century. In the early days, the Incorporation was concerned with the regulation of apprenticeships and ensuring that the level of professionalism was raised. Apprentices were required to be competent in Latin and to be sufficiently literate to read what literature was available on the art of surgery. A great deal of energy came to be devoted to ensuring that barbers did not stray into the practice of surgery, and that there should be a proper gulf between trained surgeons and the enthusiastic amateurs who offered all sorts of procedures and promised cures to the sick and gullible. The march of professionalisation continued, encouraged by the expansion of medical teaching within the universities. Eventually, in 1778, the Royal College of Surgeons of Edinburgh was granted its charter by the Crown, and the modern structures of training in surgery and its practice came into existence.

A profession requires a home and as the profession became more confident of its status, the search began to create a place that would express that status in stone. This was eventually achieved, of course, with the construction of the handsome Greek-revival building that the College still occupies today, but before that there were various buildings that housed the College during its rise to eminence. The final home of the surgeons might be a triumphant flourish, but the beginnings were humble – a tenement in Dickson's Close, leased by the Incorporation (as it then was) for £40 a year. At that time, the Incorporation's accommodation was neither suitable not stable, and it ended up moving from house to house until a more permanent building was obtained. This came in the shape of Curryhill House, adjoining High School Yards. This was more fitting for a public body growing in importance, as it had four storeys and a spacious garden. This building came to be known as Old Surgeons' Hall and was used until the early nineteenth century. By that stage, however, it had become increasingly unsuitable for its purpose, being too small for the growing numbers in the profession and for the storage of collections of books and anatomical samples. The College appointed a committee to consider their options: the existing premises could be repaired, another building could be purchased and adapted, or the College could build something entirely new.

The College decided on the third option and approached the celebrated architect William Playfair to advise on a design. While discussions were being carried out with Playfair, the clock was set running by a condition attached to a gift promised by John Barclay, an honorary Fellow of the College. Barclay, the son of a Perthshire farmer, was educated at the University of St Andrews and became a minister of the Kirk. He spent ten years in that role before he decided to study medicine, which he did in Edinburgh. In the course of his career, Barclay assembled a vast collection of anatomical specimens that he left to the College – provided that it started to build a hall to house the collection within two years of accepting the gift. This forced the College into action.

The choice of Playfair as architect reflects the determination to build something that would express the College's importance. Playfair had already designed several impressive public buildings, including the Royal Scottish Academy on Princes Street and the Calton Hill observatory. He came from an accomplished family: his father, John Playfair, was an architect, and while one of his uncles was a professor of mathematics another was a well-known engineer. His architectural practice was highly successful and round about the time he was commissioned by the College he was also working on several important New Town streets: Regent Terrace, Royal Terrace and Calton Street.

Playfair's work is instantly recognisable because of its neo-Grecian feel. The roots of this are to be found well before Playfair's time when a number of eighteenth century Scots became convinced of the similarities between Scotland and Greece, and, in particular, between the physical situation of Edinburgh and Athens. Affinity for all things Grecian occurred in a wide range of contexts – literary and philosophical, as well as artistic and architectural. In a literary context, the extraordinary works of James Macpherson enjoyed wide popularity, not only in Scotland but on the continent. Macpherson had learned Greek when he was at Aberdeen University and in his Ossianic poetry sought to create a Scottish Homeric epic set in the Highlands. This was pure romanticism, of course, but it represented a strong desire in Scottish intellectual circles to find in Scotland a Greek civic culture. This is what inspired Adam Ferguson to write *An Essay on the History of Civil Society*, and it also lay behind the educational ideal of the democratic intellect – a humanist notion that stressed the importance of a rounded education, taking into account philosophy, science and the arts. This project, with its strong emphasis on democratic debate and concern with society, has been a long-lasting ideal in Scotland, as George Davie demonstrated in his classic *The Democratic Intellect*. That ideal has not entirely disappeared, and for many it is a central plank in their sense of the distinctiveness of Scottish society and the seriousness of its claims.

The Hellenists were extremely influential and their impact on architecture in Edinburgh soon became apparent. In 1829 Thomas Shepherd published *Modern Athens: Edinburgh in the Nineteenth century* that expressed this desire to create in Edinburgh an 'Athens of the North', distinctive in style and intellectual ambitions from the rest of the United Kingdom. London might have the money, the modern Athenians conceded; it might also have political power as the centre of a vast empire; but it was Edinburgh that would represent all that was best in the classical tradition.

Surgeons' Hall must be looked at in the context of this extensive Hellenisation of the Edinburgh townscape. There it stands, right up against the public pavement and the road – without the room to breathe that a building of this size and majesty should have – but as clear and powerful a statement as one might wish for of the classical rationalism of the Scottish Enlightenment; of the belief that Scotland shares the vision of those who created the Parthenon and other great Hellenic buildings; of the determination of Scottish science to stand for universal human values. Playfair's building does not just have the pleasing qualities of a large, solid structure: it proclaims the importance of the body whose temple it is. This is the physical embodiment of the dignity of surgery. In medical circles, of course, surgeons have always had the reputation of having a good conceit of themselves: if anybody, therefore, is going to have an imposing building, then it would have to be them. This building has authority of the highest sort: look at the front door that lies behind the six great Ionic pillars. Look at the elaborate architrave and frieze, at their elegance and their confidence. All of these things proclaim the same message: this building is the home of a profession; it is dedicated to the highest standards of scholarship and practice; this building represents a wisdom that requires precisely this solidity, precision and stature.

It is interesting to reflect on the statements that buildings make. The architecture of our times is not given to the making of major statements, tending to the functional and being wary – perhaps with good reason – of the dangers of expressing ideology in stone. The twentieth century's examples of ideologically motivated architecture have not been edifying: the socialist architecture of the Soviet Union was inevitably monolithic and unsubtle, making a grand political statement or tending to stark functionality (as in numerous featureless blocks). Then there was Milan Railway Station and Mussolini's bizarre fascist city outside Rome, along with various grandiose dictatorial gestures – the elaborate palaces and vast kitsch monuments of late twentieth century Iraq spring to mind. Today, statements tend to be made through scale rather than ornamentation or style; buildings are designed to do what they have to do and not much else. Surgeons' Hall, however, is unambiguously a major statement building of its time.

Playfair paid attention not only to the exterior of the building, but also to the interior details. Again, emphasis was on grandeur, with even some of the furniture – which he designed – expressing the importance of the College and its activities. It is one of the pleasures of visiting the building today to see the chairs that were also designed for it still in use. There are twenty-five Playfair chairs, the most important being the President's chair, a very comfortable-looking mahogany armchair with red leather upholstery; office-bearers' chairs have no arms but sport a broad back rest and have fluted legs that display the same Grecian outlook to be found in Playfair's stone columns on the front of the building.

Elegant though it was, the building nonetheless had its limitations when it came to space. At the beginning of the twentieth century, major internal alterations were made. The hall was too small for the size of meetings that the College now needed to have: the College minutes of the time record 'not only is the hall too small for large meetings but it is badly ventilated and overshadowed by adjoining buildings'. As far as the library was concerned, there simply was not adequate shelving to deal with the volume of books that the College was acquiring, and many books were held in cupboards rather than on the open shelves.

A report on what to do about the space issue was commissioned from George Balfour Paul, an architect who had undertaken a number of prestigious projects elsewhere in Edinburgh. Balfour Paul suggested the moving of walls to allow for the creation of a larger meeting hall. This was done, with result that the College acquired a large, airy meeting space, topped with a generously proportioned circular cupola. This is now probably one of the most pleasing rooms in Edinburgh. A restful room in which functions – and rather less restful examinations – are held and conducted under the gaze of the portraits of past surgical luminaries.

Throughout the century, surrounding properties were acquired, including St Michael's Church, which was converted into a lecture hall. A number of surrounding tenement properties were bought by the College, allowing fellowship candidates and others associated with the College to find accommodation right next door.

Within the main College building, two suites of rooms lend particular interest to Surgeons' Hall. These are the original library, a relatively small, oak-panelled room, and the museum. The library demonstrates the classical simplicity of the Playfair interior; however grand the exterior, the rooms inside have a simple feel to them, even if there are cornices and strategically placed columns. The rooms seem almost square, which is always pleasing; the ceilings are the perfect height, the wood panelling restful in its effect. Leading off the library is the Fellows' meeting room, where College business was discussed. This is the setting for the painting executed by P A Hay at the end of the nineteenth century. The Fellows are depicted all congregated in the meeting room – solemn, powerful Victorian figures, several of them with impressive beards. One ginger beard in particular dominates the right hand side of the painting, a splash of colour among all the black jackets of the surgeons – a beard that simply would not be tolerated in a modern operating theatre on infection-control grounds. To paraphrase Edward Lear, such a surgeon might say: *It's just as I feared / Coxiella burnetii and Fonsecaea pedrosoi / Have all made a nest in my beard.*

Also in the painting is Joseph Bell, sitting in the presidential chair designed by Playfair. Bell was a fourth-generation surgeon of the College, and his father was one of the first surgeons to take effective efforts to deal with pain during surgery – efforts that were a precursor of Simpson's discovery of the anaesthetic effect of chloroform. Bell has a major claim to immortality, though, in respect of the inspiration he provided to an Edinburgh medical student, Arthur Conan Doyle. It was Bell's display of diagnostic skills that inspired Conan Doyle to create Sherlock Holmes, a debt that the author readily acknowledged to Dr Bell himself. This is what he said in a letter he wrote to Dr Bell in 1892:

> *I do not think that [Sherlock Holmes's] analytical work is in the least an exaggeration of some effects which I have seen you produce in the out-patient ward. Round the centre of deduction and inference and observation which I heard you inculcate, I have tried to build up a man who pushed the thing as far as it would go – further occasionally.*

The surgical museum requires a strong stomach. It used to be a closed collection, open only to Fellows and invited guests; it may now be visited by the general public. There are other treasures in Surgeons' Hall apart from anatomical collections. The staircase leading up to the hall has a fine stained-glass window displaying the College arms, with their numerous references to the surgeon's calling. The shield is flanked by two figures: Asclepius, with his serpent-entwined staff, and Hippocrates, turned to read a book held in his left hand. On the shield, we see Edinburgh Castle as it is usually depicted heraldically (a view of the front gate). Above the castle, lying transversely, is a naked figure, cleverly designed to represent both man and woman, and ready, in any event, for the surgeon's knife. Directly above that is a hand, fingers spread wide, with an eye in the middle of the palm. This symbol is widely used in a number of different traditions, including religious ones, as a protective symbol. That, presumably, is why it is there in the arms of the College: the surgeon protects his patient against ill-fortune. In the borders of the shield are those instruments by which the surgeon performs this task: surgical knives and forceps – and what looks like a barber's razor, a reminder of the fact that barbers once worked hand in hand with surgeons. There is no Barbers' Hall, of course.

The College's collection of paintings, displayed throughout Surgeons' Hall, provides in itself a visual history of surgery in Edinburgh. Many of these paintings are of individuals who took pioneering steps in surgical treatments, but at least one – the portrait of King James IV that hangs in the main hall – is of an enthusiastic amateur. James IV did his best to raise the intellectual and artistic standard of the Scottish court, and it was under his reign that the first charter was given to the Incorporation of Barber Surgeons. James was interested in medicine and surgery, as well in alchemy, and would even pay his subjects to allow him to extract a troublesome tooth. The evidence of his surgical and dental practices is slight, being restricted to entries in the Lord High Treasurer's Accounts. These entries, however, reveal that he practised blood-letting, tooth extraction, and, in one recorded case, paid for cloth to be used as surgical swabs for procedures on one of his subject's legs. According to the entry, the king healed the leg, which one suspects may have a result of good fortune rather than skill. At the other end of the spectrum is a portrait of Joseph Lister, who came to Edinburgh after his graduation from University College London and who worked under another prominent Fellow of the College, James Syme. In 1867 Lister published in the *Lancet* his 'On a New Method of Treating Compound Fracture and Abscess etc with Observations on the Conditions of Suppuration': this was to transform the profession by ushering in the era of antiseptic surgery. Lister was familiar with the work of Pasteur, who discovered the action of air-borne micro-organisms; he used this insight to develop the use of carbolic acid as a means of preventing infection in surgical wounds. The effect on survival rates was dramatic.

Surgeons' Hall is one of those buildings whose facade conceals much more than the casual passer-by would imagine. Behind Playfair's implacable front, there lies one of the world's great surgical training centres, educating practitioners from around the world, preserving Scotland's reputation in this field. Examinations lie at the heart of its activity, and these have always been rigorous as befits any test administered in such a formidable setting. Here is George Wilson, a Fellow of the College, writing to his brother in 1837:

> *Mine good brother and friend, – give me hold of your right hand; there, shake it stoutly, and congratulate me on having passed Surgeons' Hall. Ah! Ha! Ha! It is but two hours since the memorable metamorphosis took place, and here I am ready not merely to perform all kinds of bloody operations, which is small matter, seeing diplomaless folks can haggle wonderfully well, but ready, prepared, and resolved to take fees, and be independent of the subsidies of any one ... I had to sit up till one, spelling over all the mysteries of bones, muscles, nerves, &c.; and all next (that is, this) day, I have been busy reading over half a book of chemistry, and the whole anatomy of the leg and arm, from the shoulder and haunch to the fingers and toes; and well it was I did so, seeing I was examined on the arm, and I was all the more expert at answers from having looked over it ... I was ushered to the grandees, whole four inquisitors. There they fell to; shoved me Gregory, made me translate, twice write a prescription, tell them as much about drugs and chemistry as would fill a pharmacopoeia, and so much about the anatomy of the arm, skull, neck &c the surgery of the same part, and the philosophy of broken skulls, and the method of coopering such casks, that I might rival Syme, Liston or Lizars. 'You may depart, sir' said the President. I was kept for a moment in a small side-room, and then pulled in to be told, 'that my examination was highly creditable to me, and that they were very much pleased.' – Rejoiced in my heart, here I am, your affectionate brother.*

Examinations, standards, scientific knowledge – but ultimately this imposing edifice is about something very human: the relief of suffering, the excision of the bad to give the good a chance.

17

The Greatest Wonder of the Century
James Robertson

The Forth Bridge, 1881

On a cloudy, cool morning in late April, a small group of us assemble under the arching red curves of the Forth Bridge in North Queensferry. Nobody else is about. Every few minutes a train passes overhead, then all is still again. We are already keenly, and somewhat nervously, anticipating being taken – allowed – onto the vast structure above us, but the town doesn't seem to be paying it, let alone us, much attention. Maybe after 127 years you get used to having a giant in your midst.

We are waiting for Craig Bowman, senior communications manager for Network Rail, who is to be our expedition guide. That's what it feels like, an expedition. We have been advised to wear an extra layer of clothing, and walking or climbing boots. To walk on the Forth Bridge is not a privilege afforded to many, and we know it.

I remember the author Iain Banks telling me that he lived in North Queensferry until the age of nine and every morning when he looked out of his bedroom window there it was, the rail bridge, looming in front of him, and further west the road bridge in the process of being built. His father's job took the family to Inverclyde but a daily, formative experience like that doesn't easily leave you. It would inspire Iain's third novel *The Bridge,* published in 1986, a nightmarish fiction which is partly set on an inhabited, city-sized version of the rail bridge. This complex society turns out to exist in the mind of Alex, a civil engineer, who is lying in a coma after crashing his car on the Forth Road Bridge. Just before the accident, Alex looks admiringly over at the rail bridge:

> *What a gorgeous great device you are. So delicate from this distance, so massive and strong close-up. Elegance and grace; perfect form. A quality bridge; granite piers, the best ship-plate steel, and a never-ending paint job ...*

So much did Iain admire the Forth Bridge that he returned to live in North Queensferry in the early 1990s, and made his home there until his death in 2013. When the bridge opened in 1890, though, not everybody was so pleased with it.

*

The London correspondent of the *New York Tribune*, for one, did not mince his words: 'The contractor, designer, engineer of the Forth Bridge ought, each and all, to be hanged from the topmost angle of its cantilevers. That is the only thing that would improve the appearance of this hideous structure, except dynamite. It totally ruins some of the most beautiful scenery in Scotland or the world.' He went on to describe the bridge as 'monstrous, horrible, huge, shapeless and ugly beyond the ugliest dreams of Dante ... a nightmare in granite and iron.'

Hardly less violent in their antipathy were William Morris, designer, poet and doyen of the Arts and Crafts movement, and the art critic John Ruskin. Morris declared that 'there never will be an architecture of iron, every improvement in machinery being uglier and uglier until they reach the supremest specimen of all ugliness – the Forth Bridge.' For Ruskin, the bridge was the ultimate proof of his belief that 'industry without art is brutality': it made him wish he had been 'born a blind fish in a Kentucky cave'.

Even Wilhelm Westhofen, the German-born engineer who oversaw construction of the central cantilever, admitted that 'this bridge or any other bridge must be a discordant feature in a pastoral landscape.' But, given the massive and permanent intrusion into its surroundings that the new edifice was, negative reactions to it were surprisingly few. Overwhelmingly, people were enthusiastic in their approval. The bridge filled them with awe. In Scotland, there was huge national pride and satisfaction at what had been achieved.

Almost immediately, and far beyond the shores of the British Isles, the Forth Bridge acquired iconic status, to the extent of being called the 'eighth wonder of the world'. Gustave Eiffel, whose wrought-iron tower had been erected for the World's Fair in Paris the previous year, couched his praise in similar terms, generously declaring the bridge to be 'the greatest wonder of the century'. For some decades it was arguably the most famous man-made structure on the planet, and certainly its most celebrated bridge.

In 1935, Alfred Hitchcock used it as a location in his version of *The 39 Steps*, manufacturing a breathless scene (entirely absent from John

Buchan's original novel) in which Richard Hannay escapes arrest by slipping off a train halfway across the bridge. The latticework of girders might have come straight from the kind of German Expressionist film set that had influenced Hitchcock in the 1920s. 'Here, here, what for did ye pull the communication cord?' the guard demands of the police, as Hannay hides behind one of the bridge's tubes. 'It's against all the regulations to stop the train on the bridge!' Even after the train has moved off, the camera lingers for fully thirty seconds on a shot of the bridge in profile against a lowering sky. It is as if the director cannot bear to move on to the next, inevitably less dramatic location.

In 2015, the bridge was awarded UNESCO World Heritage Site status. The UNESCO report praised the bridge's 'distinctive industrial aesthetic ... the result of a forthright and unadorned display of its structural components.' It was 'innovative in style, materials and scale', and marked a 'milestone in bridge design and construction during the period when railways came to dominate long-distance land travel'. The award put the bridge into an elite group alongside the Pyramids of Egypt, the Great Wall of China and – in Scotland – New Lanark, the St Kilda archipelago, Edinburgh's Old and New Towns, Neolithic Orkney and the Roman Antonine Wall.

It is almost impossible, now, to imagine the Firth of Forth without that trio of great red spiders' webs straddling it. Alfred Hitchcock and Iain Banks celebrated the bridge in their art; its image has appeared on posters, postcards, bank notes, tea towels and every conceivable kind of souvenir, and has been exploited by Scottish manufacturers of oatcakes, soft drinks, hosiery, whisky and any other product that can be said to combine strength, taste and style. It is, and has been for its entire existence, instantly recognisable.

I first saw the bridge from the family car at the age of six, early in 1965, as we drove across its neighbour the Forth Road Bridge, which had opened just a few months earlier. We had moved home from Kent to Stirlingshire between Christmas and New Year and everything was new and interesting. My father explained how a suspension bridge worked and extolled the Road Bridge's clean, modern lines and lack of fussiness. I suspect, though I cannot now remember, that the rail bridge received less praise, perhaps because, in the age of the car, it represented the past. Throughout my childhood, whenever we travelled to Edinburgh we went either by car or by train from Stirling, a route which did not involve crossing the Forth Bridge. It was not until I was in my twenties that I had that experience. Yet long before then it had entered my consciousness as something both miraculous and solidly rational; both historic and modern; both thoroughly Scottish and of the wider world; and – despite what Ruskin thought – both a triumph of engineering and a thing of remarkable beauty.

With the newly finished Queensferry Crossing, there are now three bridges over the Firth of Forth, and they are all examples of fine design and top-class engineering. But whatever the qualities of the two road bridges, they are trumped by the qualities of the rail bridge. It is their venerable great-uncle, tough, unyielding and upright. People respect it. The older it gets, the deeper grows the respect, not just for the bridge itself but for the men who built it.

*

The Victorians were proud of their ability, through strength and forethought and ingenuity, to overcome natural obstacles. It had long been held that the Forth estuary was simply too wide, and the geology of its bed too unstable, for it to be spanned. There had been ferries sailing between Fife and Lothian for centuries, but from the early nineteenth century various plans for tunnels and bridges were proposed – and subsequently discarded on grounds of impracticality or cost, or both. What concentrated minds on finding a way to create a fixed, permanent crossing was the coming of the railways, and the intensity of competition among rival companies from the 1840s onward.

To circumvent the firths of Forth and Tay, trains travelling north from Edinburgh had to go via Stirling and Perth, and this led to a constant battle over routes and capacity between the North British Railway Company, which by the 1860s controlled most of the lines on the eastern side of the country, and the Caledonian Railway Company, which owned the western routes. One way of avoiding the long detour via Stirling for trains going between Edinburgh and Fife had already been established in 1850. From that date a paddlewheel-driven ferry, with rails on its deck, operated between Granton on the south shore of the Forth, and Burntisland in Fife. Railway goods wagons were loaded on and off at each end by an engine which pulled them up a ramp, the level of which was adjustable to cope with the rise and fall of the tide. Passengers, however, had to walk on and off the ferry and endure whatever weather was flung at them during the half-hour crossing. Despite this discomfort, the ferry was enough of a success for another to be commissioned on the Tay between north Fife and Dundee. The journey time between Edinburgh and Dundee was thus shortened and routes owned by rival operators avoided. Nevertheless, the stop–start nature of the journey was frustrating, and furthermore the ferries could be delayed or halted altogether by poor weather or sea conditions. The North British Railway Company's directors remained keen to find a more permanent solution: if only the firths could be bridged, then the company would have unrestricted control of east-coast routes south from Edinburgh and north through Fife to Dundee, Aberdeen and beyond. While increasing passenger numbers was part of their ambition, the greater opportunity for profit lay in the transportation of coal, timber, livestock and other freight throughout the entire island of Great Britain.

The train ferries were the brainchild of an engineer called Thomas Bouch. Bouch was convinced that both Tay and Forth could be spanned. In 1869 he got his first and, as it turned out, only chance to prove it when his design for a bridge over the Tay was approved and its brick-pier and iron-girder construction jointly funded by the North British Railway Company and the city of Dundee. This – the longest rail crossing in the world at the time – was completed in March 1878 to great acclaim. Even before it was finished, however, Bouch was putting forward plans for a chain suspension bridge across the Forth, centred on two 600-foot steel towers on the rocky island of Inchgarvie in the middle of the firth. The four railway companies with a direct interest in the east-coast route between London and the north backed the creation of the Forth Bridge Railway Company, and the foundation stone for one of the piers was laid on Inchgarvie by Mrs Bouch in September 1876. Nothing, it seemed, stood in Bouch's way to further triumph, and early in 1879 he travelled to Windsor to be knighted by the Queen.

Then, on the night of 28 December 1879, during a severe gale, the central section of Bouch's Tay Bridge collapsed, taking with it a train with seventy-five passengers on board. Nobody survived. An inquiry into the disaster concluded that the bridge was 'badly designed, badly constructed and badly maintained and that its downfall was due to inherent defects in the structure which must sooner or later have brought it down. For these defects both in design, construction and maintenance Sir Thomas Bouch is in our opinion mainly to blame.'

Understandably, Bouch was shattered by these events. His hair turned white during the four months of the inquiry and, less than a year after the disaster, he died of 'acute melancholia'.

Work on the bridge across the Forth halted as soon as the accident occurred, and Bouch's design was abandoned. Any replacement would have to be built to the highest specification and under the most rigorous scrutiny in order to allay the fears of both investors and the travelling public.

The design put forward by civil engineers John Fowler and Benjamin Baker, who had worked together on the first of the London Underground lines, was subject to a Parliamentary Act which required inspection at every stage of construction and the use of the best possible materials so that the installation should 'enjoy a reputation of being not only the biggest and strongest, but also the stiffest bridge in the world'. It had to be able to withstand, simultaneously, the worst possible wind conditions and the stress of an abnormally heavy rolling load. The Forth Bridge was consequently made to be far more robust than it needed to be. The construction contract was won by a joint bid from Falkiner & Tancred of London and Arrol of Glasgow. The overall supervision of the project was undertaken by Arrol's founder and owner William Arrol, who in due course would be knighted for his achievement.

The statistics are biblical in a Victorian kind of way. The bridge took seven years to build at a cost of over three million pounds. It is more than 8,000 feet in length. The three towers which support its cantilevers are 360 feet high. The railway track is 158 feet above the water. The structure is composed of 55,000 tons of steel, 140,000 cubic yards of masonry, and – at a conservative estimate – 6.5 million rivets. During the recent ten-year refurbishment of the bridge – including a new three-coat painting regime which should mean that the top coat lasts a minimum of twenty years – every one of those rivets had to be painted by hand to ensure the correct level of thickness was applied around their edges.

And then come the human statistics. 'It is impossible,' Benjamin Baker wrote, 'to carry out a gigantic work without paying for it, not merely in money but in men's lives.' In the peak years of construction, some 4,600 workers – or briggers, as they became known – were employed. Wilhelm Westhofen recorded in 1890 that fifty-seven lives were lost, but recent research suggests that the figure was seventy-three and possibly higher. Of these, thirty-eight men fell to their deaths, nine were drowned, nine were crushed by machinery or masonry, eight were killed by a falling object, three died in a fire in a bothy, and one man died of caisson disease or 'the bends'. Five men died of causes unknown. As the work progressed and the structure grew higher, so injuries and deaths rose in number. From 1886 onward, on average one man was killed every six weeks.

'Health and safety' was not a term in everyday use in Victorian times, but the clearly dangerous nature of the Forth Bridge construction meant that considerable attention was paid to minimising the risk of accidents. Secure staging, gangways, hand-rails and wire netting were installed where possible, and lifeboats, on constant patrol in the waters below, managed to rescue at least eight men who fell and would otherwise have drowned. Nevertheless, injuries or deaths caused by falling or from being struck by falling objects were not rare occurrences, especially as it was common practice, though forbidden, for workmen to throw tools or bits of timber to one another. The scaffolding stages were cluttered with hammers, nuts, bolts and riveting equipment, all of which were potentially lethal if they fell onto men working hundreds of feet below. There were some lucky escapes: Benjamin Baker reported that one spanner which fell 300 feet passed through a four-inch-thick piece of timber; he also witnessed a dropped spanner enter a brigger's pocket and exit at his trouser leg, causing no injury but ripping the man's clothes from him. Inevitably, some of the briggers grew careless over time. 'It needed the sight of a wounded and mangled fellow creature, or his bloody corpse,' Wilhelm Westhofen wrote, 'to bring home to them the seriousness of the situation.'

Following a six-month period in 1887 during which seventeen deaths occurred, the *Dunfermline Journal* ran a story headlined 'When will this slaughter stop?' Baker responded that the accident rate was tiny compared with what went on in the coal industry, and that the number of fatalities was proportionately much lower than that of guards and brakesmen on the railways. If that now seems callous or defensive, it is also an indication of how far we have come and how little we expect, in modern Scotland at least, that even dangerous work should result in the kind of personal and family disasters that were commonplace only a couple of generations ago. In proportion to the total number of men working, the death rate for the rail bridge was no worse than that for the road bridge constructed seventy years later.

William Arrol was responsible for building not only the Forth Bridge but also the replacement Tay Bridge, a project which lasted from 1882 to 1887. A man in his mid-forties, he had an astonishing capacity for hard graft and long hours. His day started at six o'clock at his engineering works at Dalmarnock, Glasgow, where he would review the previous day's progress on both bridges and brief his senior staff on what needed to be done next. After breakfast he went by train to Edinburgh and then to the Forth Bridge site, where he was engaged until late afternoon. At 6pm he took a train to Dundee to scrutinise work on the Tay Bridge. Late in the evening he took a train home to Glasgow and would be back at the Dalmarnock works for six the next morning. On Fridays he went to the Tay first, then to the Forth, before catching a sleeper to London for meetings there, returning to Glasgow on Saturday nights. Such a regime would have exhausted many a younger man, but Arrol claimed to thrive on it: the more work he did, he said, the better he felt. Undoubtedly he placed great demands on his key staff and had high expectations of all whom he employed. But his own humble origins – he was the son of a Renfrewshire spinner and had started work in a cotton mill at the age of nine – also instilled in him a strong sense of duty of care. He described his own character, when receiving the freedom of the town of Ayr a few days before the official opening of the Forth Bridge by the Prince of Wales, as 'representative of the working classes of Scotland, as one of those who had been able to raise themselves by their own energy and industry.'

His fellow-contractors came from more privileged backgrounds but shared Arrol's sense of fairness. 'We never ask a workman to do a thing which we are not prepared to do ourselves,' Benjamin Baker said. Temporary housing was provided in nearby communities for many of the men, a reading room and dining room were built for them, and from the outset of the contract Arrol established a Sick and Accident Club, membership of which was compulsory for any man working on the bridge. Every man contributed one hour's pay per week to the Club's funds. Arrol's firm contributed £200 per annum, and paid for free medical care for workers and their immediate families. A man unable to work because of sickness or injury was paid a weekly allowance by the Club, and lump-sum payments were made to the families of men killed or permanently disabled while at work. Funeral costs of those killed were also covered. By the standards of the day these were good terms and conditions of work, which took into account the dangerous nature of the job. Over the seven years of construction, there were very few delays or disruptions caused by strikes or demands for increased pay.

*

Who were the briggers, the men who created this astonishing working monument to their own physical efforts? The bulk of them were Scots and Englishmen. Experienced steelworkers and riveting squads came from the shipyards of the Clyde, and others with particular skills arrived from all over central Scotland and northern England, attracted by above-average wages since much of the labour was piece-work. Great numbers of Irish

labourers, mainly unskilled, were also hired. There were also workers from other countries, of whom the most recognisable today is probably Kaichi Watanabe, a Japanese postgraduate of Glasgow University who would go on to have a highly successful career in his own country's ship-building and railway industries. In 1887 he was photographed as part of a human cantilever which the contractors had devised as a means of explaining to the public the physical principles upon which the bridge was being built. Kaichi, sitting on a plank, represents the central girder of the bridge, and is supported by two men on chairs who represent its towers, their outstretched arms holding broomsticks which together represent the cantilevers, the whole edifice being anchored at either end by piles of bricks. It is an image which perfectly achieves its aim, in part because the three men are so obviously demonstrating, not posing.

According to Wilhelm Westhofen, some of the briggers were

> *mere birds of passage, who arrived on the tramp, worked for a week or two, and passed on again to other parts, bringing a pair of hands with them and taking them away again, and having in the meantime made extremely little use of them except for the purpose of lifting the Saturday pay packet and wiping their mouths at the pot-house … But apart from these, it is no exaggeration to say that no one need desire to have to do with a more civil lot of men. Always ready to oblige, always ready to go where they were told to go, cheerfully obeying orders … and above all things, ready to help others in misfortune, not with advice but with hands and purses.*

Drunkenness, William Arrol said repeatedly, was a great problem throughout the project. He blamed many of the on-site accidents on alcohol, although theoretically anybody found under the influence was stopped at the gates and barred from working until they had sobered up. Arrol was of the view that 'the further a public house was from a public works, the better'. There is no question that many of the men, when lowsed, retired immediately to one of the nearby taverns, of which there were plenty on both sides of the firth – and some were probably not at their most alert when they started back at work. The Hawes Inn in South Queensferry would line up 200 pints at a time when a shift was ending on pay day. But when or where in the world of hard physical labour involving large squads of well-paid men has this kind of thing not been the case? And Westhofen's praise of the regular workforce is striking: these were men doing difficult work in challenging conditions and forming – again, as is usually the case – strong bonds of camaraderie and support with their fellows.

The caisson workers were a special contingent, who worked quite separately from most of the other briggers. They were an international, itinerant team – mostly Italians, Austrians, Germans, Belgians and Frenchmen – under the direction of a Monsieur Coiseau. They came to Queensferry from such huge undertakings as the construction of Antwerp's docks and the Suez Canal, and moved on when their part in the Forth Bridge project was over. The concrete legs of the bridge's towers had to be fixed to the seabed, and this required caissons – enormous cylinders not unlike gasometers – to be made, towed out and sunk on the precise spots where the legs were to stand. The caissons were the moulds into which concrete would be poured below the surface. Each caisson was designed with a cutting edge shaped to the contours of the seabed, so that when it settled a seven-foot high chamber was created between the seabed and the bottom of the caisson. The water was pumped out of this space and compressed air pumped into it, enabling men to enter, excavate the rock and build up the piers which would eventually support the weight of the bridge. It was difficult and dangerous work, in conditions which caused serious damage to the health of those who did it. Caisson disease was not then widely understood. The pressurised conditions in the chambers created gas bubbles which then dispersed into the arterial system and tissue, resulting in agonising attacks of cramp, temporary paralysis, earache, dizziness and other symptoms. Some of the caisson workers would spend parts of their days off in the excavation chambers because their pain reduced under pressure, but of course this did not improve their longer-term health. William

Arrol himself suffered from permanent partial deafness after spending too many hours in the caissons.

*

Craig Bowman arrives, greets us warmly, checks our footwear, and kits us out with high-viz jackets and hard hats. A few rules are gone over about obeying instructions, not leaning or stretching out over spaces, and holding on to our hats if it gets gusty, and then we are off. The whole visit, which lasts about an hour, is conducted with scrupulous attention to safety, and despite our earlier anxieties there is no real sense of risk. Not so long ago a tour of the bridge would have involved scaling ladders and negotiating exposed walkways, but no longer. A caged hoist controlled by Greig Newbigging, site operator for contractors Balfour Beatty, takes us up the outside of one of the huge tubes of the northernmost tower, and we step out onto a wide and firm viewing platform. And there we are – on top of the Forth Bridge.

There is no way, really, of describing what this feels like. The bridge is so familiar in profile, or from the window of a train passing through its red Meccano canyon, that nothing quite prepares you for this new perspective. The most startling thing, perhaps, is to see how slender and straight the bridge is. Like an enormous rollercoaster, it sweeps down and up in breathtaking dives so perfectly aligned that you cannot see the third, southernmost tower beyond the central one. What seems so sturdy and muscular from the road bridge or from either shore has an almost delicate grace viewed from above. And yet its strength is also highly visible: the frame, balanced and braced at every point, the taut limbs of the girders, the countless rows and columns of rivets – not even the fiercest gale, you feel, could make such a mighty gymnast tremble. So, if the Forth Bridge was built to be rigid, why do the long arms of the cantilever stretching down to the middle part of the bridge seem to ripple and bend? I ask Craig if this is an optical illusion, and he reminds me that steel expands and contracts, albeit only slightly, as the temperature rises and falls. So, yes, over its lifetime the bridge has, as it were, constantly flexed and relaxed its muscles. I look again. Far from the distortions in the metal looking like faults, they make the whole edifice appear even stronger.

We take the cage back down and get out at a level directly under the tracks. Again, this is an entirely new perspective, an intricate weave of red steel stretching one and a half miles across the water. There are a couple of bothies, erected in the 1930s, into which workers can retreat in poor weather or when the wind picks up: if the wind speed gets above 40mph then it is deemed too unsafe to be out on the bridge. Trains rumble above us, causing only slight vibrations. I imagine a 40mph wind would make me feel distinctly uneasy.

We go back up again, to track level, and here the whole purpose of the structure is revealed: all this to hold up two sets of rails and the trains that run on them. We are encouraged – no, instructed – to acknowledge with a wave the engine drivers as they go by, and all but one of them gives us a cheery wave back and usually an accompanying blast on the horn. These three- or four-carriage passenger trains seem like toys against the scale of the bridge, but the traffic does cause wear and tear over time. Less so, however, than in days gone by: back in the 1920s the beds on which the tracks sit had to be replaced because they had buckled so much under the weight of frequent and much heavier freight trains.

Iain Banks was revisiting long-established mythology when he wrote of a 'never-ending paint job'. What the bridge needs – and this is why there will always be gangs of workers on it – is a continuous care and maintenance programme. When a weakness is spotted, it is strengthened. If a part has corroded beyond saving it is replaced. And, of course, painted. The underwater structure also has to be regularly checked, and any serious repair issues down there would pose major challenges. But neither Craig nor Greig has any doubt about the long-term viability of the bridge. It was built to such a high specification using such quality materials that, with good management, it should outlast them and us and serve many future generations.

There is something honest and assured in their assessment. Like others who have worked on the bridge, they have a genuine fondness for it and a strong sense that they are curating a very special work of both art and science. You can tell that they feel privileged to have that responsibility, and that there is a genuine, profound respect for the bridge's human story too. It is an almost entirely male story – our guides can think of only one woman currently working on the bridge, a member of the abseil team which fixes the safety nets – but it shows men in a far better light than a great deal of other history. The men who built the Forth Bridge, I suspect, were themselves built much as these men who now look after it.

18

A Little Girl Remembers
Alistair Moffat

Glasgow School of Art, 1896–1909

When the Glasgow School of Art opened in 1899, I remember a grey shady afternoon. Not a big crowd but quite an assembly of people arriving at the School and going into the first hall. After we'd been there a bit, a certain amount of talk and then we were all shooed out. Everybody stood out on the steps. Then there was another pause, then I'm afraid there were speeches. I don't remember what they said, I just remember waiting. Then I was shepherded up holding a small, oblong, pale, pearly silk cushion with a silver fringe round. It was oblong so as to be suitable to hold the special key of the front door. This cushion was made by Mrs Mackintosh and my mother. Thinking about this lately, the formal ceremony would be arranged by my father who had a touch of pageantry. He liked formal things done properly. Then the door was unlocked and in we went. There was a feeling of cheerful achievement. I don't remember Mackintosh being present at the ceremony, but I am sure he must have been there somewhere in the building. When he did the work on the Glasgow School of Art, he was only a draughtsman in Keppie's office. Then he was made a junior partner. But in all these jobs, Keppie always maintained that they were done by the firm.

Mary Newbery Sturrock was the daughter of Francis Newbery, the Head Master or Director of the Glasgow School of Art, and Jessie Newbery, the Head of the Department of Embroidery. I met her several times in the early 1980s after I began to work at Scottish Television. Working in Glasgow, I became fascinated by what Charles Rennie Mackintosh had created and wanted to know more about the man. It was a unique pleasure to talk to someone who knew him well and whose family were intimately involved in the making of his masterpiece.

Mary lived alone in a small Georgian terraced house in South Gray Street in Edinburgh and each time I visited, she made me Earl Grey tea and put down a plate of home-made biscuits. Her sitting room was decorated with art, with her watercolours (her paintings still sell at auction) and other beautiful objects. I remember particularly the embroidery on her antimacassars and on her clothes. More than ninety years old when I first met her, she was always immaculately, thoughtfully dressed, once wearing a Chanel-style suit but with flowers appliqued on one side of the jacket. When I admired them, Mary told me that her mother had taught her to sew and make things. Hers was the house of someone who loved and lived art.

Talking quietly and with precision, sometimes correcting herself, she brought Charles Rennie Mackintosh to life, recreating the artistic milieu in which they all lived. Although she was a little girl when the first phase of the School of Art opened, Mary had come to know Mackintosh when she was a young woman and an artist herself. There were others, I discovered, but such was the long interval since his death in 1928 that they had only known him late in his life and while they were children. Mary's testament was unique, and it began with the memory of a little girl staring at a key on a cushion before she was led up the steps to the main door to present it.

> *I think Margaret Mackintosh must have got the cushion home because it would have been very suitable for us to play with. But the cushion was very fine. The thing is the Mackintoshes were perfectionists and they couldn't have an ordinary key. The door had a special plate and to open that interesting door of the new School of Art, there had to be a proper key and that key had to be laid on a cushion, and they couldn't have just bought a Victorian cushion for a Mackintosh key. That's the thing – Mackintosh wasn't all that fussy, as they said he was, but to get things right he had to design them. I remember the key quite clearly now, shining pale in this grey afternoon when it was raining slightly, a drizzle, a real Glasgow afternoon. I was six.*
>
> *By the time the Glasgow School of Art opened, my mother and father were friendly with the Mackintoshes, not just as an employer and his architect. It was much more than that because Charles Rennie Mackintosh had worked with my father as a student, and then for two years on this very big building. They got to know each other well as they considered the details of the School of Art.*

In the early 1980s access to public buildings such as universities and colleges was much more relaxed and when I asked Francis Newbery's successor, Tony Jones, he told me I could come any time to the School of Art and should feel free to wander around, without, of course, disturbing teaching. Scottish Television's studios and offices were only a few hundred yards away and often at lunchtime I would walk up Garnethill. The site must have seemed awkward, narrow and sloping. The gradient up Scott Street is steep, but Mackintosh made his building look planted, massive, solid – even monumental – making use of its elevation over Sauchiehall Street. The facade faces approximately north on Renfrew Street, and there was probably no other option. But north light is steady and suits studios for painting and drawing.

So that he could maximise exposure to this light on the Renfrew Street facade, Mackintosh created a traditional Scottish area, a lower storey below street level that would also capture north light. It was lined with wrought-iron railings linking chunky stone stanchions, and the main doorway where Mary Newbery Sturrock carried her cushion up the steps is set in a dramatic break in the asymmetrical facade of huge studio windows, three on one side, four on the other. To the left of the main door, on the first floor, is a small bay window and that was the Director's Room.

Inside the building, Mackintosh everywhere played with light. Even corridors are bright, and many doors, including the one leading into the Director's Room, have stained-glass panels of exquisite plant-like forms. Known as the Chicken Run, one corridor at the top of the building has glazed walls that send borrowed light into the building's interior. And all over the building there is thoughtful detail. Mackintosh had been an art student and he knew what art students needed.

> *My mother always tried to get more jobs for Mackintosh but at that time he didn't really need to be promoted a great deal. He was gifted, he'd done a good job, he didn't really need that. He only needed to be appreciated and recognised and that was his difficulty. When they saw the School of Art, it was too much – forty years ahead of its time. But that was the appearance of the Glasgow School of Art, inside it worked so well – it was a splendid working building, the people who objected or couldn't swallow it, didn't go inside and see what it was like. They just saw this curious castle-like place from Sauchiehall Street. It's still rather an odd building. Maybe a businessman wouldn't order a building like that. Even today when people look at the furniture, and say how modern it is – not only that but the carpets, the lights – all look very suitable for today, they could have been designed yesterday.*

After a time, I began to see the School of Art through Mary Newbery Sturrock's eyes, and the more I looked and the more I researched, the more I wanted to make a film about this remarkable man and his work. Mackintosh was certainly Scotland's greatest artist, and yet even as late the 1980s, he was not recognised as he should have been. Convincing my bosses at Scottish Television to finance a regional programme was difficult, and in any case I agreed with them as they fobbed me off with encouragement to seek a network commission. I thought Mackintosh's work should be seen on a British stage. But I was worried that we would lose Mary. After all, she had passed her ninetieth birthday.

An idea occurred. Scottish Television had a second outside broadcast unit to cover football and, depending on fixture lists, rights to broadcast and the weather, it was sometimes available for other projects. The crew were being paid anyway, working or not, and I persuaded my bosses that they should drive the unit through to Edinburgh and park it in South Gray Street outside a small terraced house. I wanted to tape an interview with Mary as soon as I could. It looked crazy, a mile over the top, a narrow residential street clogged by big outside broadcast vans and cabling leading in through a front door and a window to shoot an interview with a white haired old lady. Mary loved it. And for two hours she talked wonderfully, sometimes tearfully, about Mackintosh, glad to commit her memories to tape for posterity. Even though she was very tired by the end of the recording, Mary kept asking me if she had got it right. It mattered very much to her and she knew that she was the last living person who had known Mackintosh well.

The outside broadcast crew packed up their gear and I promised Mary that we would make a good film. By that time, I had visited every building Mackintosh had designed, including the remodelled interior of 78 Derngate in Northampton, his last commission. But I kept being drawn back to the School of Art. I liked that the priceless original fittings were sometimes scuffed or well worn and that rooms and corridors were littered with stuff that had nothing to do with the original design. This was no shrine or museum but a living and breathing building – one occupied by art students, not known for their deference. Even though Mackintosh's own circle lived an almost self-consciously ordered, artistic way of life surrounded by beautiful objects, I think he would have smiled at the clutter. Mary told me that when she visited the Mackintosh's house at South Park Avenue in Glasgow, the magazines on the low tables were always squared in the corner at the same distance from the edge on both sides. It was a telling detail. But in the working building that is the Glasgow School of Art, order is not always easy to find, and nor should it be.

And yet it is very much his building, designed in the 1890s. Someone once said to me that since Mackintosh was a junior partner in the firm, there must have been other people working on the designs for the School. I said, but you didn't know Mackintosh. If anyone else touched his work, he'd have literally torn them apart. While he was away once, while the School was being built, Keppie, who was the head of the firm, arranged for a cornice to be put at the top, just above the stairs. Mackintosh didn't like cornices, he liked the walls to reach the ceiling, and when he came back, he bounced with anger and fury and passion and he had it all cut out – put the workmen on to cutting it out. And there is still no cornice.

You see they were his ideas and it was his work. I knew architecture students who thought he was a god. He was a marvellous teacher and really understood materials. He knew how to cut wood. He taught an old man who worked on his first house to use an adze. Anything he did in metal, the metal wasn't maltreated. If you beat silver one way, then you mustn't beat it on the other side. I think the best things he did were his wrought-iron pieces. Just a few things – the bird on the top of the School of Art, the bell in the School of Art and one or two lights in the Hill House seem to me to be quite outstanding. Mackintosh was very interested in the old simple Scottish ways with whitewash and cutting wood with an adze and not mangling metals.

Thinking back now, I can see that the Glasgow School of Art alarmed people and after the second phase, he never really got work. Le Corbusier did some very odd things in France but went on doing them. But Mackintosh didn't get the chance. He might have got more orthodox, you really can't tell. The Glasgow School of Art was so ahead of its time, he just had to wait for people to assimilate his ideas.

In 1983 the Burrell Collection opened in Glasgow. After many years in storage, the shipping magnate's vast and eclectic collection was put on display in a purpose-built museum in Pollok Park and since this was seen as an event of national significance, Channel Four commissioned Scottish Television to make a film. I took the same approach as I did with my Mackintosh project and tried to find people who knew this enigmatic, almost hermetic man. Since William Burrell died in 1958, it was much easier and I assembled some revealing recollections of a collector 'with an itch he couldn't scratch'. And the film worked so well that Channel Four asked us what we wanted to do next. There was only one answer.

By that time, Mary Newbery Sturrock had died but I had found nine other people who had met and remembered Mackintosh, a remarkable number since it was almost sixty years since he himself had died. Inevitably, all of these were the memories of children and of his later years. It was, as Mary had said, mainly a time of disappointment and decline. In the late autumn of 1914, Walter Blackie, the publisher who had commissioned Mackintosh to build the Hill House in Helensburgh, received a note from Margaret Mackintosh asking him to call on her husband. He complained to Blackie that he had received little or no recognition for his work and that his partnership in the architectural firm of Honeyman, Keppie and Mackintosh was dissolved. In response, Walter Blackie told him plainly, perhaps bluntly, that he could not expect recognition since he had been 'born some centuries too late: that his place was among the fifteenth century lot with Leonardo and the others'. The outbreak of war in Europe also closed down opportunities for new work and Mackintosh told Blackie that he and Margaret were leaving Glasgow.

The Newberys had spent summer holidays at Walberswick, a village on the Suffolk coast near Southwold, and in 1914 they invited the Mackintoshes to stay with them.

> The Mackintoshes used to come to see us in the evenings and discuss the war. He was very patriotic, Mackintosh. We went back to Glasgow and they stayed on in the same place. They were quite happy. Whatever they really felt, they didn't show it. They were dignified, they never moaned.
>
> Walberswick was an artists' colony and mother got them a studio along the riverbank. They gave tea parties in their studio, not in their room. It was really only a fisherman's shed, very much open on one side to the river. They liked the conditions and went on working there. They were doing the decorations for Miss Cranston's last tea room – it was called the Dugout because it was downstairs.

At Walberswick Mackintosh began to paint watercolours, exquisite studies of plants, flowers and some landscapes. A sad incident compounded his disappointment. Because he was a Scot with a pronounced Scottish accent and fond of taking walks along the shoreline in the gloaming, Mackintosh was suspected of being a German spy. Their house was searched by soldiers and Mary was told by local people that he was taken into custody, spending a night in a cell. People vouched for Mackintosh and eventually they were told that, like all artists, they could not live in Norfolk or Suffolk because they might be able to pass drawings of installations or other aspects of the war to the Germans. It was crazy and the

Mackintoshes left for London and rented a studio and a flat. Mary stayed in touch with them.

> *I remember going to the Mackintoshes' studio in Glebe Place, in Chelsea. I was working in London at that time, in Hampstead, and I used to take a bus right down and have tea with them on a Sunday afternoon. I remember a big oval patch of ground where Mackintosh planted potatoes. He was nothing if not practical, but I'm afraid cats used it too much. They didn't live in their studios because they weren't rated for that. They had bed and breakfast in Oakley Street, nearby. They spent the day in the studio and went in the evening for supper at the Blue Cockatoo where they had quite a collection of friends.*

By 1923 Mackintosh had given up hope of winning any architectural commissions and he and Margaret decided to go and live in France. The exchange rate was very favourable and they could afford to stay in the Hotel du Commerce in Port Vendres on the coast not far north of the Spanish border. Mackintosh painted landscapes and hoped for an exhibition in London. They needed the cash. But by 1928, he had become ill and was forced to return to London for treatment. A cancerous lump was discovered on his tongue and when he was in hospital students came to draw it, as they did in the days before manageable cameras. Mary remembered that he scolded the students, telling them that they were not drawing the construction of the tongue properly and he did it for them: 'That shows the true Mackintosh – brave, truthful and wanting to get things perfect.' He died in London on 10 December 1928, and his body was cremated the following day at Golder's Green Cemetery.

> *Looking back now I feel terribly, terribly sad at the waste. Here we have this brilliant man whom it would pay you to use. And he wasn't given any real use at all, apart from the Glasgow School of Art and the odd jobs he got in Glasgow. Of course, if he had got Liverpool Cathedral, if he'd got the Dough School, if he'd got these studios in London, he could have gone ahead from that. Because I think, almost by the end of the Second World War, other architects were using his ideas, such as those for the Art Lover's House, to build their houses. They used the detail which they got from photographs from Country Life, and other magazines. So if Mackintosh had managed to live those extra years, he might have been employed again.*

Mackintosh could have designed anything, but he just didn't get a chance. Perhaps he did all he was going to do, but I'd like to have seen his fiftieth house. I don't know how many houses Robert Adam did but his fiftieth house mustn't have been a bit like his first. I would like to have seen Mackintosh's fiftieth house, with all the edges rubbed off and all his experience and development brought into play. We could have had somebody as good as Corbusier but we weren't able to do it.

Thinking back now, the tears come to my eyes and I feel so sad that the genius was wasted. I feel great sadness. When I hear of these high prices [for his watercolours], I think that if the Mackintoshes could have got a hundredth part of the money, how happy they would have been and I would be now. I've got a lot of pleasant friendly memories but I must say I could weep at the waste of his genius.

In May 2014, a fire raged through part of the Glasgow School of Art and Mackintosh's wonderful library was reduced to ashes, a blackened shell. As firemen fought the blaze, some of those watching from the street wept at the destruction. The Glasgow School of Art has become a building that is loved. But restoration has begun, led by Park Page architects, and when complete, something unlooked-for will emerge. Over the century since it opened, the library, perhaps his greatest achievement, had been much changed with new bookcases added, dark wood fitted and a staircase built to the mezzanine floor. Park Page have gone back to Mackintosh's original drawings and with some concessions to modernity such as underfloor heating and wifi access, it will look exactly as it did when the second phase of the School of Art opened in 1909. The fire was an expensive disaster, no doubt, but it will allow us to see the library as Mackintosh intended it to look. His vision will rise from the ashes. Perhaps when they open it, a little girl will come forward with a key on a cushion. A special key and a special cushion.

*A History of the Nation in
Twenty-Five Buildings*

13 – 25

13 **Glenlivet Distillery**

14 Bell Rock Lighthouse

15 **Abbotsford**

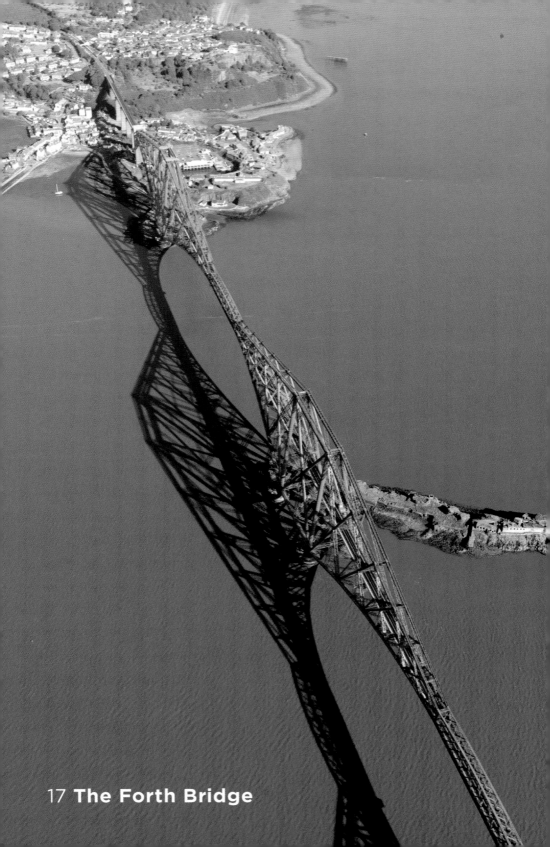

17 The Forth Bridge

18 **Glasgow School of Art**

19 **Hampden Park**

21 **Inchmyre Prefabs**

23 **Sullom Voe**

24 Maggie's Centre

25 **Sweeney's Bothy**

19

The Bewteis of the Futeball
James Crawford

Hampden Park, Glasgow, 1903

On family car journeys when I was a child we would listen to cassette recordings of Billy Connolly. We only had three of them: two originals and one copy made on a black TDK SA60 with the title scrawled in biro on the peeling A-side label. And so we played them over and over, until we knew all the jokes and songs off by heart. Phrases and punchlines still pop into my head: always in Connolly's voice, with those unmistakable intonations in his delivery. One of his descriptions made a particular impression on me – a digression about Hampden Park, Scotland's national stadium. 'You'd get 100,000 people in Hampden,' he said. '*That's 200,000 eyes …*' He stretched this line out into one long hiss, followed by a crackle of dead air. The pause gave you time to think. Mostly about the weight he placed on the presence and importance of those eyes: that instant doubling of the capacity. It implied gravity and undisguised menace, a massed fixation on watching and demanding to see. Who did those eyes belong to? And what did they want to see? 'Of course they're all Scottish,' he said. '*Because no one else goes there*. The English have an unwritten rule: they only go to places they might get back from.'

Connolly conjured a vivid picture in my young mind. As early as I can remember, Hampden to me was a thing of nightmares, a many-eyed monster waiting to devour the unwary – and in particular the non-Scottish. At least, I supposed, it was a monster that was on *my* side. But still … Years later, almost by accident, I came across a passage in the autobiography of the World-Cup-winning English goalkeeper Gordon Banks that resurrected my childhood vision of the Hampden bogeyman (and name-checked Billy Connolly in the process). Banks described the slow journey of the England team bus to the stadium through the massed Glasgow crowds for a home nations match in 1966. As the throng smashed their fists against the side of the bus, the England captain Bobby Moore reassured his worried team that 'it's just the traditional Clydeside shipbuilders' welcome'. This prompted Banks to embark on a florid description of the shipyards themselves:

I can still hear the evocative sounds of the Clyde at full tempo: an army of hammers echoing in the empty bellies of hulls, the fiendish clatter of riveters at work, the sudden squeal of metal tortured in a spray of bonfire-night sparks that died of cold as they fell. Ships could be seen lolling in cradles from Greenock to the very heart of Glasgow. Some were just keels, like whale skeletons; others, gaunt hulls of rusty red smeared with rectangles of airforce-blue paint ... These were the shipyards of Billy Connolly and the Labour activist Jimmy Reid, boiler-suit blue and testosterone driven.

For Banks sitting in his team bus, 'it appeared as if all those Clydeside shipyard workers were on their way to the match, as well as a good many of Glasgow's other artisans. They numbered in excess of 135,000 and at no time did I spot the friendly face of an England supporter.' 135,000? *That's 270,000 eyes* ... 'The din of fists on the side of our bus matched the din of those shipyards,' he continued, 'hammer, hammer, thump, an incessant racket that could unnerve even the strongest of constitutions.'

Banks depicted Hampden as an extension of Glasgow's great industries – another sparse hull, wrought in steel and concrete, to be filled on matchdays with a cacophonous, grinding wall of sound. Clydeside to him was somewhere both awe-inspiring and unknowable to the outsider, a vast and alien landscape populated by people like Connolly (whose comedy the English struggled to understand) and Reid (whose politics the English struggled to understand). In his description of the football crowds Banks was invoking the radical Glasgow of 'Red Clydeside' – and the ghost of the 1919 mass political demonstration which prompted Winston Churchill to order troops to the city to quell a feared 'Bolshevist' uprising. Reid was the contemporary face of this movement, an engineer, trade unionist and Communist Party member who would go on to lead a world-famous 1970s shipyard 'work-in'. Hampden had acquired – and cultivated – a similar air of defiance, of anti-establishment vigour. It was always on the edge of spilling over into something. If the stadium was a part of Glasgow's industrial machine, then it was the pressure valve, the place where it was all let out. Or at least it was if the result was right.

Think about all those eyes, over and over, looking down at that pitch with no control over what they see, but so much invested in what they see. What must it do to a single piece of ground to be so stared at, so known? A patch of grass, 100-or-so yards long by 70-or-so yards wide, bored into by an unwavering collective gaze that is by turns harsh, hopeful, enraptured, furious, joyful and despairing. Drill down into the ground beneath Hampden and you can imagine striking a vast psychological oil well, the concentrated deposit of all the competing emotions that have fed, saturated and sunk below this one rectangle of turf.

*

Just over a century and a half ago, the grass was there, but little else. Then, Hampden was an unassuming field among a sea of unassuming fields stretching south past the nearby village of Cathcart all the way to Galloway and the Borders. Set between a farmhouse and a brick and tile works, it was bisected by the slow trickle of Mall's Myre Burn, and overlooked by a hill called Mount Florida (topped by the ruin of a mansion house going by the same name). No stands enclosed it, just an irregular boundary of dry-stone walling. The field's only significance, as recorded in the mid-1850s by the Ordnance Survey, was that it had been walked over by the forces of Queen Mary en route to the Battle of Langside. There would have been no reckoning that – just over a hundred years later – one of Scotland's most well-respected sports journalists, Bob Brown, would describe it as standing 'four square with Bannockburn in the Scottish psyche'. Over the course of the twentieth century it had grown so significant, Brown said, that it was 'for the Scots ... irreplaceable'. That's quite a transformation.

At the outset, however, it was replaceable – or at least moveable, because there have been three Hampden Parks. The first was established in 1873, occupying empty ground on the eastern side of Cathcart Road at the foot of Prospecthill. The name came from a line of recently built Victorian tenements overlooking the site: Hampden Terrace begat Hampden Park. (Rather ironically, the terrace itself was named after John Hampden – a seventeenth century *English* parliamentarian who had been instrumental in ousting Charles I and starting the Civil War.) It was the home of Scotland's first ever football club, formed six years earlier by a group of 'gentlemen' who held regular kickabouts on the Queen's Park recreation grounds on the south side of the city. They called themselves – what else? – Queen's Park.

To begin with, they had no-one to play against. But other clubs soon followed. In August 1868 they sent a letter arranging a fixture with Thistle FC of Glasgow Green – reminding them to be 'good enough' to bring their ball with them 'in case of any breakdown'. Another four years on, and they were representing Scotland in the first full international match with England. The English, who had established a Football Association in 1863, could draw on players from around a hundred clubs to form their team. Scotland had less than ten clubs – but in any case, the entire national squad was made up of players from Queen's Park. The match was held at the West of Scotland Cricket Club ground at Hamilton Crescent on St Andrew's Day 1872.

Watched by a crowd of over 4,000, the result was a seemingly uninspiring 0–0 draw. But for the English in attendance it was a revelation. Queen's Park played a style of football that they had never seen before. It focused on collective endeavour as opposed to individual brilliance. Where the English dribbled and ran with the ball, the Scots passed it. This was a striking physical metaphor for the differing evolutions of the game in the two nations. South of the border, football had developed through the public school system, with its institutional focus on personal skill and attainment. In Scotland, it had always been more of a working class game, an outlet for pent-up energy and aggression in breaks between shifts. On the pitch, players became cogs in a different machine, working together to move the ball quickly and efficiently around the field. 'Like so many innovations inspired by the Scots,' wrote the social historian James Walvin in *The People's Game,* 'coherent teamwork spread rapidly throughout the English game and by the late 1870s such teamwork, based on passing rather than dribbling, had come to dominate English football'. Or, as a commentator in 1888 put it, this 'one change … so far revolutionised the game that we may fairly say that there have been two ages of Association play, the dribbling and the passing'. This was industrialised, Clyde-built football.

The match also marked a turning point for Queen's Park – although for entirely different reasons. The club had taken the financial risk for the fixture, hiring the ground and paying all other expenses. In return, however, they could retain the ticket receipts, which came to over £100 (around £45,000 today). Football was clearly now more than just a passion and pastime for those involved on the pitch. More and more – and along with the likes of cricket, rugby, horse-racing, athletics and boxing – it was feeding a mass desire for spectator entertainments. Rapid urbanisation, increased working-class spending power, and the development of Saturday afternoon leisure time, laid the foundations for the emergence of an entirely new type of building within the Victorian city: the sports stadium. Queen's Park recognised the economic necessity, and opportunity, in developing a home of their own – something more than an empty space on a recreation ground.

The original Hampden Park opened in 1874. When first established, it was still on the periphery of the city. But the tendrils of Glasgow were reaching out rapidly. Expansion by the Cathcart and District Railway Company saw a planned new line running over the top of what was then the ground's west terrace. The club was forced to move, and was fortunate to lease another space, barely 200 yards away, from an iron manufacturers. The second Hampden opened ten years after the first, and over the next two decades was developed into a 25,000 capacity ground, including a two-storey brick pavilion with changing rooms, baths and a gymnasium. Even this, however, proved too small to meet the demand. As a sports journal wrote in the mid-1890s, 'Scottish football cannot be described as anything else than a big business.' By this time Rangers and Celtic had emerged from the city's Protestant and Catholic communities, with Ibrox stadium, set in the heart of the Govan shipyards, capable of holding over 40,000. At the turn of the century Queen's Park resolved to end their lease and buy their own piece of land: 12 acres on the other side of Prospecthill.

The third Hampden was in development for three and a half years. Two main steel-built stands offered covered seating. But the key innovation was the use of the site's natural setting on the side of a hill to create banked-earth terracing (removing the need for unstable wooden terracing, which had collapsed at Ibrox during a 1902 match, killing 25 spectators and injuring hundreds more). The pitch was set some 30 feet below the main entry points on Somerville Drive, and so fans emerged from the turnstiles into a vast, sunken, oval bowl, 'grand in conception and great in area' as the *Evening Times* described it on 31 October 1903 – the official opening of the stadium for a league match against Celtic. The Caledonian Railway Company had to put on extra trains from the city centre to Mount Florida to cope with the demand for tickets. This was more than just a new home for Queen's Park. The men from the south side recreation ground had built the biggest football stadium in the world.

*

In the late afternoon of 21 May 2016 – Cup Final Day – Hampden sat empty. Bright sunlight still poured in over the west stand. In front of the east stand was a scene of dishevelment. There was a series of long gouges out of the pitch, scars of brown earth in the otherwise pristine green turf. The goal posts were broken – one post had collapsed completely, and the other was propped up in a triangle by the snapped crossbar, its broken end biting into the ground in the centre of the goal line. The net had snagged and flopped loose.

Hours earlier, Hibernian fans had flooded the pitch after a dramatic 3–2 injury-time victory over Rangers – their club's first win in the Cup for 114 years. Thousands ran from their seats past the security and stewards. The goal posts were scaled and selfies were taken from the spar before it broke in half. Some fans tore at the grass, looking for physical momentos to smuggle home – patches of Hampden to be transplanted into Edinburgh lawns. Others surged towards the opposite end of the ground, to be met by a smaller, but no less vociferous, tide of Rangers supporters. The BBC sports reporter Richard Wilson described a scene that was 'a mass of contradictions: gleefulness, tears, vindictiveness, violence'. As fighting broke out, police, including mounted officers, spread across the pitch in an attempt to bring the chaos under control. It took the best part of an hour before the Hibernian players could re-emerge for the trophy presentation. The stadium was three-quarters empty and their fans were back in the stands – but enclosed by a hi-vis ring of police and stewards.

The 2016 Cup Final saw mounted police deployed at a Scottish football ground for the first time in three and a half decades. The previous occasion had been at Hampden again, for another Cup Final – Celtic against Rangers in 1980. The circumstances were much the same: a hot May afternoon, and a 1–0 extra-time win for Celtic in a tight, hard-fought match. As the Celtic players received the trophy and held it up to their fans on the east terracing, some started to scale the ten-foot-high perimeter fences which had been erected, running on to the pitch. One young supporter, decked out head to toe in green and white, brought on a football, sprinted to the opposite end of the ground, and booted it into the goal. For many of the Rangers fans, this was too much. Within seconds, they were pouring over the fences as well. Punches, kicks, cans, bottles – even bricks – were thrown. Thousands thronged the Hampden turf. In his television commentary the broadcaster Archie Macpherson likened it to 'a scene out of *Apocalypse Now*' and called it the 'equivalent of Passchendaele'. He was describing the national stadium as a warzone, a place where the divisions of Scottish society were spilling over into spontaneous, primitive violence. 'Let's not kid ourselves,' he continued. 'These supporters hate each other.'

This was Scottish football's infamous 'shame game'. Pictures of the riot playing out beneath the Hampden terraces were broadcast across the world. The *Glasgow Herald* bemoaned how 'years of patient effort to persuade industrialists and others that Glasgow is a desirable place to live are easily negated in a few moments on the national news'. The match was

discussed in the House of Commons and the House of Lords. Within the year, an Act of Parliament was passed banning the sale of alcohol at Scottish sporting grounds. Some argued that the banning of all Old Firm games was similarly in the public interest. For many commentators, a football match, and a football ground, had brought Scottish society to a new low.

Yet this was still not the first riot Hampden had witnessed. For that, we have to go back another seven decades to 17 April 1909, just six years after the new stadium's completion. Once again it was Celtic and Rangers meeting in a Cup Final. On this occasion, however, the result was a 2–2 draw. A crowd of over 60,000, incensed at the decision to replay the match rather than see it through to a conclusion, swarmed the pitch in protest. The fans displayed no antagonism towards each other, but rather targeted the authorities, hurling bottles and stones at the police, and attacking the stadium itself. Goal posts were uprooted, and wooden barriers torn down and set alight on the running track that surrounded the pitch. 'An infuriated crowd surrounded the blazing pile and danced and cheered wildly while willing hands seized more woodwork to feed the flames,' reported the *Glasgow Herald*. In the middle of Hampden Park, supporters enacted a scene of prehistoric pagan abandon. A small group of mounted police, supported by several hundred others on foot, finally pushed back and dispersed the crowd – which continued to filter out through the city in a trail of violence and vandalism. Like Archie Macpherson in 1980, the *Glasgow Herald* described the pitch as 'a miniature battlefield, civilians and policemen being carried over the ground in dozens of stretchers or on the shoulders of willing helpers'. In the aftermath serious questions were asked of the potency and dangerous emotional extremes of football. 'No matter under what circumstances the affair occurred,' wrote the *Daily Record,* 'public opinion would very soon demand the cessation of a pastime capable of converting a crowd of human beings into an army of savages.'

The idea of banning football was not new. The earliest surviving written record of the sport in Scotland was a banning order – passed by an act of the Parliament of James I in 1424. The Stuart kings clearly had little tolerance for the game. James II banned it in 1457 (along with golf), James III in 1471, and James IV in 1491. Hard times for fifteenth century footballers. There were signs of a change of heart, however, at the very end of the century. In 1497, the accounts of the Lord High Treasurer recorded a purchase of an undisclosed number of footballs for James IV.

Was the game itself the cause of trouble, or simply an outlet for tensions built up elsewhere? The early accounts saw it as popular and pernicious in equal measure. One of the characters in Sir David Lindsay's famous 1540 play *A Satire of the Three Estates* was a football-obsessed minister. An anonymous poem from the late sixteenth century offered a wry take on *The Bewteis of the Futeball*.

> Brissit, brawnis and broken banis
> Stryf discord and waistie wanis
> Cruikit in eild syn halt withal
> Thir are the bewteis of the futeball

What football is best for, it suggests, is fighting, bruising, broken bones, fierce arguments and desolation. It is Archie Macpherson's lament once again.

Nevertheless, the game's popularity could not be contained. The 1708 book *The Present State of Great Britain* said 'the common people of Scotland' were 'addicted' to football. Near the mid-point of the eighteenth century the Reverend John Skinner produced what may be the first poem dedicated solely to the merits of the game. Sections of *The Monymusk Christmas Ba'ing* read not unlike a transcript of a modern football commentary:

> The hurry-burry now began,
> Was right weel worth the seeing,
> Wi routs and raps frae man to man,
> Some getting, and some gieing;
> And a' the tricks of fit and hand,
> That ever was in being;
> Sometines the ba' a yirdlings ran,
> Sometimes in air was fleeing

In the early nineteenth century two of Scotland's most famous literary figures, James Hogg and Walter Scott, found themselves caught up in the excitement. The 1815 Caterhaugh Ba' Game, held on open ground where the rivers Ettrick and Yarrow meet, set teams from Selkirk and the Vale of Yarrow against each other, with sport acting not as an incitement to disorder, but as a peaceful, symbolic substitute for generations of bloody Borders conflicts. Special poems by both men commemorated 'The Lifting of the Banner of the House of Buccleuch, at the great football match on Caterhaugh' and were printed and distributed among the 2,000 spectators (this match, incidentally, has also been cited as the origin point for the game of rugby). Here, the game's explicit purpose, as Scott and Hogg explained in verse, was to *heal* social divisions – a civilised and non-violent (well, comparatively non-violent) means of asserting community pride and winning bragging rights. Or, to invert the *Daily Record's* fevered response to the 1909 Hampden riot, the very idea was to convert an 'army of savages' into a 'crowd of human beings'.

Compare 2,000 people at Caterhaugh in 1815 to 149,547 at Hampden in 1937, for the Scotland against England match: still a record attendance for any fixture in Europe. Two events separated by time and scale. *4,000 eyes to nearly 300,000.* The old fashioned ba' game, with hundreds of players on the field, to modern rules football with eleven against eleven. Two crowds of human beings. It took another Scot, Bill Shankly, Liverpool manager from 1959 to 1974 and a passionate devotee of Robert Burns, to sum up best what Scott and Hogg had implied. In what is the most famous quote in the history of the sport, Shankly asserted – admittedly with tongue in cheek – that football was more important than life or death. It was a provocative way of saying that it wasn't simply a game. That for large portions of the population, and in particular among the male industrial working classes, it was all-consuming.

As a result, over the course of the twentieth century, the football stadium gained a unique status: nowhere else in Scotland's towns and cities could compare to it as a place for regular massed public gathering. Not churches, not markets, not civic squares, not cinemas, not parks. Every Saturday afternoon at 3 o'clock many hundreds of thousands would pack out spaces which became synonymous with shared and competing local, regional, religious and political loyalties: Ibrox, Celtic Park, Tynecastle, Easter Road, Pittodrie, Tannadice, Dens Park, Brockville, Love Street, Firhill, Somerset Park, Cappielow. The weekly pilgrimage of the fan was handed down the generations – grandparent to parent to child, and on again. Stadiums have become the focal points and shared spaces for countless family traditions. They are where history is made and then remade. It is a potent mix – buildings enshrined in modern folklore, inscribed with personal and local identities, where new stories are always unfolding, and new myths are always waiting to be forged. But of course, there are good myths and there are bad myths, great tales of both triumph and disaster. The one factor that remains out of the control of the stadium and the spectator is what happens down on the pitch. Every week, fans place their self-worth at the feet of eleven men. Every week they leave with their pride either gilded or tarnished. Prejudices are sustained, grievances are formed, conspiracies are cultivated and wraths are nursed – and sometimes unleashed. For good or ill, what happens in the stadium shapes our society. Today, what other buildings can claim such impact?

Take Hampden on the evening of 25 May 1978. Scotland had qualified in style for the World Cup in Argentina, beating the reigning European Champions Czechoslovakia in the process. The new national team manager was an incorrigible optimist. When he was appointed the year before, he had introduced himself to the squad with the immortal line, 'My name is Ally MacLeod and I am a born winner.' He had a side containing some of the greatest players in the history of Scottish football: Kenny Dalglish, Alan Hansen, Graeme Souness, Archie Gemmill, Sandy Jardine and Joe Jordan. The team's World Cup song, performed by the comedian Andy Cameron, was unequivocal

We're on the march wi' Ally's army
We're going tae the Argentine
And we'll really shake them up
When we win the World Cup
'Cause Scotland is the greatest football team

The excitement grew as the tournament approached – stoked by the Scottish media and MacLeod's always-quotable soundbites. The players, the manager (and even the manager's wife) were fronting advertisements for everything from cars, televisions and carpets to beer and cigarettes. The Scottish Football Association decided to arrange a grand send off for the team at Hampden. Some 30,000 fans came. It began at 6.30pm, with ten of Scotland's 'best known' pipe bands marching into the stadium. Andy Cameron then introduced the squad one by one; they performed a lap of honour, and then boarded an open-top bus which 'toured' the stadium before exiting to take the team to Prestwick for their flight, that same evening, to Recife in Brazil. (The souvenir programme even included details of the in-flight menu that 'Ally and his men will be tackling while you are in bed tonight': cocktails and canapés followed by smoked salmon, chateaubriand steak with braised endive and garden peas, strawberry cheesecake, international cheeseboard and liqueurs). 'The great thing is that we are contenders in the main event, in the forefront of World football. Good old Scotland!' wrote SFA president Ernie Walker in the programme introduction. 'We know that all of you at home will be thinking about us a great deal. We will surely be thinking of you.' You could be forgiven for believing that the team was on its way to war (as many young men would be just four years later, travelling to the same part of the world at the onset of the Falklands conflict). That evening at Hampden combined hope, patriotism, idealism, naivety and even arrogance, all decked out in the tartan pageantry of a Bay City Rollers concert. It was also the opening scene for what remains the greatest calamity in all of Scottish sport – and what many consider to be a watershed moment in the history of the nation.

What unfolded 8,000 miles away in Argentina in the summer of 1978 has entered modern folklore as a tragedy of Greek proportions. The passion and hype that fuelled the pre-tournament excitement set the Scottish psyche on an inexorable collision course with hubris. There is no need to dwell over the events themselves, as they are gouged into the consciousness of a generation. Simply put, Scotland lost to Peru, drew with Iran, beat eventual finalists Holland with the best goal ever scored, and then failed to qualify for the quarter-finals on goal difference. At a press conference after the first defeat, a mongrel dog wandered up to MacLeod. The manager addressed the mongrel as 'the only friend I have got left', tried to pat it, and it bit him. Bad omens abounded. Winger Willie Johnston was sent home for failing a drugs test. The media and the fans turned on the team. They slunk into Scotland on their return, although could not avoid a jeering crowd on the tarmac at Glasgow airport: 'HOME BY THE BACK DOOR' thundered the *Daily Record* headline. They were not conquering heroes, but cowards and wasters. MacLeod became a haunted figure. 'With a bit of luck in the World Cup I might have been knighted,' he said. 'Now I'll probably be beheaded.'

I can't confess any memory of the events in Argentina at the time – I was born just a couple of months later. But I am certain that my father's ire at what was unfolding on the television screen crossed the placenta. And so I emerged into a different Scotland. A Scotland that had developed a pathological mistrust, even fear, of optimism. A Scotland that favoured doom-laden predictions and creeping fatalism over gallus self-confidence. 1978 was like the seventeenth century Darien disaster all over again – it resurrected tragic yet glorious failure as a persistent national narrative; a moral obligation even. Pride, in turn, was the greatest sin. I had lived through it, even though I hadn't lived through it. *Remember Argentina? Bubbles were made to burst.* 'Had I raised the level of national optimism just too high?' MacLeod later wondered. If you believe some – genuinely serious – commentators, then the South American debacle even influenced the low turnout in the 1979 devolution referendum and the ultimate rejection of the proposal to establish a Scottish Assembly. Of course, this is just speculation. But it brings us back to Hogg and Scott and Shankly – football always was, and is, more than just a game.

*

Hampden for Ally MacLeod's fateful 1978 send off was part political rally, part hanky-waving dockside. Over the years, the stadium has come to represent many things – garden, prison, theatre, factory, concert hall, cathedral. It acts as a surrogate for some of the old pillars of society, and a mirror for the state of Glasgow, even the nation. In the 1980s what Hampden came to resemble most was a slum. My father wouldn't take me to Scotland matches there – I remember distinctly him referring to it as a 'concrete toilet'. The stadium was in its seventies (in fairness, surpassing the life expectancy of the average Glaswegian male at that time by almost a couple of decades ...), and was in an advanced state of dilapidation. In 1980, as contractors prepared to demolish the north stand, the government withdrew a pledged £5.5 million to assist with reconstruction. Writing in November of that year, the *Daily Record* wondered grimly if 'Hampden could be dead and buried before Scotland's next game'. The stadium limped on throughout that decade and into the next: dirty, ramshackle and increasingly unloved. Some suggested that it had had its day and that other grounds – like Ibrox or Murrayfield – could take its place. What was certain was that Hampden could not last without redevelopment. 'It would be a bereavement to God knows how many thousands of people if it was never rebuilt' said the then Scotland manager Andy Roxburgh.

Work finally began in 1992, and progressed through several stages over the following seven years. Sometimes other grounds stood in for Hampden, other times matches and even Cup Finals were held amid the bizarre setting of a partial construction site. The last phase of redevelopment was boosted by the £59 million injection of National Lottery money. Hampden reopened in 1999 as one of European football's top class stadiums, with all the extensive modern facilities that entails: lavish changing rooms, indoor warm-up areas, executive boxes, media rooms, corporate offices and even the Scottish Football Museum. Almost nothing of the original remains beyond its distinctive bowl shape. The 1989 Hillsborough disaster required every new British ground to be all-seater. Hampden's capacity today is 51,886 – just a third of the crowd that filled the terraces for that record attendance in 1937, back when it was the world's largest ground (a title it held until the construction of the Maracana Stadium in Rio de Janiero in 1950). But it has survived.

And with it has survived something more important than concrete, steel, bricks and mortar. It is the space that matters to people. The sense of continuity. You walk into Hampden and you feel the presence of those who have gone before: another crowd from last year, or fifty years ago, or a century ago. Your dad once stood here. Or your granddad. Or your great-granddad. They sang and shouted and swore and jeered and cried and danced on the same spot. Hampden is a place of remembrance, a historic landscape. If you follow the logic of Caterhaugh, it is a substitute battleground – the site, for large chunks of the population, of some of twentieth century Scotland's greatest triumphs and tragedies, a wellspring for both pride and shame (not just a modern day Bannockburn, but Flodden and Culloden as well). Perhaps it is more than that too, something that transcends tribalism and nationalism.

The comparison between football and religion is persistent and well-worn: the weekly congregation, the performance of set rituals, the observance of long-held traditions, the sanctity of rules (although rather less respect than in the kirk for the central figure wearing black), and the supremacy of faith and belief over rationalism. As the sports sociologist John Bale puts it, football and religion 'have in common both the striving for perfection built on discipline, and the aim of integrating body and soul … it is almost something spiritual'. Beyond winning and losing, there is the search for football's divine – the perfect player, the perfect team, the perfect game. Hampden lays claim as the site where, over half a century ago, all these things came together at once.

On 18 May 1960 the stadium hosted the final of the European Cup between Real Madrid and Eintracht Frankfurt. Madrid were the undefeated, four-time European Champions (the continental competition was only established in 1956) with a side containing two of the world's most celebrated players, the Hungarian Ferenc Puskás and the Argentinian Alfredo Di Stéfano. Frankfurt, for their part, had astonished Scottish pundits with their aggression and endeavour in demolishing Rangers 12–4 to reach the final. Tickets went on sale at the stadium just a week before the match: 130,000 were sold in one day – to an almost entirely local Scottish crowd. The estimated European-wide television audience was some 70 million.

Reporting on the game that evening for the *Scotsman* was Hugh McIlvanney – a then fledgling reporter now acknowledged as one of the greats of sports journalism. He described what he saw as 'a watershed for me, as it was for so many … Here was the game as it could and should be played.' Those who witnessed it would later recall the events with a brand of beatific praise normally reserved for religious converts. The match commentator Kenneth Wolstenholme thought Real Madrid 'played as if they were touched by angels'. Jimmy Johnstone, then just a junior for Celtic, said, 'it was like a fantasy staged in heaven. I had never seen football like it, nor would I ever again. I'll recite the names of that Madrid forward line till the day I die.' For Billy Bremner, 'it was awesome; nobody could believe what they were seeing, and in the end there was this incredible, indescribable buzz all round'. Watching on television, Bobby Charlton expressed disbelief: 'these players are doing things that aren't possible, aren't real, aren't human'.

Of course, it is one of the pleasing ambiguities of the sport that – despite the boorishness and the bluster, the relentless machismo and 'hard-man' culture – football fans are arch-sentimentalists prone to the most ardent streaks of rheumy-eyed romanticism. That, however, is exactly why the stories that they tell – and retell, and retell, over and over – are so potent. Over the course of 90 minutes, Madrid put the ball in the net seven times, Frankfurt three times. And from that you get Jimmy Johnstone reciting a forward line like an invocation; Bremner and Charlton claiming witness to the miraculous; and Hampden transformed into a site of stunned, adoring worship. McIlvanney summed it up best in the opening to his match report, produced on a typewriter high up in the press gantry:

> The great Glasgow stadium responded with the loudest and most sustained ovation it has given to non-Scottish athletes. The strange emotionalism that overcame the huge crowds as the triumphant Madrid team circled the field at the end, carrying the trophy that they had monopolised since its inception, showed that they had not simply been entertained. They had been moved by the experience of seeing a sport played to its ultimate standards ... Scots in the ground could not conceal an awestruck appreciation of the glories that had been paraded before them.

McIlvanney's language is almost biblical. He recalled how the crowd remained for an hour in the stadium after the match. As if leaving would break the spell. But it wouldn't, it hasn't. It remains there, every time you go to Hampden. It remains like a fine dust, like a promise delivered as a whisper. That if you're lucky, the fabric of the stadium will split open once again to offer a glimpse of something indefinable, a secular salvation. 'Have faith,' it says, 'have faith'. And, despite it all, we still do.

20

Far From Home
Alexander McCall Smith

The Italian Chapel, 1940s

I went to the Italian Chapel on the Orcadian island of Lamb Holm on an egregiously raw spring day. Orkney is well known as a place of winds, and that week gales had roared in from the west, lashing the Pentland Firth into a maelstrom of angry waves. These gales lasted for several days, with only occasional periods of calm while the weather gods regrouped for a fresh onslaught. Going through my mind was that irredeemably dyspeptic poem by a naval officer, Hamish Blair, posted to Orkney during the Second World War. Entitled 'Bloody Orkney', it is a rant against everything in Orkney, including the weather, and includes the memorable lines: 'All bloody clouds, and bloody rains'. Blair was obviously a churlish guest of these charming and friendly islands and would seem to have deserved the anonymous reply penned by one of his Orcadian hosts: 'Captain Hamish "Bloody" Blair / Isna posted here nae mare / But no-one seems to bloody care / In bloody Orkney.'

Hamish Blair would have been dispirited by the unrelenting gales, but I found that even if they made being outside a challenge, they had a spectacular impact on the landscape. Perhaps Orkney, beautiful though it may be on a fine day, comes into its own in difficult conditions; it is a place of high winds and turbulent seas; it is a landscape of flattened hillsides and bent, discouraged trees. This is not Highland Scotland, but something quite different; it is a halfway house to Scandinavia, where low-lying islands and a cold sea are the backdrop to daily life.

I drove down from Kirkwall on the road that runs to Scapa Flow. It was too early for lambing, and the sheep were standing about waiting for their time to come, indifferent to the winds to which they were so accustomed. The farmhouses along the side of the road, like many of the buildings on the island, had a low, huddled look to them, as if they were keen to burrow back into the protective earth. Had they been brochs, rather than houses, they would not have seemed out of place.

The road ran straight, even if it went up and down as it followed the gentle folds of the Orkney countryside. No journey in Orkney is all that long, the blessing of an island being that it is, usually, a place of short distances. Such a landscape never suffers from the loneliness that can infect those that go on forever. The American West and the Australian Outback are melancholic places because of their distances. Orkney is not like that at all; it may be relatively sparsely populated, but I suspect it would be hard to be lonely there.

The road ends where the sea begins, and you turn off, should you wish, to make the journey over the barriers to one of the outlying islands, to Burray or South Ronaldsay. That route is hard in these windy conditions, as the sea is whipped into plumes of spray as it meets the sides of the causeways. But I did not have far to go, as my destination was just over one of these causeways, on the island of Lamb Holm, and I could already see the squat, white-fronted building, so tiny in the distance. The Italian Chapel. And next to it, energetic in the gale, the Italian flag. Again, a line of a poetry came to my mind, and I thought of Auden's description of a flag in the wind in his 'Journey to Iceland'. He describes a flag as 'scolding', and it seemed just right. Here was the Italian flag, scolding in the wind.

I crossed the barrier and stood before a building I had seen many times before in photographs. It was so small, as buildings – and people – so often are when you seem them in the flesh. But it had such presence that it would have seemed wrong for it to be any bigger.

I went in.

The story of the Italian Chapel starts with the disaster of the Second World War. Scapa Flow, a large, sheltered bay at the southern end of the mainland of Orkney, was the base of the Royal Navy in the First World War. It had been used by other navies before that, including by the long ships of the Vikings, and was also the graveyard of the German Imperial Fleet, scuttled by its commander, following the end of hostilities in 1918. On the outbreak of the Second World War in 1939, it still fulfilled a major role for the Royal Navy, for whom it was an important sanctuary not too far from the European theatre of war. Scapa Flow was protected by block ships, old vessels that were placed in such a position as to prevent sea access from unguarded angles. This, though, was only an illusion of security; aerial photography allowed the enemy to see exactly where obstructions were and to plan accordingly.

On 14 October 1939, only weeks after the beginning of the war, a German U-boat under the command of Captain Gunther Prien took advantage of a dark night and high tide to sneak past the defences and torpedo the British battleship, *Royal Oak*. The loss of this ship meant more than a considerable loss of life involved – over eight hundred men died in the attack – it was a gift to Nazi propagandists and a profound shock to the British public for whom the war, at that stage at least, was a rather unreal affair.

The political reaction brought Winston Churchill to Orkney to review the situation. Churchill was then First Lord of the Admiralty, and he decided that the security of the fleet would require barriers to be built between the string of small islands that sheltered Scapa Flow to the east. The scale of this operation was considerable and involved major engineering challenges. The flow of the tide between the islands could be vicious, and anything intended to block it completely would have to be much stronger and more substantial than the existing ship hulks. In May 1940 the bulk of the civil engineering workforce arrived and took up residence, along with a vast amount of engineering equipment. Over two hundred workmen were boarded on a ship anchored off Holm, and these were joined by a number of specialist engineers from the construction firm to whom the contract had been awarded. Work began, and lorries started to bring quantities of rock from the quarries allocated for the purpose. This rock was dropped into the sea to create continuous causeways and barriers between the islands. One can imagine how impossible the task must have seemed to the workmen charged with performing it – dropping bundles of rock into a stretch of sea that looked easily strong enough to sweep away any of the works of man.

Reasonable progress was made with the shallower sections of the barriers, but marine topography was not the only problem: labour was in increasingly short supply as men working for the contractors joined the armed services or found themselves drawn to equally pressing defensive work closer to their homes further south. But if local labour was in short supply, and too busy, there was one source of under-employed male manpower in Britain at the time – prisoners of war. And who better at carrying out engineering works than those consummate craftsmen – the Italians? That question resonates with me: as a boy, I had a chess set that had been made, my father told me, by Italian prisoners of war 'because the Italians are so good at making things'. And they were: the chess set was beautifully fashioned out of hardwood and came with a fine marquetry board. I might have thought – but never did – of the hands that made it; of the man who, far from home, wiled away his captivity in the making of an object of beauty.

The Italians who provided the labour for the completion of the barriers and who were, in due course, to build the chapel, reached Lamb Holm by a very long and tortuous journey. They were originally taken prisoner in North Africa, where the defeat of Mussolini's forces in the desert campaigns resulted in the incarceration of many thousands of tired defeated troops in prison camps in Egypt. From there, they were shipped via the Cape and West Africa to Britain, where a number were sent to Edinburgh. There they found themselves mustered at Waverley Station and being given into the charge of men from the Pioneer Corps. They were informed that they were going to Orkney, a destination that must have seemed as remote to these southern Europeans as the Arctic Circle.

The Italian prisoners were accommodated in a camp known as Camp 60, on Lamb Holm. Conditions were better than those they had experienced in Egypt, but it must have been a shock to these men of the South to have to cope with Orkney's wind and rain. Some of them were sustained by their faith in the eventual triumph of the Axis cause; others were relieved at being out of a conflict that they never wanted. These were for the most part small farmers and artisans, villagers, ordinary young men – not SS bullies or strutting *fascisti*. In spite of that, though, there was discontent, and in particular there were arguments as to whether they should be obliged to work on any military project, something that was forbidden by the Geneva Convention. If the barriers were seen as defences against enemy attack, then their construction was military work; if they were seen as a means of allowing islanders to travel more freely between their homes and the mainland, they were acceptable civil projects. After negotiation, it was the latter view that prevailed.

The ingenuity and spirit of the men interned in Camp 60 found expression in numerous ways. They constructed a bowling alley and a billiard table – both made out of concrete. They acquired – or made – musical instruments and put on concerts and operettas, sometimes attended by local people. They painted and made metal and wooden objects – ashtrays, toys, and other items that were useful in a time of shortage. All the while, the news from Italy got worse and worse – at least from their perspective. Sicily was invaded, Mussolini fell, the Germans poured down the peninsula, ready to make their country a battlefield. Far away from all this, unsure as to the fate of friends and family, the prisoners clutched at what small scraps of beauty and spirituality came their way.

A priest arrived – a Father Gioacchino Giacobazzi. He spoke to one of the prisoners who was an artist, and who had created a cement statue of St George and the Dragon in the camp. They agreed a church was needed and a request to this effect was put in to the camp authorities. Permission was granted: a church could be made out of two Nissen huts bolted together. Nissen huts are half-cylindrical huts made out of corrugated iron. They were common in army camps, such as the sprawling Cultybraggen camp just outside Comrie, and they can still be seen in the Scottish countryside, occasionally sold on by the army to farmers as a cheap and convenient way of storing equipment or housing hens.

A Nissen hut as a church might have satisfied protestant souls accustomed to the stark simplicity of many Scottish kirks, but it was a far cry from the setting in which Italians would have attended Mass at home. The skills for which the Italians are famous were well represented in the prisoner of war population. One of the main creators of the chapel, Domenico Chiocchetti, was an artist; others included a blacksmith and those with woodworking skills. The challenge for them was to transform both the exterior and interior of the two joined-together Nissen huts into something that could, with just a small imaginative leap, be an Italian church. That meant smooth walls, ornamentation in pillars and screens, and murals that would evoke the religious paintings the men had seen in their native towns and villages.

Concrete would be the material to achieve this feat of architectural legerdemain. The facade of the chapel conceals the half-cylindrical shape of the main body behind it: two small pinnacles, each topped with a fleur-de-lys, complete the square outer pillars; crockets parade along the inclined top of the facade, giving a crenelated effect; an inlaid red pastille featuring the suffering face of Christ is to be seen immediately above the entrance, and on each side of the door is a small pillar, painted white like the rest of the front wall. All this is concrete, a substance that, in the wrong hands, can be bland and dispiriting (think of the architectural crimes of the 1960s and 1970s) but which can be coaxed into pleasing shapes when used on a small scale.

Inside, the walls are lined with plasterboard, curved to follow the shape of the tin behind it, and this surface is painted with *trompe l'oeil* tilework. An elaborate metal screen, the work of Plaumbo, the blacksmith, separates nave from chancel, and beyond is the altar – also concrete, painted white, performing the work that in Italy would be performed by marble. Behind the altar, a mural of Madonna and Child – again reminiscent of the images to be found in virtually any Italian church, lowly or otherwise.

The striking thing about the Italian Chapel is the impression it gives of being made with very limited materials, which have nonetheless been used to the greatest effect. Tin cans were twisted into the shape of candleholders;

stones from the beach were painted and laid for flooring; wood and metal from wrecks were salvaged and pressed into use. And, as is often the case with the make-do item, all of these things acquire a particular beauty when wrought in this way.

Some items have been added later. In 1964 Domenico Chiocchetti, the artist, returned to Orkney with his wife, Maria. He brought with him the wooden stations of the cross now hanging on the walls: a personal gift to the chapel – but also a gift by a former prisoner to his former captors. The mayor and Comune of Moena and Trento sent a crucifix and Venetian glass altar cruets. There was a subsequent visit by eight former prisoners in 1992, to mark the fiftieth anniversary of their arrival in Orkney. By all accounts, this was a moving occasion, and not surprisingly. By and large, Italian prisoners of war were treated with consideration by the people of Orkney and friendships were formed in spite of the festival of strife and hatred that was being celebrated at the time. The Italian Chapel speaks to that – to the ability of people, in the midst of conflict and darkness, to create something of simple beauty – a building that celebrates forgiveness and humanity. If buildings can bear messages on their brows, that is what this one says.

After my visit to the Italian Chapel, I returned to Edinburgh. The winds were still high, but the pilots who fly the planes between the mainland and the islands are not put off by a bit of a gust. We rose above the clouds and headed south. As I looked out, I thought of the next chapters I had to write in the novel that appears each year in the *Scotsman* newspaper, chapter by chapter, until it is later published as a complete book. It is a format that allows for digression, and I wanted now to compose a scene set in Orkney that would be about this tiny chapel on its windswept islet. I chose to do so through the eyes of two young men, students from Edinburgh and St Andrews, who had taken summer jobs as ghillies some decades ago in an Orkney hotel, roughly modelled on Merkister House, where my wife and I stayed on our visit. It had been the family home of the great Orcadian novelist Eric Linklater, and a plaque in his memory is to be found in its lobby. I started the section with the two students in the bar, where they hear some Scottish folk songs.

> The hotel bar was busy, and a group of folksingers was expected. They arrived late, but to a rousing cheer from the locals who were drinking in the bar. David bought Angus a pint of Guinness; he blew the froth across the top of his glass. The folksingers struck up as somebody in the bar called out, 'Callum, you're the man! You're the man!

'My love's in Germany,' announced Callum.

'Germany!' somebody shouted.

The musicians started. *My love's in Germany, send him hame, send him hame ...*

Angus listened to the words. *This is very sad*, he thought.
My love's in Germany, fighting brave for royalty,
He may ne'er his Jeanie see;
He's as brave as brave can be,
Send him hame, send him hame ...

They finished, the last chord dying out in silence. There was applause, and shouts of appreciation. David looked at Angus. 'It makes some want to cry, that song,' he said. 'It's about ... Well, what do you think it's about?'

'About being separated from somebody you love?'

'Yes.'

Angus looked down at his glass. Had it ever happened to him? Had he ever been separated from somebody he loved? No.

'Or not being able to speak about how you feel,' said David.

Angus was not sure what to say. He was nineteen; what time was there to be separated when you were still nineteen? Separation, he thought, would come much later.

'Where does that come from?' asked Angus.

'Here,' said David.

'Here?'

'Yes, the music was written by an Orcadian. He was called Thomas Trail. And the words are from a poem written way back. Seventeen-something, I think.'

Angus was impressed. 'How do you know about that?'

'I just do. I listen to songs. I learn the words. I know who wrote them.' He paused. 'Sometimes I feel that the people who wrote these songs – you know, the people way back ... I feel that they're talking to me. Personally. I feel I know them.'

Angus raised an eyebrow. 'Although ...'

'Although it was a long time ago. I still feel that.'

Angus took a sip of his Guinness. The singers had moved on. *Love is teasing.* The words were clearly articulated; they were full of longing. *I wish, I wish, I wish in vain, I wish I was a young lad again, But a young lad I will never be, Till apples grow on an orange tree; For love is teasing, and love is pleasing; love is a pleasure when first it's new ...*

He looked at David. There was a smile playing about the other young man's lips. 'Do you wish you could stop the clock?'

Angus asked him what he meant.

'I mean, keep the feeling of a particular moment alive. Right now, for example. Wouldn't you like to keep hold of this moment. Us sitting here in Orkney, with these people singing these particular songs. Scotland. The whole works. Keep it as it is.'

Angus did not reply.

'Because I would,' said David. 'I like where we are, if you see what I mean. I find that just as I get used to something, the future comes and takes it away. So when you're happy being nineteen – that's us – somebody says: *But you're going to be thirty, one of these days, oh yes you will, and then forty.*'

Angus leaned forward. Without knowing why, he put his hand on David's forearm. David looked down, and Angus withdrew his hand. You did not do that, even in a bar in Orkney, with songs being sung about being away in Germany and friendship, and talk about being nineteen, and loss, and the still evening and the light, the light, reminding you where you were.

Two weeks later the manager of the anglers' hotel gave them both a day off. There was a break in the hotel's bookings, with one set of guests leaving the day before another large party arrived.

'You boys have been doing a good job,' he said. 'Go fishing.'

They both laughed. Even David had had enough.

They caught the post bus to the other end of the island and got off at St Mary's Holm, a small village on the edge of Scapa Flow. 'Now?' said Angus.

David pointed. 'Over there. You can just see it. That low white building.'

'Everything's low here,' said Angus. 'The hills, the houses – everything.'

'The wind.'

'And no trees.'

'The wind.'

They walked slowly along the road that led to an island causeway. On the other side, barely a few hundred yards away, was the island of Holm, and on it the small building David had pointed out.

'The barriers,' said David. 'Churchill Barriers. They built them to keep U-boats out during the war. They managed to sneak in at the beginning and get our ships. The Italians built these – Italian prisoners.'

Angus looked up at the sea. The wind had risen again, and there were waves against one side of the barrier. 'Aren't you glad,' he asked, 'that you weren't around then?'

'Why?'

'Oh, everything,' said Angus. 'Having to join the navy, for example. Having to be in a ship on that …' He gestured towards the sea, 'Knowing that there was somebody out to sink you, to kill you.'

'And nobody wants to kill us now?'

Angus shook his head. 'Not immediately. They're not actually hunting us down.'

'I suppose you're right,' said David. 'I imagine they didn't think about it too much. You did your duty. You just did it, like everybody else.' He paused. 'How brave would you have been?'

Angus smiled. 'Not at all. I expect I would have been scared stiff.'

'I don't think so,' said David.

'I do.'

They walked the rest of the way in silence – each alone with his thoughts. Angus thought of the sea, and of its colour, a blue that shaded into emerald in the shallows. And then there was the land itself, with its intense Orcadian green and the greys of the stone dykes, stretching across the fields in the gentle curve of the hillsides. And black rock at the edge of the sea; angular black rock. There would be a palette for this place, he thought, that would be different from the palette he used for other parts of Scotland.

Once on Lamb Holm they had only a short distance to walk to reach their destination.

'The Italian Chapel,' said David.

Angus looked at the building before them. It had been built around a curved tin Nissen hut of the sort used in older military camps. The facade, which was only slightly higher than the low-slung hut, would not have been out of place in an Apennine village: a white church front, pillars to each side of the front door, with a small arched recess for a bell. It was very small.

Angus felt awed. 'They built this while they were prisoners? Here … in the middle of nowhere?'

David smiled. 'Yes. The prison camp was over there.' He pointed to the field behind the chapel. 'That was full of these huts. They're all gone now. This is all that's left.'

They went inside. The arched roof had been painted with *trompe l'oeil* brickwork and stone arches. Behind a screen of elaborate metalwork, an altar had been set against the back wall of the hut; a mural showing the Madonna and Child, along with saints and angels as envisaged by the Italian imagination, was the backing of the altar.

David went forward to the screen. He crossed himself. Angus caught his breath. It had not occurred to him.

'You're Catholic?'

David nodded. 'Yes. Should I have told you?'

'Not at all.'

David moved forward. 'Look at these lovely paintings.'

Angus winced. It was typical Mediterranean religious art; over-stated, sentimental, naïve.

David noticed. 'You don't like the subject? Graven images?'

Angus tried to make light of it. 'Some people like this sort of thing.'

David looked serious. 'But these men were so far from home. They were just trying to create something that would remind them – trying to make something beautiful.'

Angus reassured him. 'Oh, I can see that. And, look, I understand what this means.' He paused. 'Do you want me to leave you here for a few minutes.'

David looked amused. 'So that I can pray?'

'If that's what you want.'

David shook his head. 'I haven't been to mass for over a year. I stopped when I was eighteen – when I left school.'

'I see. So you no longer believe.'

'Not in all this,' said David. 'Yet for me it's still the thing I don't believe in, if you see what I mean. It's where I'm from, I suppose.' He stared at the mural behind the altar. 'I think this place is all about forgiveness.'

Angus frowned. 'Why do you say that?'

David did not answer. 'We should be getting back,' he said. 'We're going to have to hitch back to Kirkwall.' And then he said something that Angus did not at first understand, but came to do so years later. 'The Church doesn't really want me, you know.'

They left, and fifteen minutes later were in the back of a chicken farmer's van, heading for Kirkwall. When they arrived back at the anglers' hotel, they walked down the staff corridor to the rooms they occupied at the back of the building. David stopped. 'Thanks for today, dear friend.'

Dear Friend. 'That's all right. I enjoyed myself too.'

'It's going to rain tomorrow.'

Angus made a gesture of acceptance. 'It always does.'

The next day, heavy squalls moved across the loch, whipping the water into white-topped wavelets. A recently arrived angler, impatient to begin fishing, persuaded David to take him out in one of the boats. In the middle of the loch, a gust of wind tipped the boat and David and his charge fell in. They might have drowned, but David was a strong swimmer and dragged the fisherman to the shore.

He was blamed, and dismissed by the manager. 'I cannot have you risking the lives of our guests.'

Angus said goodbye to him in the car park behind the hotel. David was on the point of tears, ashamed and embarrassed. Angus put his arms around him. 'Dear friend,' he said.

And now, with this mention of Orkney, so many years later, he thought of all this, of the trip to the Italian Chapel; of forgiveness; of friendship; of the future that takes the present away from us.

21

Arcadia
Alistair Moffat

Inchmyre Prefabs, Kelso, 1948

I have four small, slightly creased black and white photographs taken between 1950 and 1952. In the first I am in the arms of Bina, my beloved Grannie, and as far as I can tell, only a few weeks old. It looks as though I am asleep, a small hand poking out of a shawl, the palm open. On Bina's right, my big sister Barbara is standing, her glorious smile already there on the dimpled face of a four year old. She has a light coloured ribbon pinning back her parting to one side. There is no date scribbled on the back of the photograph, but beside Barbara, a climbing rose is in bloom. And roses begin to bloom in June, when I was born. Perhaps I am only a few weeks old.

In the second photograph, it is my Dad who holds me as I stand unsteadily upright on the front doorstep of our house. Barbara is beside me again, holding my hand and she has the same sort of bright ribbon in her hair. She sits on the floor of the lobby, just inside the open front door, wearing a cardigan over her frock and white socks and sandals. What looks like an old floral coverlet of some sort had been spread out on the step for my Dad to sit on as he clasps me around the waist. For the photo he has taken the trouble to put on a tweed jacket that is too big for him and he wears a pair of pin-striped trousers, probably from his demob suit. They don't match. But what lights up the picture is my Dad's smile. Even though he wears old tortoiseshell National Health specs, I can see his eyes smiling too. Mine are closed, a blink at the moment of the shutter click, but my smile is his smile. And my hair is by that time very fair indeed, much lighter than Barbara's. Like many self-conscious five year olds, she manages what she thinks is the right sort of smile when posing in front of a camera. I think my Mum took the photo in the spring of 1951.

The sun is shining so brightly in the third picture that Barbara and I both have our eyes closed. I am also clearly very tanned and thriving, with round cheeks and what seems to be an open-mouthed chuckle. Mum

has me trussed up in an elaborate harness clipped to the sides of the pram. There is a soft toy of some sort in my left hand. Perhaps that is what is making me smile. With her forearm very brown, Barbara holds on to one side of the pram and it is parked outside the front door of our house, where the earlier picture was taken. I remember its brakes very well. Operated by a foot pedal, they fascinated me when I was older, especially when they got stuck.

The final photo shows me holding the handle of the pram, a well-covered toddler in a short-sleeved summer shirt under knee-length dungarees. My independence, needing neither helping hands nor harness, meant that there was only me in the picture. My ears appear to have grown, revealed by a haircut, and I am holding on to the pram handle with one hand and carrying something with the other. Looking off camera, probably at my Mum taking the snap, I seem to be talking and that suggests a date of summer 1952. Behind me, some distance away, are the tops of trees and they are in leaf, bending a little in the wind. Above my head, washing flaps and I am standing next to a brick wall. I recognise it: it is the small gable of a garden shed, the one the roses climbed up. There seem to be leaves on the grass by the shed, perhaps it was autumn.

These four little black and white photographs are all the record I have of our time in Arcadia. To the north of Kelso, on a patch of damp, boggy ground known as Inchmyre, an estate of prefabs was built in 1945 and for seven years we lived in our own cosy, well-designed detached house. I was too young to remember details but the atmosphere of life at Inchmyre has stayed with me. It was the body warmth of a community relieved that the horrors and risks of Hitler's war had ended, living in the shattered aftermath, subsisting on rations – but starting families in their own houses, ones they could walk around, homes with tiny front and back gardens, with good heating and refrigerators. It was paradise and somehow I knew it.

Photographs sometimes stir memory and, behind the one with Bina, I can see something of the landscape of Arcadia. Stretching east towards the woods at Broomlands are rows of prefabs huddling together. Each has a garden shed, the curved corrugated iron of wartime Anderson shelters with brick-built gables. No more bombs would fall and many thousands of these air raid shelters were converted to a more peaceful purpose. To Bina's left is a wire fence that divided our back garden from our neighbour's. The posts look as though they were made from pre-cast concrete. Beside them, leaning at drunken angles, are the cast-iron poles that held up washing lines. All my Mum ever seemed to do was wash clothes, sheets and tea towels. Perhaps we had so few of each that the turnover of dirty washing had to be rapid. The garden ground beneath all that flapping was small and well tended. During the war everyone grew as many vegetables, potatoes, berries and fruits as they could. Our front garden was a narrow grassy slope that led up to the road. In those quiet, far off days there was very little traffic.

As the war was ending, Churchill's government put in place plans to build homes fit for heroes. The Housing (Temporary Accommodation) Act of 1944 promised 300,000 prefabs to supply homes quickly while more permanent houses were being built. It was a stop-gap measure and in the event only half that number were supplied. All of the major construction companies built prototypes and these were expected to have a life of between seven and ten years. So that they could be put together quickly (one a day was the expected average), the prefabs were modular and standardised. I can remember the colours. Made from concrete and asbestos, the outside wall panels were an off-white and the timber door surrounds were painted a gloss green. Magnolia was the colour used for the interior walls but some people relieved the uniformity by using wallpaper, if they could afford something that was not a necessity.

Insulation was good, much better than draughty older houses, and I am sure that the front door had a sill against which it closed. Perhaps I tripped over it often. There was a coal fire in the sitting room with a back boiler from which central heating pipes could draw hot water to keep the prefab warm. And while the fire burned, there was constant hot water for washing and a bath large enough to allow an average man to immerse himself completely. But the fire had to be kept burning and coal was not cheap. In the long and bitter winter of 1947, when the snow lay on the ground until April, my Mum found Barbara freezing in her cot with ice forming on the quilt. Perhaps the central heating was faulty or pipes had burst in the extreme cold.

For my Mum and Dad many of these fittings and features were luxuries. Both had been brought up in tenements in the centres of Hawick and Kelso that had only running cold water and, for a hip bath, water had to be heated with kettles on a stove. And prefabs also had inside flush toilets, something tenement dwellers loved. They had been forced to share smelly stairhead toilets or use freezing outside lavatories. To have everything under one roof and not have to share facilities gave dignity and privacy.

What was known as a service unit was standard. Each prefab had a fully fitted kitchen that backed onto a bathroom. This concentrated the main pipework in one place and greatly reduced construction time. Ovens were built in and all of the shelving and work surfaces were part of the prefabricated unit. What I remember most clearly was the fridge. Small and with a chrome handle, it meant something simple. Women did not have to go shopping every day. For me, its principal gift was ice lollies. Made in grey plastic tubes with a makeshift stick plonked in (it usually fell to one side before the lolly had time to freeze) and pushed into the tiny freezer compartments, they were flavoured with the orange juice supplied by the NHS for children but considerably diluted with water. In order to persuade the lolly to drop out, Mum had to rub the plastic tubes vigorously between her palms. When we moved to a council house in 1952, it was at least ten years before we could afford to buy a fridge.

Barbara remembers the internal layout of the rooms. All I can recall is a dark corridor leading inside from the front door but my sister told me that the bathroom was at the end of it and the door to the kitchen on its left. The service unit with all its pipes and cables and both rooms took up a bit more than one corner of the rectangular footprint of the prefab. In the photograph where I am clutching the pram handle, there is a clear view of the outside aspect of that part of the building. Leading out of the kitchen, there was a back door with a step down into the garden, and to its left a double window unit that must have lit the sink and the draining board. That arrangement would allow the pipework to link with the bathroom next door.

The kitchen had no door into the sitting room at the front of the house. In the brick-built council house we moved into at 42 Inchmead Drive, only about 500 yards away, there was a similar layout. The bathroom was close to the kitchen in order to keep all the pipework at the back of the house. And the lack of a connecting door between the kitchen and the sitting room shows a cultural shift. In the 1940s and 50s, cooking smells were properly confined to the kitchen and the odour of overcooked cabbage was definitely not to be allowed to permeate the rest of the house. Nowadays, no self-respecting architect would ever force house dwellers to go out of the kitchen, into a corridor and through another door to get to the sitting room. Cooking itself has become much less of a chore and more adventurous, and cooks like to be in a position to talk to the people they are cooking for.

Our prefab had two bedrooms on the right of the dark central corridor. Barbara's was at the front and Mum and Dad slept in the back bedroom, probably with me in a cot beside them. That might at first have been a problem for my Mum. It was a matter of regret all her life that she found mothering me as a young baby very difficult. At more than 11 lb, I was a huge baby and my birth must have been very painful. I am not sure I can blame a forceps delivery, but apparently when I was born, I was ugly and my head misshapen, looking a bit like a bulldog. At first my Mum rejected me, wouldn't hold me, wanted nothing to do with me. And at the same time she suffered from mastitis. It must have been hard, and maybe Bina helped. No-one took a picture of Mum holding me as a baby, at least none that I have ever seen. Perhaps my roly-poly chuckle in the third photograph came from being a bottle-fed infant and all those calories. I don't think those early weeks and months made any difference to me, and in any case, she quickly accepted me as her mastitis abated and I began to look a bit less like a bulldog. I had an uncomplicated and complete love for my Mum. Her smile could light a room and she defended me fiercely and promoted me relentlessly all her life. But I know that she never forgot those difficult early months.

I am sure that Mum was supported by her neighbours. The photos show how very close to each other the prefabs were and, after I was born, it was high summer. Records show that August 1950 was very sunny, almost every day, and Mum would have had me out in the pram in the back garden, probably below the kitchen window where she could see me. Almost all her neighbours had young children or babies and the Nisbets next door were very friendly, as were the Ainslies whose garden backed on to ours. In those days, Mums were at home, and in good weather people sat outside in the warm evening air, probably smoking, talking with each other. Babysitting was informal: 'Can you keep an eye on them while I go down the street for some messages?' There was no TV, only the radio, and hospitality was a cup of tea that cost next to nothing. Over milk and two sugars, problems would have been aired.

I can remember small groups of mothers pushing prams or holding the hands of toddlers (reins were often used to prevent dangerous freedom of movement) to go for walks on warm summer evenings 'to get out of the house'. What had made Inchmyre boggy was a natural spring that used to drain into it at the foot of what was called the Pipewell Brae. It fed a tank and there was a standpipe where buckets could be filled. In the early 1950s droughts drove Mums to fill tin pails, sometimes queuing at the standpipe, and carrying them back to their prefabs. It was warm work as they walked slowly so that too much water did not slop out of the pails.

After we moved out of Inchmyre, the little estate continued to be occupied until the early 1960s, the prefabs far outrunning their projected lives. Perhaps it was because they were loved, simple buildings, easy to maintain. No-one worried then about living in a box that was partly made from asbestos. Housing was still managed by town councils and each employed an officer called the Burgh Surveyor. Wilbert Neill lived opposite us in Inchmead Drive and he probably oversaw the demolition of the prefabs. I remember it very well. It seemed to be a process that took much longer than building them. The off-white walls were simply cast down, no doubt putting up clouds of asbestos dust, and they lay around in heaps for a while. Any that were at an angle, we jumped up and down on them like seesaws. When they were taken away, the brick founds were revealed and the Anderson shelter sheds were flattened. Too young to be sentimental, we played among the ruins for weeks.

When the site was eventually cleared, the planners did not change the road pattern and built directly on the footprints of the prefabs. But what they built turned out to be dreadful: dreary low-rise flats used up less space to house more people but compared to the cheerful, chattering clutter of the back gardens of the prefabs with their tangles of clothes lines, potato patches and climbing roses, they were soulless, cold. After 1965, I had a paper round and delivered to the flats at Inchmyre. Trudging up and down echoing concrete stairs, shoving *Sunday Post*s through clanking letterboxes, I could have been anywhere.

Last year, I went off in search of prefabs. I found dozens that had survived sixty years beyond their allotted life-span, and they were all clearly loved. The most dense concentration I came across was in Moredun, a suburb on Edinburgh's south side. In 1947 a large estate of 565 prefabs was built very quickly and, despite the efforts of the local authority to remove what remained in the 1990s, several still sit proudly among streets of more modern council houses. At Craigour Avenue, I came across twelve prefabs and they looked to be of a very similar type to ours. What triggered that connection was the sight of a small outshot asbestos sheeting lintel above the back door of one of them, a feature designed to keep out the worst of the rain when the door was opened. We had that in Kelso.

At Moredun, many of the roofs had been replaced or updated and all had new front doors, the sort available in DIY supermarkets. The walls of three were still off-white while others had been painted cheerier colours. One was an amazing midnight blue. All were clearly well looked after, having been bought from the council by the residents. I had no way of knowing but I suspected they had stayed in families, passed on from one generation to the next. I spoke briefly to a man who came out of one of the prefabs and he believed that to be the case, repeating my parents' old pleasure in living in a detached house. But he was in a hurry to get into his car and not about to invite a stranger inside. Part of me thought it unacceptably rude to go down the street and knock on doors and brazenly ask if I could have a look inside. Like some sort of social anthropologist. It felt disrespectful to the point of those little houses. Perhaps the most poignant photograph I took that day was of two prefabs overshadowed by three massive fourteen storey tower blocks behind them.

When my Dad died in 1986, my Mum was more than bereft. She had been raised in a Hawick tenement in a family of seven sisters and a single brother. At the age of 70, on the night my Dad had a heart attack, she had for the first time to face the prospect of sleeping alone. He had suffered a very debilitating stroke in 1974 when the surgeons made a mess of their first attempt and he had had a second stroke after his operation. Overnight, a dominating man shrivelled into an invalid unable to walk without a stick. He needed a lot of care and, brutally, I thought his death twelve years later might be a merciful release for my Mum. But it was not. Always a politically principled woman, she had thought it wrong for the government to sell council houses in the 1980s ('are they building new council houses for young folk who haven't the money to buy?') and when Dad's death left one person living in a three-bedroom house, she though that wrong too. The idea that she was occupying a house meant for a young family appalled her. There were smaller flats at Inchmyre and one of those would do.

My sisters and I thought it would mark a break, be the start of a new life. But instead, Mum began to decline, living alone, withdrawing into herself, losing confidence after she herself had a minor stroke, almost setting fire to the flat with a careless cigarette. Her smile was fading. Looking back now, I see that she had come full circle by moving back to Inchmyre. But those dismal low-rise flats were not the sunlit, neighbourly muddle of the prefabs built in a post-war atmosphere of hope and decency. When Mum died, my sisters asked me to give a short, informal eulogy in the tiny sitting room of her dark little flat. I managed to get the words out without my voice catching, but when we spilled out onto the pavement, only yards from where our little prefab stood, that was when the tears came.

22

Views and Vision
Kathleen Jamie

Anniesland Court, 1968

Take the bus from the city centre along Great Western Road, passing the Botanic Gardens at the top of Byres Road and grand Kelvinside mansions, eventually you'll pass under a railway bridge and find yourself among the handsome red sandstone tenements of Anniesland. Jump off the bus here and you're down among the usual parade of small city shops: barbers and betting shops, pharmacies and hairdressers. Soon, you're at the busy junction where Great Western Road, the Crow Road, Bearsden Road and Anniesland Road all meet to form Anniesland Cross. From here the city opens out westward, with the Argyll hills in the distance.

Just at the junction on its north-east side, officially at 833 Crow Road, there stands a solitary high-rise block of flats. It's a slim and elegant rectangle, white with a few evergreen trees growing at its base. There are no other similar buildings nearby. In that sense only, Anniesland Court is isolated, rising alone among its neighbours ('like a sore thumb', its residents say, fondly enough). Its neighbours on the Crow Road are traditional tenements, a branch of Morrisons supermarket, and a late Victorian Gothic-style parish church.

They make an odd couple, architecturally speaking, the sandstone, pitched-roofed church with decorative pinnacles, and its austerely elegant 1960s neighbour. Only sixty years separates them, but change is quick hereabouts. The church website notes that 'at the end of the nineteenth century Anniesland was an area where coal-pits and quarries, blaes bings and brickworks existed side by side with agricultural land. In 1899, at the Cross itself, there was only a smithy standing in an open field, with farmlands to the east.'

No smithy now. It's one of the busiest road junctions in Europe, or so it's said, with this high-rise block standing sentinel above.

Anniesland Court is Scotland's only listed tower block. Category A means it is of national importance. The official description calls it 'a landmark for the area, a striking composition of banding and lift shaft with generous 2-storey flats.'

It's raised on a plinth or podium above street level, and at twenty-two storeys you have to stand back quite a way to see it whole. Its design has rhythm: broadside on, the north or back elevation rises in thin layers, like a wafer biscuit. Three layers of square windows, then one of enclosed drying areas, then three layers of windows again, and so on seven times up. Hardly a skyscraper by Manhattan standards, but against scudding clouds it's tall enough to look as if it's swaying. There are actually two conjoined towers: stair and lift-shaft are in a separate one, linked across every three storeys. The tower's narrow sides are picked out in salmon-pink mosaic. It is not ugly. In fact, having actually looked (and personally I'd never really looked at a tower block before, not properly), I thought it elegant, stylish even – from the outside, at least. Tall, but not grandiose.

Of the walkway at the base of the tower, some parts are covered, other parts open, and the whole catches the almost inevitable Scottish wind. There are offices and a public library accessed from this podium. When I arrived, it was school's out time. Mothers with buggies and infants and shopping were making their way into the block's surprisingly modest street door, set on the narrow side. There they tapped their security cards on the reader to unlock the door. Within the tower is a residents' warden with security TV, anyone hanging around within the block without authorisation will soon be challenged. There are 125 flats: the block is fully occupied. Here at least, things went according to plan.

In Scotland, if we look at tower blocks at all, it's often with prejudice. Like many others Anniesland Court is a child of the 1960s. Many were built, and many have already been pulled down, soon deemed failures. But the story of tower blocks – of all post-war mass housing – is a tale of passion and vision.

*

There is a line by the poet Liz Lochhead: 'After the War / was the dull country I was born in.' We are now firmly within living memory, and when it comes to post-war housing developments, especially in Scotland, we are also deep into living social history. 1950s Scotland may have been a 'dull country', but it was one in the grip of a building boom like it had never seen before.

Lochhead's poem evokes an overcrowded dwelling, with a young married couple sharing space with their in-laws, their baby's cot crammed up against their bed.

Many of us lowland Scots who are now middle aged can remember our grandmothers' tenement flats with the shared toilets and back courts and smell of coal, as we grew up in our parents' new homes on post-war schemes. Many of us remember the sight of half-demolished streets as 'slum' tenements were cleared en masse. We recall inner walls with fireplaces and peeling wallpaper being exposed to the weather, and we remember the phrases current at the time: 'slum clearance', 'overspill' and, a new one, 'high-rise'. 'Progress' was another favourite. Unstoppable 'progress'. Blocks of flats were going up on the city skylines. Frightening or exhilarating, they were without doubt modern. They offered novelties that people were clamouring for: fresh air, sanitation, health. Entire new schemes were planned from scratch, even whole new towns.

In my own primary classroom in a 1960s school, itself built amid a swirl of post-war council and private housing, we learned to chant the names *Cumbernauld, Livingston, Irvine, East Kilbride, Glenrothes.* They were the five New Towns created to house the 'overspill' populations, as tenements were demolished and populations in the crowded inner cities fell.

In the case of Liz Lochhead's family: 'By International Refugee Year / we had a wee front green and a 12" telly.'

We had those things too. By the time I reached secondary school in the early 1970s, our history teacher could make a grand Socialist declaration. Standing by the windows, he could gesture eastward and cry, 'Scotland has more social housing than anywhere else between here and the Urals!'

Did we know what or where the Urals were? Communist Russia was what he meant.

Then came the oil crisis of 1973, sending the cost of construction soaring, and Margaret Thatcher's coming to power in 1979, with her anti-union attitude, and the shrinking State and privatisation and 'right-to-buy'.

So much change in so short a space of time. Perhaps it's worth remembering why this happened at all, and asking why Scotland has so many post-war schemes and why tower blocks were built, both in the city centres and especially at the edges, even in our climate.

*

A trenchant feature in the *Picture Post* of 31 January 1948 caught the spirit of the times. With famous photographs by Bert Hardy, it concerned the Gorbals, the inner-city area on the south side of the Clyde where 40,000 people then lived in nineteenth century tenements hastily thrown up and sub-divided as more and more workers and immigrants arrived, heading for factories, yards, mills.

By that time, after the War, the situation was deemed desperate. The feature noted that people lived:

> *five and six in a single room that is part of some great slattern of a tenement, with seven or eight people in the room next door, and maybe eight or 10 in the rooms above and below ... The windows are often patched with cardboard. The stairs are narrow, dark at all times and befouled not only with mud and rain. Commonly, there is one lavatory for 30 people, and that with the door off.*

There were smart fashion-conscious girls and dance halls, but there was also an undertaker on every street, open all hours. The link between poor housing and poor health had been long understood. There was little in the way of nostalgia, in those days, for tenement life. The *Picture Post* writer concluded: 'Local folk say the area is ripe for dynamiting. Certainly nothing short of an over-all slum clearance would meet the case.'

And so 'slum clearance' became the universally agreed solution to the housing crisis of the cities. In areas of Glasgow, Edinburgh, Dundee and the other Scottish industrial towns, nothing short of total demolition and rebuilding would do, if the people were to be decently housed. Planning had won the War, it would win the Peace. Commissions, government committees, local authorities and city corporations were mobilised. The new Welfare State was in action. It was all systems go, lift-off into a hoped-for better future.

Of course, all the new building meant it was a heyday for architecture. Art schools were turning out socially committed welfare-concerned architects, who took to designing the schools, churches, and low-rise and high-rise blocks never seen in Scotland before. Concrete was their material of choice. It must have been an exciting time for these young professionals, coming into practice sure that architecture could solve social ills.

For many architects of the day, their inspiration was Swiss-born Le Corbusier. His Unité d'Habitation in Marseilles, built in the late 1940s and best photographed under blue bright Mediterranean skies, offered a model of concrete building younger architects were keen to develop. 'A machine for living in' was Le Corbusier's famous phrase. Raw concrete offered opportunities for design that traditional stone could not. (The unfortunate name 'Brutalist' is derived from the French 'brut', meaning raw.) Concrete needed a lot of energy to make, but energy was cheap in those days and seemed never-ending. Concrete had advantages: it could be made in situ, by pouring the liquid concrete into wooden moulds, or it could be fabricated off-site, with pre-cast panels taken where required, as at Anniesland. Concrete could be capable of great architecture in some cases – and of quick solutions in others.

A mass building boom, cheap energy, concrete, health and happiness. It was all to be a great future, but as is well known, much soon soured. In Glasgow, as slum tenements were cleared wholesale, peripheral schemes were built from scratch but the very names Pollok, Castlemilk, Drumchapel and Easterhouse soon became bywords for deprivation. The new houses were often damp and ill-maintained, the lifts broke, people felt banished without transport or amenities, their old communities disrupted, their children bored. Even inner-city developments, like Basil Spence's high towers which were built on the cleared Gorbals site, are already demolished. The infamous Red Road tower blocks are likewise gone to dust. They came quickly, and went quickly too.

Such high-rise towers would have been the first time that working-class housing announced itself, or was allowed to announce itself, on the landscape. One can't help wonder if that was also a factor in their demise.

*

Which brings us back to the survivors, like the slender profiled Anniesland Court, with its lowly neighbours the station and the supermarket; the passing buses and the parish church. Here we have a tower still standing, fully occupied and apparently popular, well into the twenty-first century. If it's a success, that's partly down to architecture, but its neighbours and busy junction may also be the reason why.

Anniesland Court was designed by Jack Holmes & Partners. Jack Holmes was born in 1918 in Ardrossan, and studied at Glasgow School of Art, going into private practice after his war service. The photo on the Dictionary of Scottish Architects website shows a plain man in 1960s spectacles, with a knitted tie and broad lapels.

The list of Holmes & Partners' projects is exclusively Scottish, mostly in the west, and it is very much of its 1960s 'white heat of technology' age, including hydro dams and electricity showrooms. The list also includes a number of schools, including, in 1963, primary schools in Wyndford and Maryhill. Holmes lived until 1999, long enough to see his Anniesland Court receive its Grade A listing. The official description of Anniesland Court, given on that listing document, notes that it is made of 'horizontal bands of pre-cast mosaic-clad concrete panels', and here Holmes was also of his day.

During the great post-war boom, there was another tactic. There was certainly a housing crisis, but not everyone believed that the best solution lay in wholesale clearance and peripheral scheme building. In fact, as tenements were rapidly pulled down and the population fell, an anxiety grew in Glasgow that actually too many people were being sent outwith the city boundaries. Glasgow Council began to fear depopulation and, partly for reasons of prestige and political clout, partly for rates, a desire grew to keep people within the city. Another proposed solution, therefore, was to build new working-class homes within the city, wherever small pockets of land could be found.

Hence Anniesland Court, standing alone, but not without its community and amenities. It may be up on a windy plinth, but its neighbours are shops and tenements, a library, a railway station, frequent buses into town.

Which is all very well and good. We don't live in visions, or even history, we don't even live in architecture. Most people, most of the time, live in our homes. What is it like inside?

*

Donnie Blair was that day's duty warden and, after he had admitted me, we travelled in the lift up to the top floor – I felt my ears pop – and stepped into the main building via another secured door. We were immediately in a corridor, facing east with a row of plain front doors on the right, and on the left, heavy windows with frosted glass and access doors onto outside drying balconies. I couldn't think what it reminded me of at first, but the clue was in its name, 'deck'. The light and air, the use of space, was like a ship. Le Corbusier was keen on ships. Basil Spence had a fantasy that, on wash day, his high-rise towers would look like galleons under sail. And here there was something of it, as though we were looking at a row of cabin doors opening onto a port deck. If Jack Holmes was an Ardrossan lad, maybe it was a CalMac ferry he was half thinking of.

I said 'cabin' but I was soon to discover that was not the right word.

There, on the 22nd floor, Donny rapped on the first of the doors. It was opened by its owner, long-term resident Alan Stewart who had kindly agreed to show me his apartment. I say 'apartment' not 'flat' because his home had a continental feel, and it wasn't flat. Immediately within the door a flight of stairs led upward to a light-filled hall. From there, Mr Stewart, rightly proud of his home, led us across a narrow living room, and moved aside his dining table, to show off his south-facing windows which spanned the full width of the room, and the views.

The views were astonishing. Both living room and kitchen looked clear over the Clyde southward to the Ayrshire hills, westward downstream to the Erskine Bridge, even to Arran. You could trace the route of the Clyde. From the two north-facing bedrooms, over a couple of old gasometers to more hills, even a field of Highland cattle, and eastward over the spires of Glasgow itself. From this room, you could see you were part of the city and that the city was part of the land. Even if it was only visual, this was surely the first time since the Industrial Revolution that ordinary folk had had such a connection with their land.

The flat was quiet and draught free, the original single-glazed metal-framed windows having been replaced with double-glazed PVC units. No more condensation.

For a single person with a head for heights, or a couple with a love of wind and weather, the flat would have had an enviably spacious, almost glamorous feel. Nautical and continental. Mr Stewart had chosen a light, bright decor, with yacht-like whites and pale greens. For other residents it might feel imprisoning; who would want to spend a week here in the rain with small children – but isn't that true of any flat?

Walking east along the access deck later, the port side, if you like, I noticed homely touches. Each door had its nameplate – Scottish, Chinese, Polish names. A few pot plants – there being enough light – an ornament, a toddler's buggy and wellies. Donnie the warden explained how the inner architecture worked. We were passing a wall of doors, and had seen how Mr Stewart went upstairs directly from his door to reach his flat. His next door neighbour, however, would go straight along a short hallway to reach hers, and the third door along would descend a stair. Then repeat. The interior space clicked together like a puzzle.

The stairwell was swept and painted fresh cream and maroon, the lift was speedy enough. No graffiti, no litter, no foul smells.

*

I went back to Anniesland the following week to meet some of the residents. A few folk gather every week for a cup of tea and a blether in the ground floor community room. I joined half a dozen elderly ladies, salt of Glaswegian earth, in a plain room with a kettle and cakes. They told me there was a male friend too, but he was unsteady on his feet nowadays and didn't like the wind; he wouldn't come out today. We spoke about the effect a high wind had on the building. How water in the toilets slopped and gurgled. Very nautical. Some could recall Anniesland before the tower was built; there were prefabs where it now stands. Old smiddy, prefabs, tower block. All in the space of sixty years.

Perhaps rudely, I was a little surprised by the elders, surprised that there were elders here at all. Somewhere in my mind I still thought of tower blocks and high-rise concrete architecture as they had been presented to me when I was a child myself and these things were being built. Modern. Progressive. Chic. Young, all that. To find their inhabitants becoming a little infirm in body but with long cultural memories was odd, I don't know why. Perhaps it's odd to think these 'modern' tower blocks are now half a century old, those that have survived. And that they can provide accommodation suitable for old folks too, with lifts and single person walk-in flats.

The community room was low ceilinged and not in the least architecturally exciting, and over tea the ladies told me how things had been in the first decades of the tower block. There was more community spirit, they said. A residents' bus trip to Blackpool had been arranged every year, the bus came right to the door and the tower block decanted itself and went to the seaside. But not now. No-one wants the responsibility. There used to be barbeques on the patio, but young ones are not interested.

This was striking. These elders were lamenting a community spirit which survived well into the tower-block era, a spirit which such architecture is generally accused of having destroyed. A building may be convenient to blame, but there must be other factors at work in perceived community breakdown, and you can bet they are economic, not architectural.

I thanked the ladies for their tea and cake and made my way down a few steps and out onto Great Western Road to catch the bus back into town. A bus came almost at once, and I spent the journey wondering if we weren't just too hasty. Too quick to destroy the old streets, though the need was urgent, too quick to build tower blocks out on the moors, too quick to destroy them again, all like some weirdly accelerated film. With high-rise blocks, have we abandoned a housing solution simply because we didn't execute it very well the first time round?

If the build was sound, with modern insulation and environmental safe-guards, and the maintenance up to scratch, and social deprivation actually tackled, not merely shunted around like a bad penny, we could have both tenements and towers. We could have Scottish cities, and not wastelands of identikit suburbs.

We can do 'vision'. We've proved it. The fact remains that very many Scots now living were raised in one confident post-war housing development or another. Not the tenement or croft of fond nostalgia, but high-rise and low-rise flats and post-war schemes and New Towns. We are children of political passion and ambition – and architecture, did we but know it. Where is it now?

23

Homecoming
James Crawford

Sullom Voe, Shetland, 1974

'It was jaw dropping' my father said. 'Just … wow. Look at this amount of earth. Look at the amount of equipment that's here. And it was mud. Everybody covered in mud. Land Rovers covered in mud. Diggers and excavators covered in mud. The temporary accommodation was in Nissen huts – and they were just housing a bunch of people who were trying to get all this mud cleared. And it was isolated. It was away from everything.'

*

The cloud cover was breaking up. A few more minutes passed and then it was gone. I put down my book and looked out of the window, down past the blur of the aeroplane's propeller to the sea. The water was glinting in the mid-morning sun. The surface was creased and rutted with waves, but it looked somehow motionless, like a slab of wet rock. There was no land in sight. I glanced across the cramped, pencil-thin cabin out the other side and it was the same. Just the sea. The engine noise was a steady, gentle rhythm that sounded like waves lapping on a shore. A new cloud-bank appeared low on the horizon ahead. We had started our descent. Minutes passed, we dropped lower and lower, but still no land. Gradually the cloud-bank started to resolve. Behind it were solid blue silhouettes. Soon I had my first glimpse of coastline, a slender hook of rock outlined in white. I peered out the other side again. A massive cliff had emerged, hundreds of feet high and topped by the distinctive creamy globe of a radar station. Below us it was still sea. We were almost touching the waves, close enough to spot birds bobbing in the swell. At the last moment the runway slipped past, the tarmac reaching towards us from the very tip of the land.

Out of the aeroplane door, the wind hit me straight away: strong, warm, and heavy with the scent of brine. Forty years ago, almost to the day, my father stood on this same spot. On 1 May 1977 he flew from Glasgow to Shetland's Sumburgh Airport. He was twenty-nine years old and had just started a job as a mechanical construction engineer on what was, at that time, one of the largest building projects in the world. Some fifty miles north, on an uninhabited peat-bog peninsula accessed by a deep-water sea loch, work had begun breaking the ground for an oil terminal – a facility to receive pipelines running from two newly discovered North Sea oil fields. He had never been to Shetland before, but would spend almost all of the next two years on the islands.

I was born the following summer. My family was one of a small number of families who migrated to live within sight of the rapidly emerging terminal buildings. We left when I was just six months old, not long after the arrival into the terminal of 'first oil'. I hadn't been back to Shetland until now.

*

It is a little known fact that the origin point for today's multi-billion-pound global oil industry can be traced back to, of all places, Bathgate. It was there, in 1851, that James Young, the son of a Glasgow cabinet-maker, opened a distillation plant for oil production. Young, who took evening classes in chemistry at Anderson's University (now Strathclyde University) while working as a joiner, succeeded in developing and patenting a means of extracting oil from cannel coal – from the Scots for 'candle', so-called because of the long, luminous flame it produced when burned. The works at Bathgate were built right next to an abundant seam of this coal. When it was exhausted, Young adapted his technique to derive oil from boghead coal – named after the South Lanarkshire village where it was first discovered – and shale. He opened a new plant in West Calder in 1865, and by 1885 it was producing a million barrels of oil a year. Young was Scotland's first oil man.

My father left school at seventeen to work in these same West Lothian coal mines. He started a mechanical engineering apprenticeship with the National Coal Board, and for four years worked underground, mostly at Kinneil Colliery near Bo'ness. The Coal Board offered to fund an engineering degree at the University of Edinburgh – on the condition that he worked for them during holidays and remained tied to them for another three years after. By this time, however, he had been supporting himself financially for long enough to apply for a mature student grant. And besides, he could see that the coal industry was in decline. He began studying mechanical engineering at Strathclyde University in 1967. Four years later, straight after graduating, he was offered another mining job – not coal, this time, but minerals. It was in Zambia, in the region known as the Copper Belt. So, in the summer of 1971, he moved with my mother from Glasgow to Africa.

It was at this same time that the first major oil discoveries were being made in the North Sea. For around a decade, drilling rigs had been boring holes in the seabed, searching for gas and oil. They had found the former, but the latter was proving more elusive. It prompted some, including the then chairman of British Petroleum, Sir Eric Drake, to predict that there would be no major oil field found in the North Sea. You can't help but enjoy the irony of this rather impatient reaction to a search that relies entirely on patience. And we're not just talking here about the patience necessary for a few years of exploring. Oil demands patience on an entirely different scale. The sort of 'deep time' patience that James Hutton, another Scotsman who knew a lot about rocks, first described in the eighteenth century. Because oil is a long, long, long time in the making.

To put it in very simple terms, oil is formed out of the decayed mass of vast amounts of organic material – plankton, algae and other marine organisms – that accumulated on beaches and coastlines many millions of years ago. While it can be found in lots of places, mostly these are too small or too inaccessible to make commercial exploitation viable. That requires even greater geological luck: the formation of huge underground sandstone or limestone reservoirs where oil can collect in large quantities, but can't escape as a result of being surrounded by much harder, impermeable rock. In October 1970, a BP drilling rig a hundred miles off the coast of Aberdeen hit one of these flukes of nature – a domed chamber in a layer of sixty-million-year-old Paleocene rock at a depth of nearly 11,000 feet. It was called the 'Forties' field, after the shipping forecast region in which it was discovered. With an area of 90 square kilometres, and holding an estimated volume of over 2,000 million barrels, it was the North Sea's first 'giant' oil field. A year later, in June 1971, a second massive field, known as 'Brent', was found on the Continental Shelf a hundred miles east of Shetland. All of a sudden, the North Sea was being hailed as one of the largest and most important 'oil provinces' in the world.

My father remembered the news of the discoveries. 'When I saw "Forties" and North Sea oil I thought, "that's the industry I want to work in"' he said. 'I had been in the coal industry and it had died – or was dying. I was in the copper and metals industry and I couldn't see a future there either. And anyway, it was too much mining for me. My mind was made up. It was time to go.' My parents returned from Zambia to Scotland in December 1976 and by March the following year my father had a job as a mechanical construction engineer for BP. After a couple of months working at the oil refinery at Grangemouth – within sight of his old colliery at Kinneil, which would finally close five years later – he received the posting to Shetland. 'It was exciting' he said. 'Absolutely exciting. It was the biggest job in Europe. The biggest job BP had ever undertaken. And it was a matter of pride. It wasn't daunting – it was challenging. I just thought this is great. Massive.'

*

I collected my hire car and began the drive up the long thin finger of Shetland's South Mainland. Rather worryingly, I first had to cross the Sumburgh Airport runway to reach the main road. The barriers were up, allowing me through, but I still couldn't help checking left and right just to make sure no planes were about to take off or land.

In places the road was almost totally obscured by drifts of white sand, which skittered and whirled in the incessant wind. A beach was obviously nearby, although I couldn't see it. I drove north through a sparse and taut landscape: hump after hump of treeless hillsides, punctuated by stones and everywhere strewn with clumps of sheep's wool – like one great, stretched, bobbly green-and-white jumper. Grey clouds were massing, and when the sun slipped behind them the colour leached from the surroundings. The sea off to my right, which had been sparkling happily moments before, suddenly became a darker, rather more menacing expanse. It was a reminder that the land here was outnumbered and outgunned by the elements. Water in particular was everywhere, appearing to inundate any hollow or dip, however big or small.

As I passed Lerwick and drove on towards the north-west, the palette of the landscape changed, with greens giving way to the purples and browns of peat moor and heather. Everywhere the familiar and the unfamiliar were intermingled. It was Scotland but not Scotland. You had Scottish road signs directing you to Old Norse place-names. Houses were dotted haphazardly, alone and in tight clusters. Some were boxy and harled in off-white stone chippings, like you'd see almost anywhere on the mainland. Many others were in wood cladding and painted in blocks of bright colour – mint greens, mustard yellows, icy blues – and all topped by red-tile roofs. One minute you felt you were in the Scottish Highlands, the next in coastal Scandinavia. It was all pleasingly disconcerting.

I was approaching the village of Brae, set on the narrow isthmus that joins Shetland Mainland to the peninsula of Northmavine (and where, a little further on at a bend in the road called Mavis Grind, there are barely a few metres of land separating the North Sea from the Atlantic Ocean). Brae was where my parents and my elder brother lived when they all moved to Shetland – and where I lived too. I drove up to the house, just for a look. I'd seen photos of it newly built, a picture from a helicopter of a surprisingly suburban estate transplanted into an empty, heathery space surrounded by water. Brae had been a tiny fishing village right up until the 1970s, before the oil came. Now it had its own school, swimming pool and supermarket. Shops, hotels and restaurants had spread along the main road. The spaces had been filled up between my old house and the others built back then. Now everything was tightly packed, huddling in against the wind and the weather.

I drove off again and crossed the tiny land bridge of Mavis Grind into Northmavine. I was still waiting for my first glimpse of the oil terminal. I had decided to take the route up into the hills opposite, on the western side of the deep-water sea loch which provides sheltered mooring for supertankers, and gives the terminal its name: Sullom Voe ('Sullom' from the tiny settlement on its east shore, 'voe' from the Old Norse *vágr*, for 'creek', or 'inlet'). The road climbed up through a place called Stanes Moor, where I pulled into a lay-by and got out of the car. Below me, my map told me, was the Loch of Burraland, a neat little stretch of water attended by one solitary farm building on its shores. Beyond were the waters of the Voe. And beyond them, was the terminal. I had stopped at a laughably opportune moment. While grey clouds were all around, the sky above the peninsula was clear, and the sun caught the terminal like a spotlight. It was a bizarre sight. The scale seemed wrong. Several lines of white cylinders were gleaming in the light – the tanks for storing all the oil. Even from a distance, they looked colossal, almost too big to make sense of in their surroundings; like an optical illusion. My first thought was that it was as if some vast desert facility had been dropped accidentally onto a peaty island hillside. Someone had made a mistake, got their latitudes and their longitudes mixed up and put the terminal in entirely the wrong hemisphere. Of course, there was no beauty. What else would you expect from a series of structures that are all about function? But from the sheer size alone, you could feel a kind of awe – an uncomfortable jolt at your own smallness when set against such indifferent monumentalism.

*

On 15 May 1981, *The Shetland Times* ran a special edition of its newspaper to celebrate a joint British and Norwegian Royal visit to the completed terminal the previous weekend.

> *Shetland's Royal Day dawned foggy, miserable and wet, but, just before the Queen, King Olav and Prince Philip stepped ashore at the Sullom Voe construction jetty, the sun peeped through the clouds. It quickly went in again and most of Saturday was a raw, grey day. It could have been worse, and the fog held off for most of the time. The Royal yacht* Britannia *had crossed from Stavanger with a southeast wind on her starboard quarter, which must have made the voyage less than smooth ... The atmosphere was informal but not wildly enthusiastic, with the cheering and clapping ragged and no-one quite sure what to do next.*

The jetty had been converted into a giant red carpet – which had been wrapped in polythene until the last minute, in a vain attempt to keep it dry. The party greeted the waiting crowds then stepped into two Rolls-Royce cars – a first for Shetland – to be taken on a tour of the terminal. While they were entering the engineering services building to the accompaniment of a military band, there was a distant noise, described by one of the few who heard it as 'like a large sliding door being shut quickly'. Days later it was confirmed that the IRA had detonated a bomb in a waste heat boiler in the terminal's power station. No-one was hurt, the damage caused was relatively minimal, and the Royal tour barely broke stride. But it demonstrated how a remote peat bog was suddenly at the intersection of so many volatile aspects of the modern world: money, multi-nationals, pence-a-barrel, politics, power.

Indeed, the dramatic nature of this change in circumstances was at the heart of the speeches given at the inauguration ceremony. 'This year', said the Queen, 'the oil recovered from the British sector of the North Sea will be worth some £11 billion. Much of this wealth remains within the British economy, so the significance of this for the prosperity of Britain as a whole is immense ... Shetland is a vital link in bringing this oil wealth ashore for Britain ... I can well understand the hopes – and fears – which this has aroused among the people of Shetland. The impact of such a development on the economic life of these islands is considerable.' Alexander Tulloch, convener of the Shetland Islands Council, followed. 'One thing is certain' he said. 'In this energy-dominated world in which we live, Shetland will play an important and vital part in the supply of energy to our nation.' But, alluding to the Queen's words on the impact, he responded, 'we have hopes that the wealth of oil flowing through this great terminal will create a better Britain for people to live and work in. We have fears for the Shetland it will leave behind.'

∗

Just seven years earlier, there had been nothing. The first people on the site, arriving in the spring of 1974, were the surveyors. There were no access roads, and even Land Rovers couldn't get far into the thousand acre mass of deep heather, peat and bog. As a result, one of the largest surveying jobs ever undertaken had to be carried out mostly on foot – in wellington boots and oilskins, in often extreme weather conditions.

The peninsula had once been home to a thriving crofting community, the four townships of Rattleton, Orka, Calback and Crooksetter, but a lack of modern amenities had led to a dramatic population decline at the start of the twentieth century. By the 1950s, the area was completely abandoned. All the surveyors found on the peninsula were a few clusters of ruined farm buildings and a scattering of military structures down by the water: the remains of a Second World War Coastal Battery.

The clearing work alone took three years. It required the removal of 10 million cubic metres of peat and rock, often in huge tracts running 6 metres deep. Everything had to be taken down to solid ground before any building work could start. An entire landscape was being removed and flattened. My father arrived just as this first phase was nearing completion. The priority was the development of the site's essential infrastructure, most importantly the jetties. 'Everything for the construction of Sullom Voe came in by sea', he said. 'There was no other way. So we were building the construction jetty, and building roads from the jetty throughout the site, then building "lay down" areas so lengths of pipe and steel could be brought in and stored for installation. And it would go on like this, over and over again.'

The statistics for the materials used in the terminal are so huge as to become almost meaningless: 300,000 cubic metres of concrete; 100,000 tonnes of tarmac for 25 miles of road; 26,000 tonnes of steel for the container tanks; 2,200 miles of cable; 150 miles of pipes joined by 35,000 individual welds. I asked my father how they tackled something so complex. 'First you had to step back and grasp the enormity of it', he said. 'And then, to get there, you just had to go bit by bit, bit by bit, bit by bit.' Once the construction jetty was operational, huge, pre-assembled steel pipe units and pipe racks were delivered every single day. As *The Shetland Times* put it, at first, the people of the islands 'knew little and saw less' of what was happening at Sullom Voe. All that changed, however, as 'the pieces of the steel jigsaw loomed over the horizon on barges or on heavy lift ships'. Construction yards across Britain were commissioned to build these pipe assemblies – it would have been near impossible to do the work on site – and so a procession of ships ferried them northwards. Once they arrived, the challenge was to fit the maze of pipes together.

Throughout 1977, there was a rapid increase in the number of workers. 2,500 in June of that year had risen to 4,000 by December, and then 5,000 the following summer. The peak came in July 1980, with 7,237 people on site. Providing the accommodation required a construction project all of its own. Two workers' camps, Firth and Toft (the latter built on the site of a former Viking settlement on the far side of the peninsula from Sullom Voe), provided 1,800 and 2,400 beds. When these reached capacity, two accommodation vessels, the *Rangatira* and the *Stena Baltica,* were chartered, and moored up on a jetty overlooking the construction site.

'We generally worked every day,' my father said. 'It would be seven in the morning to seven, eight, nine at night. Maybe on a Sunday we'd finish at lunchtime, take a drive up somewhere. In the summer we'd play rugby in the afternoons. And you could read the paper at midnight. I even played golf at midnight.' As no workers were allowed to leave the camps during the week, Sundays were also the busiest time at the nearest off-site bar – the Sullom Voe Hotel. 'It went hell for leather', my father said, 'from twelve noon till two o'clock, just for those two hours. Then it was everybody out. You had the drinking bar and the lounge bar and you couldn't move in either of them. In the winter they'd just set up this huge long line of whiskies on the bar, all topped with snow from outside to save them making ice.'

At twenty minutes to seven on the evening of 25 November 1978, the critical moment came – the 'first oil ashore'. For months, devices known as 'pigs' – short for 'pipeline integrity gauge' – had been checking the lines for faults. A pig was a metal cylinder pushed through a pipeline by high-pressure water, registering any rents, buckles or tears. Finally it would come to a stop in a special section of pipe known as the 'pig trap'. That evening in November, however, it wasn't water that was behind the pig, it was oil: oil travelling from the Brent field one hundred miles offshore. 'We were all waiting for it,' my father said. 'Tracking the pig in, all the way to the pig trap. Then the pig had arrived, the trap signal is up. The oil was there! But you don't see it. You can't see it. It's diverted to one of the tanks, and the tanks start filling up, and that's it.' The next day, my father said he was going to check the line, to make sure there weren't any leaks. 'There were drain valves on parts of the pipeline, on the low parts. And I knew a part to go to. So I took this bottle – a glass Barr's lemonade bottle – and I've got it tucked inside my Parka jacket. I knew the line. I knew the valves there.' He released one of the valves, just for a few seconds, and caught what came out in the bottle. 'I've got oil! You couldn't show it to anyone. It was a private thing. I just wanted to touch what it was all about. I wanted to see it. I wanted to smell it. I'd never seen oil up to that point. The first chance I got was to steal it and see it. And I thought it was brilliant.'

*

This, of course, was the essence of the whole place. Sullom Voe was designed to store up to 1.4 million barrels of oil – which, at that time, was two thirds of the oil needs of the whole of Britain. All of that planning and earth moving and concrete pouring and pipe assembling. All of that fiendish complexity. All of the estimated 55 million man-hours spent in construction (while the pay-roll peaked at just over 7,200, the actual number who worked on-site at one stage or another was around 25,000 – and if you include those involved in pre-fabrication on the mainland, the total rises to over 50,000). All of this was in the service of one comparatively simple task. 'Fill a tank, fill another tank, fill as many tanks as you can', my father said. 'Then decant them into the tankers moored at the jetties. Then take it to be sold.' And so it goes on, four decades later – oil flowing almost non-stop from the underground reservoirs offshore, travelling along seabed pipelines to Sullom Voe, and brimming to the tops of sixteen giant container tanks. Empty the tanks, fill them, empty them again, fill them again. Keep going, don't stop. Until, that is, there's nothing left. What do you do then? Well, you just move on.

We've waited for the oil for millions of years. And now we've found it, we can't use it quickly enough.

*

I kept driving north, heading away from the terminal. There were far few-
er houses now, just bare, rounded hills and wide stretches of peat moor.
The road narrowed to a single lane – with regular little bulges, like Adam's
apples, offering passing places. On my left was Ronas Voe, a long rib of
Atlantic Ocean curling deep into the land to mark the narrow entry point
to the Mainland's final peninsula, North Roe. A handful of ruined stone
buildings – some farms and an old mill – sat at the head of the Voe. Above
them was Shetland's highest point, the 450-metre Ronas Hill, a big brown
lump topped by a prehistoric burial cairn and a couple of tall radio masts.

The route skirted east around this high ground and came almost instantly to the opposite side of the peninsula, running right alongside the
waters of the Sound of Yell – the wide, sheltered entry point for ships heading down to the jetties at Sullom Voe. I drove through a cluster of houses
and a primary school – the tiny village of North Roe itself – then on into a
hollow surrounded by hills. On my right there was the utterly bizarre sight
of small aeroplane fuselage sitting outside a house set back from the road
up a long gravel pathway. A magazine cutting, pasted into a makeshift
wooden display at the foot of the path, explained that it was the fuselage of
a 24-seater French 'Potez' airliner, which the owner of the house had decided to salvage after it had crash-landed at Sumburgh in 1981. It had, according to the article, been brought in two pieces by road all the way from
the southernmost tip of the island. I drove on past this towards a group of
modern farm buildings, where the road came to an abrupt end. I parked
next to a little curved barn and continued on foot.

Off to my right, on the breast of a hill and silhouetted rather evocatively
against the sky, was a walled graveyard – all that now remains of a twelfth
century chapel that once stood on this spot. I passed through a gate onto
a stony path leading up through the hills. The grass around was matted
and yellowed, and everywhere stones were poking through, breaking the
surface, straining at the skin of the land. When I'd started out walking, the
sky had been completely grey. After twenty minutes it was almost completely clear, blown through by a strong, relentless south-westerly. I stood
to watch the whole cloudbank shift rapidly across the sky and off over the
horizon. On reaching the top of another rise, I saw my destination – the
very last stretch of Shetland Mainland, known, somewhat confusingly,
as the Isle of Fethaland. The path ran down past more roofless old farm
buildings towards a bright curve of shingle beach. Beyond was a rocky
wedge, sloping left to right down to the sea, and topped by the bright white
box of a small lighthouse beacon.

Groups of sheep watched me pass, some clustered for shelter behind stone dykes, but all giving me hard, inquisitive stares. The sun was high and bright as I walked along the last stretch of coast to the beach, and the water in the bay was an inviting, beautiful turquoise. On the grass verge above the beach was a jumble of twenty or so ruined drystone houses. A community lived here once, not that long ago – a community that was a kind of predecessor to the terminal at Sullom Voe. Fethaland (from the Old Norse for 'fat land', or 'rich pasture') was Shetland's busiest *haaf*, or deep-sea fishing station. In the nineteenth century, over sixty boats operated out of here – six-oared, open wooden boats called *sixareens*, built in the traditional Norse style. It was work for the summer months, with fishermen venturing forty or more miles out to sea to spool out seven-mile-long lines for cod, ling and tusk. What started as subsistence work became a major industry. Fish were cured, split open and dried on the beach, then packed for export to foreign markets. Go digging a little in the shingle and you can still find the fish bones. There were houses for each of the crews, around seven men per boat, and they were roofed with wood and turf, which was removed at the end of each season to avoid damage from winter storms. The industry collapsed in the last decade of the nineteenth century, rendered uneconomical by competition from advanced commercial fishing. By the start of the twentieth century, Fethaland was all but abandoned.

I sat down in one of the old houses, framing my view out through the doorway to the wind-rippled waves lapping on the beach. A visitor in 1822, Samuel Hibbert, described a bustling, noisy site 'with all the disorder of a gypsy encampment'. It was hard to imagine as I sat there. I felt like I was inside a structure that had been abandoned for longer than a century. There was just the wind and the calls of the sheep and the gentle breaking of the tide. Everything here was just crumbling steadily away – erosion and the elements taking buildings and beach at the same time. A little plaque set up overlooking the site told a brief story of the *haaf*, and explained that in this area you could find some of the oldest stones in the world – quartzites and schists and Lewisian gneiss. Fethaland lies on the collision zone of two 500-million-year-old continental shelves – another accident of geology that allowed the Shetland fisherman access to deep, abundant seas. Until others came here too, and the old ways grew too dangerous, and the money went away.

I headed up to the lighthouse beacon on the towering cliffs on the other side of Fethaland. It was set up in 1977 to aid with navigation into Sullom Voe – lifted in by helicopter, as any other access here would have been too difficult. The automatic beacon was spinning round and round in its glass casing, ready to come on once the light dimmed. I kept on up to the very tip of the land. Nesting birds wheeled below me, loud adult calls mingling with the high piercing cries of new chicks. Buffeted by the wind, I glanced over the final precipice, down 50 or 60 metres to a rocky inlet. I was shocked to see the huge white body of what looked like a sperm whale bobbing in the swell. It was rolled on its side, clearly dead, with a solitary seagull standing on its body, pecking absently at the flesh. It was a sad, mournful sight. Once, of course, it would have been a bonanza for the islanders – blubber, bone, skin. And, of course, *oil*.

I walked back to the car, into the wind, blasted head-on by strong gusts for the hour or so it took to return. I drove south and the sun cut in and out of the clouds, lighting up moorlands and hillsides and the innumerable lochans that drifted past. There was a stark, petulant beauty to it all. Heading back through Northmavine, I started to catch sight of the terminal again, looming out of the landscape, an over-sized oddity.

'A commitment was made to reinstate the land after Sullom Voe was finished,' my father told me. 'At the time, they weren't looking thirty, or forty, or fifty years into the future. They didn't think the terminal would be needed for that long. It's still going, but it's on a downward curve now. And when there is no more gas and no more oil coming through it, they are going to return it to peat bog.' The idea, presumably, is that the oil industry will move on, and they will put the land back just as they found it, like an apology – all of that concrete and tarmac and steel either dismantled, broken up, or buried beneath new peat.

Will there then be a plaque, set somewhere at the end of a road that peters out to nothing, that tells the story of Sullom Voe? That laments the passing of a community – local and global – that worked a resource until it could be worked no more? Or will it all just be forgotten? The 25,000 people on-site and the other 25,000 around Britain who helped build it; the tens of thousands more – and their families – who have been somehow connected to it over the decades; the millions who have used its oil.

But then, of course, if you speak the language of 'deep time', maybe there really is nothing to say. It all came and went so quickly. It never registered at all.

24

Caring for the Carers
Kathleen Jamie

Maggie's Centre, Fife 2006

In Kirkcaldy, the Victoria Hospital stands like a fortress behind a moat of car parks. Like a fortress, or perhaps a walled city. There's a tower block to the left of the main portal, which could house hospital wards, or anything. There are the other inevitable hospital buildings, anonymous affairs with metal chimneys or flues, more car parks, barriers.

A new wing, five storeys high, tries to be more architecturally engaged; its facade, the length of a short street, is deeply sinuous and pierced with irregular windows, but one still feels embattled merely reaching its main doors. Even for one in good health, it is a daunting journey. Within and around the doors there's a constant busyness, all humankind present, all trades practised, the halt and the lame. Within the foyer, with its chain coffee shops, lengthy signboards direct arrivals to foreign-sounding destinations. Frightening destinations. To reach them, there will be corridors and corridors, bland and clean.

One walks a hospital corridor feeling a curious mix of gratitude and dismay. Gratitude that one was born in this day and age, in a time of modern Western scientific medicine, accessible to all. A modern hospital, its staff and friends, humanity at its best. If your child is sick, if your son comes off his motorbike, if you find a sudden lump, the hospital will gather you in. It may not feel like an embrace, more like a process. But dismay seems churlish. Dismay at what, exactly? A kind of grimness. Corridors and corridors, wide enough for trolleys. Angles designed to be kept clean. More corridors. Bland white spaces. Frightening curtains. (However did we learn to fear curtains?) No windows, no trees or sky. Of course. How else could it be?

We accept such architecture, or non-architecture as a price worth paying, for who would choose to go back to the olden days? How glad we are to live in the era of medical science, of anaesthetics, antiseptics and antibiotics, sterile instruments in well-trained hands. We've become accustomed to the idea that modern medicine means modern hospitals, even 'super hospitals', supposed models of efficiency and complexes of buildings which are often far away from home. Like medieval pilgrims, we make long journeys there. We appreciate the medicine, and put up with the architecture, which is often vast and soulless, somehow fearing that to find fault with the buildings and decor is to find fault with the staff. Not true, not true! We have to care for the carers as well. Why shouldn't they work in uplifting surroundings, when we demand they give of their best?

Few people have the architectural knowledge to articulate their unease in hospitals. We are not taught architectural vocabulary, though we are surrounded by it. Of hospitals, many people say 'I don't like the smell.' But there is not much smell. Perhaps such people's non-specific unease is to do with the architecture, an architecture driven by scientific pragmatism and serious financial constraints. It means the 'spaces', as architects say, the 'spaces' wherein treatment is given, and sometimes where bad news, the worst news, might be shared, are pretty awful.

*

What might a therapeutic space look like? A space designed for well-being?

Last year, for a few weeks I joined archaeologists excavating the prehistoric settlement at Links of Noltland, Westray. The site, under huge Orcadian skies, is right at the seashore behind a broad north-facing bay with powerful surf waves. Until recently, it was all sand dunes but, latterly, the winds have changed and increased. The dunes are quickly being obliterated. Beneath them, an extensive settlement has been revealed, with layers of houses and field systems belonging to the Neolithic and Bronze Ages: people lived and farmed there for a long time. Were it not for the excavation, now in its ninth season, the archaeology would also be destroyed.

In 2015, the archaeologists turned their attention to a large mound at the seashore, just outwith the settlement. Being covered in sand and bent-grass, it looked a bit like all the other nearby sand dunes.

However, the team soon discovered that, under the sand and grass, the mound was actually a huge accumulation of burnt and heat-shattered stones. They've since calculated that there are hundreds of years' worth of discarded stones. They worked on and down until a stone floor emerged. Then excitement grew: it wasn't a floor they were standing on, but a roof. They were standing on the roof of a substantial chamber, half sunk into the earth. The heap of burnt stones had piled up around a sophisticated building. Built all of stone, with a central chamber and a fireplace in a cell at one side, and with several other side-cells, the structure had been sited to benefit from a natural spring, which still flowed. The spring-water replenished a tank or cistern set into the ground at the centre of the chamber.

As the archaeologists worked, you could stand at the lip of this chamber, looking down and in. As site co-director Hazel Moore explained to me, the architecture of this little building had a sense of drama. To enter, you would have had to stoop, even crawl along a passageway for some nine metres, long enough to block out the daylight. It was still possible to make that little journey, the structure was so well preserved. At the turn, just before you reached the chamber, with its small cells off, you would have passed the fireplace or furnace, vented out to the open air; the heat must have been considerable. Once within, there were private side-cells, as well as the more open, central area with the water tank.

The fire or furnace heated the stones, which were then trundled into the water tank one after another until the water boiled, and hissing clouds of steam filled the space. You can only roast a stone so many times before it breaks; the mound's enveloping heap of burnt stones was testament to centuries of use.

With typical restraint, the archaeologists called it a 'ritual' building. But they are pretty sure this was a therapeutic place. Ritualised maybe, but they are confident it was a place of healing or well-being: a retreat for the sick, or possibly it was a birthing chamber, or a hospice for the dying, or all of those. Maybe there were attendants, specialist healers, cleansers, midwives, certainly someone to stoke the fire and manoeuvre the roasting stones. Were there smells? Herbs, oils and unguents? It's hard to imagine there were not. Was it a place for intimate conversations and shared confidences? There is much we can only surmise. But it is an evocative thought.

The archaeological record shows that they were difficult times, the far-off Bronze Age days. Layers of sand laid down over the fields show that the balmy climate of the Neolithic was changing; then as now winds were rising and wind-blown sand was becoming a perpetual nuisance, making crops more difficult to grow. Associated disease such as arthritis, maybe eye problems, would have increased too, and general malaise. In time, conditions deteriorated too much and the settlement was abandoned altogether, overwhelmed by sand, forgotten until now.

Upon its rediscovery, the press called the building a 'sauna', but that word, with its modern, leisured connotation doesn't cover the therapeutic possibilities, or the importance of the building to its community. The archaeologists are sure it was used, and maintained, for centuries, an important 'space'. The builders of Bronze Age structures are lost in time. But it's intriguing to wonder how and why the idea first arose in that small farming community, that a therapeutic space was needed, and where the 'sauna' idea had come from.

And if this building was indeed a place of therapy, at the edge of the village, does it mark the beginning of the long separation of buildings we are so familiar with now, and sometimes regret? A gulf that grew, with the general hospital often far from home, at the edge of town.

The Bronze Age 'sauna' or therapeutic site is again filled with sand. Having been carefully excavated, it has been backfilled by the same archaeologists; there was nothing else to do with it but put it safely back underground. Two of the strongest diggers spent days last August heaving wheel-barrows full of sand up ramps and tipping the sand into the space, packing the passageway to keep it intact, filling the passageway and cells. They heaved so many tons of sand their own backs and shoulders ached, and they too were in need of therapy, healing oils, saunas.

From the Bronze Age well-water, heat and intimacy, to the cool modern super-hospital. The question is, must we choose? Can't we have both? Can't we have our state-of-the-art treatments, with clean instruments in highly trained hands, but also have buildings, which in our hour of need, are not frightening, spiritually dead, anonymous or vast? Places like the Bronze Age structure, which offer intimacy and support as we come to terms with what's happening to us or our loved ones, or undergo gruelling treatments?

*

In her 1995 essay 'A View From the Front Line' Maggie Jencks bravely recounts being told, five years after apparently successful treatment, that her breast cancer had returned and had spread to her liver, bone and bone marrow. She would have just months left to live. She was in her early fifties, with teenage children. The doctor meant well, but it was a busy clinic. Having been given the news, she was asked to go sit in the corridor. In the event, 'extremely powerful chemotherapy' granted her 18 months remission, during which she wrote her account and laid down her vision for cancer care. She speaks about diet, and supplements and non-Western approaches, of the need to engage with one's treatment, not be passive. The daughter of a Scottish merchant family, Maggie had grown up in Hong Kong and was familiar with Chinese medicine. 'Yoga, Qigong and guided relaxation all helped me during my treatment' she writes. But chiefly, and here began the movement that would bear her name, 'no patient should be asked to sit in a corridor ... immediately after hearing they have three or four months left to live'. She continued, 'even after the less devastating diagnosis of primary breast cancer, most people need adjustment time before going home to do the washing up'.

Even unwell, she must have been energetic and persuasive. Soon, she had convinced the Western General Hospital in Edinburgh that what they needed was a cancer care centre, where 'thoughtful lighting, a view out to trees, birds and sky, and chairs and sofas arranged in various groupings could be an opportunity for patients to relax and talk, away from home cares'.

That first centre opened a year after her death in 1995, at age 54. In the two decades since, Maggie's husband Charles Jencks has striven to open many more 'Maggie's Centres'. There are eight now in Scotland and more appearing across the UK and abroad. The Maggie's Centres raise their own funds – it is not NHS money – and build at the invitation of the NHS, usually where there are oncology departments. Charles Jencks was and is a landscape architect and architecture critic. He and Maggie counted amongst their friends many now-famous architects. Maggie herself had the blueprint. After her death, Charles had the clout, contacts and vocabulary to take the project forwards.

The Fife Maggie's Centre has had to find space in the congested site of the Victoria Hospital, and in the bewilderment of signs and destinations, you might not notice it if you weren't looking for it. It's rather like something in a fairy story, a little building which only becomes visible when you need it, and even then it's not as you might expect a 'caring' centre to be. The single-storey building has a dark, angular, mineral look, like folded sandpaper. It's not what you'd call touchy-feely. The walls are pierced with triangular windows that look as though they'd admit no light. If you find your own way there, or are nudged toward it by clinicians or friends, you must enter by a long, dark, walled-in ramp. Here, similarities with the Bronze Age structure on the Orkney beach begin and possibly end. In both, the entrance passageway is deliberately dramatic. It tells you that that you are leaving one space, and one state of mind – the huge hospital, buses, car parks, corridors, and language you barely understand – and entering another kind of space. The wall protecting the entrance looks and feels gritty but it guides and protects the traveller and announces an arrival. It's like the embrace of a benign but powerful witch.

The dark hard slanting walls may discomfit some, but people who find their way into the Maggie's Centre are not perturbed. You have to be brave when you have cancer, or are caring for someone who has cancer; entering a strange building is the least of it. If you're courageous enough to approach the building you are rewarded. 'Its apparent aggression is all bluster' said critic Edwin Heathcote. Crucially, you have to enter the building to know that, after the dark passageway, there comes the transformation of light. Inside, the darkness is banished and the space is open-plan, but with turns and curves like a seashell. At the centre, there is not a fire or spring, but the modern equivalent: a domestic kitchen, with a big communal table for informal meetings. Around the perimeters there are not cells because there are no walls, but instead there are comfortable, more-private sitting areas for conversation and activities or just thinking.

There are pink sofas and creamy rugs, plants and artworks. On a shelf stand a row of playful animal sculptures by Eduardo Paolozzi. The walls are white, but soft white, not clinical. The triangular, deep-set windows offer no view of the hospital or car parks, rather they admit changing spangles of sunlight.

The real surprise is a whole long wall of glass, shielded and unseen from the entrance passage, which opens onto trees, almost at canopy level, meeting with the leaves and birds. Beyond the window, accessed by sliding doors, a balcony runs the whole length of the building. Although it's only yards away, the looming, multi-storey hospital is not to be seen.

*

Mostly, Maggie Jencks's vision was about enabling people to be active in their own care, and the Maggie's Centres seek an architecture that enables this. The professional staff run drop-in support sessions all day, and plan a weekly programme of meditation sessions and confidence-building sessions – helping you face the world when you feel rubbish and your hair falls out – and sessions on the financial repercussions of cancer, and sessions especially for youngsters. The centres are intended as places to go when the stress of cancer, its treatments and aftermath can get on top of you. Charles Jenks called the centres 'a house which is not a home', offering relief which is often not available, even in the happiest house.

The staff, nurses and counsellors, know their building. There is no reception desk, and no uniforms. But the staff know where to sit so the door is visible to them, so they can tell the moment someone arrives who has not been before, perhaps someone in crisis who can be led to the kitchen table, or to a secluded sofa if needs be.

I asked one of the centre staff if she felt uplifted herself, coming to work, if it is indeed a building which cares for the carers. Before, she told me, she'd done the same kind of counselling and support work in the corner of a library and I was reminded at once of Maggie Jencks being asked to go and sit in the corridor. Out of sight. Corners and corridors. The Maggie's Centre motto is 'people with cancer need places like these'.

'Yes,' the nurse said. 'It still has the "wow" factor. I feel I can do my work here. But I do have centre-envy! The new Lanarkshire one is fantastic.'

As Charles Jencks notes in his recent book about the centres, *The Architecture of Hope*, architects can be competitive. One wonders if each Maggie's designer is upping the ante, just a little.

The Fife centre was the work of the late Zaha Hadid, the Iraqi-born British architect who became the first woman to win the Royal Gold Medal from the Royal Institute of British Architects, twice won the Stirling Prize, and was knighted in 2012. Hadid died suddenly in 2016, leaving some of her major projects uncompleted, so her London-based practice continues in her name. There is the Al Wakrah stadium in Qatar which is intended as a stadium for the 2022 World Cup, and a skyscraper on 6th Avenue, both a far cry from the little centre in Kirkcaldy. But Maggie's Fife, small and intimate, was Hadid's first permanent structure in the UK and with her passing becomes more noteworthy. 'It's an architecture which is about well-being,' she said. The present centre director, Alison Allan, knows the building now needs some attention; the surrounding trees are lovely but green resin or algae is staining the building's dark facade, and there are one or two other issues which mean that Zaha Hadid's office has to be approached before work can be undertaken. I wish them luck. Dealing with cancer patients is one thing, temperamental architects quite another. It makes you wonder, if a Maggie's architect goes on to become a 'starchitect', a famous name like Frank Gehry or Zaha Hadid, with huge global projects, will they inevitably forget their more humble commissions'? What will become of the buildings, if the original architect has passed on and the personal connection with the Jencks family is lost?

It's the question of care, again. How to care for the unique buildings which care for the carers who care for the sufferers? It ought to be a cycle of virtue, and it needs to be achieved if the buildings are to function as metaphors, where peeling paint or a weather-stain or a bit of breakage takes on great symbolic weight.

*

I spent a little time at the Fife Maggie's Centre, sitting on the sofas, looking out at the trees, speaking to two of the staff between their other duties. They always have one eye on the door. The place was unflustered, I heard the murmur of voices from the kitchen and the sound of the kettle boiling, and when I left I took something of its atmosphere with me. Calmly I set off to leave the hospital complex down the route I'd approached it by earlier, or so I thought. Soon I was lost. Everywhere was car parks. Then the back of a sinister building with metal chimneys. Then a pile of discarded stone behind a crush-barrier. I was calm no more. Then came an unofficial gap in a fence I was glad to squeeze through to reach the street, itself lined with work-a-day unloveliness: a convenience store like a concrete shoe-box, a housing scheme with neither curve nor tree. It's not just hospitals. Most people, most of the time, put up with grim buildings because we know of no alternative. Having squeezed through the gap and reached the street, a terrible thought struck me: if you don't ever have cancer, you might never encounter brilliant small-scale modern architecture, ever. You might live your whole life in this country and never enter a bespoke, well-designed modern building. Not a house, not a school, not a pub, not a leisure centre or library, certainly not a hospital. The Maggie's Centres have many virtues. One is that they are free to use, and democratic, if that's the word. As indiscriminating as cancer. Anyone can step inside and be received.

Is it utterly impossible that our public hospitals could be scaled-up Maggie's Centres? With stellar architects vying for the commission, architects encouraged to dream about more than cost and efficiency? Can't hospitals be about nature and well-being, places of character and atmosphere? Here intimate as a Bronze Age sauna; there views of trees and sky? Apparently not. I crossed the road by the traffic lights and made my way.

25

A View with a Room
James Crawford

Sweeney's Bothy, Eigg 2014

I left Edinburgh at 5.30am. It was very cold, my car cocooned in a fine dry frost that scraped off the windscreen like icing sugar. The birds were already singing in the darkness. I was heading north-west, away from the sunrise. Every so often, I caught the distracting glimpse of a pinkish glow in my rearview mirror. Ahead, the Ochil Hills and the mountains beyond were a bright white, almost glowing. I passed Stirling Castle, turned off the motorway, and by the time I reached Lochearnhead the frost on the ground had turned to snow. The road wound upwards and then straightened out to cross the plateau at Glencoe. My car was the only thing moving. Either side the orange-white mountains were reflected in lochans still as glass. It felt as if I was driving along the hinge of a pocket mirror. When I emerged out of the other side of the pass the sun was up, the snow had gone and the sky was a near cloudless blue. I passed quickly through Fort William then joined the wide empty road to Mallaig.

I parked overlooking the sea, grabbed my bags, and within five minutes was sitting on the ferry. There were only a handful of other passengers, two families and a young couple, all speaking German. We stood on the open front deck, gazing out past the Saltire hanging limp from the prow and enjoying the surprising warmth of the March sunshine. The wind was so light that the boat barely seemed to rock at all on the crossing. Instead the islands came closer as if delivered by conveyor belt. The first, nearer island was long, blocky and flat-topped; although punctuated at its far end by a great, tower-like rise. The second was the antithesis of the first – all peaks and edges, nothing flat, just a series of looming, snow-capped serrations, like a row of saurian teeth. Eigg and Rum.

The ferry pulled into the bay at Eigg, swivelled round, and lowered its ramp onto the pier's stone run-off. A jeep, a truck loaded with timber, a van and a quad bike drove out from the car deck. The rest of us followed on foot. A small crowd had gathered. I was supposed to find a man called Eddie, driving a green Land Rover. He found me first. He directed me to another man, Charlie, who would take me to the far side of the island. As we drove I remarked to Charlie about the calmness of the conditions. He laughed and told me about once being on a CalMac Ferry that was listing so severely that the wall-mounted television in the cafeteria flew off and exploded on the floor. And that was nothing, he continued, compared to his time serving in the Falklands, when a journey to Ascension Island saw his boat riding waves as tall as … he paused for a comparison and then pointed to the hundred-metre-high cliffs that surround Eigg's high plateau. *As tall as those.* I considered myself fortunate.

The drive along the island's single main road took just a few minutes. I was dropped outside a house where my host (and Eddie's partner) Lucy greeted me and we walked with her excitable dog Fiji up a steep path, passing over a couple of makeshift wooden bridges. My home for the next few days emerged over the rise, surrounded by an orange and red mass of desiccated bracken laced with thorn bushes. Its entire front wall was a window – catching the reflection of the blue sky and the darkness of the Rum Cuillins behind me. It had a sloping, corrugated metal roof, with a gleaming cylindrical steel chimney poking out at one side. In front of the window was a small wooden decking with a neat little rectangular bench. And behind was the escarpment of massive cliffs – the great half moon of rock wall that cradles the land on this side of the island. It had been just over six hours since I'd hauled myself out of bed, but now I was here, at Sweeney's Bothy.

*

I met Bobby Niven on a chill but bright morning in a timber-framed, corrugated polycarbonate structure called the Pig Rock Bothy, set in the grounds of Edinburgh's Museum of Modern Art. We sat down at a simple wooden table and talked. Bobby wore a heavy black overcoat, a purple woollen beanie and gloves. There was an oil-burning radiator under the table to fend off the cold, but we both stayed wrapped up throughout.

Bobby, in collaboration with the architect Iain MacLeod, had designed and built the space we were sitting in. It is the third structure to emerge out of 'The Bothy Project', their plan to establish, across Scotland and beyond, a network of modern, hand-crafted, small-scale, off-grid dwellings:

bothies (from the Gaelic *bothan*, meaning 'shelter') designed specifically for use by artists. Bobby is an artist himself – a sculptor, photographer and filmmaker, and a former student of the Glasgow School of Art and the Master of Arts programme at the University of British Columbia in Vancouver. When I asked him where the project came from he struggled to pinpoint any one moment.

'Sometimes it's hard to know whether you're going towards something or away from something', he said. 'I was always travelling up the west coast at weekends while I was at Glasgow. The art scene could be a bit of a boiler-house. It was nice to get out, switch off, just go for a walk or get some hill time.'

He would often stay in mountain bothies, taking his sketchbook along with him, drawing ideas for new sculptures, walking in the landscape, enjoying the fresh air, picking up bits and pieces as he went. 'I guess it was a kind of recreation in a way, creative recreation or something like that.' He enjoyed how, consciously or unconsciously, place and location could act as a source of inspiration. It was also, he said, about friendship.

'You'd use jumping on the train and getting away for the weekend for talking, for getting to know each other and disengaging from other things that had been happening during the week. Or sometimes you're hungover and you just get in the car and make it up as you go along'.

The one downside he found with the bothies was the same thing that was central to their appeal – their remoteness and lack of facilities meant any stay had to be brief. 'Sometimes it's a really intense experience, you get a lot from a short period of time, because it's really visceral with extremes of temperature and weather. But you've got to really pack up all the gear, carry in all your fuel, get your food. You can only carry enough for a night or two.'

In 2009, Bobby and Iain were talking about bothies in a pub with a friend, the environmental artist Will Foster. They thought about how they are now almost entirely the preserve of hill-walkers and mountaineers, used as shelters and staging posts for venturing out into the more inaccessible corners of Scotland. But before that bothies were used for work: by people who were building, making and maintaining things. What, they wondered, about returning to that original idea? 'Artists could go there for a longer period to undertake something, undertake practice, creative work rather than just recreation', explained Bobby. 'That's a nice shift. Maybe that's pioneering.'

They decided to turn their discussion into an open door event at Glasgow School of Art, 'We filled a room with loads of books on architecture and travelling, and all sorts of things about Scotland. People came and did drawings on tables and drawings on the walls, showing the kind of structures they'd like to stay in. We had a map out and people were putting pins in the map to mark their ideal locations.' They took the results from the event and put them up on a blog. Not long after, they received an email from the Royal Scottish Academy asking if they wanted to be a part of their 'Residencies for Scotland' scheme. The Academy had misunderstood the material on the blog. They thought that the fantasy bothies already existed, and that funded artists could stay in them. Bobby and Iain's response was wonderful. 'We don't actually have a venue yet', they said. 'But could we apply to build a residency *on a residency*?' The Academy said yes. In the summer of 2011, with a grant of £5,000, they found themselves installed in the Edinburgh Sculpture Workshop, designing and building their very first artists' bothy.

They began by mocking up a scale model – a little wooden frame with corrugated cardboard for walls. The form was simple, vernacular. To a large extent the structural design was informed by practicalities and logistics. The idea was to build the bothy on-site at the workshop, then dismantle it and reassemble it once they had found an appropriate home somewhere out in the Scottish landscape. So it had to be a panelised structure, it had to fit on the back of a lorry, and its individual sections had to be light enough to be moved and carried by a small number of people. The bothy started to take shape in the car park space outside the sculpture workshop – a timber frame with plywood walling, sitting on rubber tyres to raise it up off the ground. At the same time, work was ongoing to find an appropriate host. A friend put Bobby and Iain in touch with Walter Micklethwait, the manager and family-owner of the 200-acre Inshriach Estate in the Cairngorms National Park. Micklethwait has form as a patron of quirky and innovative ideas – the estate already offered bespoke accommodation in a converted 1956 Commer Q4 fire truck, and had turned an old horsebox into an outdoor hot-tub – and he needed little convincing. 'It is not every day', he said, 'that someone offers you a bothy, prefab, insulated, small enough to be a temporary structure, large enough to stay in.'

In the middle of August, just a couple of weeks after meeting Micklethwait, the bothy was reduced to its component parts and loaded onto a truck heading north up the A9 towards Aviemore. Using an old tractor, Bobby and Iain transported the large panel sections to a secluded spot among traditional woodland near the banks of the River Spey. A footprint for the building was roped out among the heather and juniper, and then they began digging the holes for the six concrete pillar foundations.

Much of the structural work was achieved in the first two weeks. But the fine detail took a lot longer.

'There were about fifteen people involved in the build', Bobby explained. 'All volunteers – a mixture of arts friends from Glasgow and people connected to the Edinburgh Sculpture Workshop.' They followed the same routine over some ten weekends between August and the following March. 'We'd pack the car – an old Volvo 240 Estate – loading the roof rack with materials and trying to cram five folk in as well. We'd leave on a Friday night, drive up in the dark and all stay in the bothy.' For much of this process it was half built with no windows – sometimes snow would be drifting in on top of them. 'We had a beer keg stove that this pyromaniac American guy from the Glasgow Sculpture Studios had made. We'd sit around that and try to keep warm.' Other times the weather was kinder. 'If you get a high pressure sunny day and you're building outside you'd get a really magical feeling. It's a lot different to being in a carpentry workshop with the sound of nail guns and tunes pumping away. The woodland smells are amazing, the fire's going, somebody's taking care of the tea and the toast, some of you are having chat, some of you are just working alone. And enjoying that, being out in nature.' Then, come sunset on the Sunday, they'd pack up their things and drive back home again in the dark.

They were operating on a shoestring budget, so they worked the building out as they went along. Much of the aesthetic of the bothy was the result a scramble to get material donated. They wrote a lot of letters to suppliers explaining the project and asking for discounts or freebies. The structure's standout feature – its corrugated, galvanised-steel cladding, 'the spaceship look' as Bobby puts it – was gifted to them by a company called Cladco after a mis-order had left a pile of it lying unused in their yard. The narrow, floor-to-eave sash and case windows came from Bobby's own Glasgow flat – two were fitted on either side of the building, with one on the gable end. Iain custom-designed and fashioned special clipped gutters. The bothy's floor and mezzanine level – a bed in the roof space reached by ladder salvaged from the Glasgow School of Art – was formed out of reclaimed ash, while the gables were clad in locally sourced Scottish larch. The insulation came from sheep's wool. 'It smells good, it's nice to work with, it's non-toxic and non-abrasive, unlike the glass fibre stuff', Bobby explained. 'It helps you feel like you're in a much more natural space.'

They fitted out a kitchenette below the double bed, installed a wood-burning stove with an oven, built a mini library, and furnished the bothy with two basic wooden tables, an old leather armchair and a desk chair. Lighting was provided by wall mounting a solar-powered anglepoise lamp, and hanging glass-lanterns to hold tea lights. Their shower was out-doors, a curve of the corrugation providing a partial screen for suspending a water bag heated by the wood-burner. When the Inshriach Bothy was finally completed in the spring of 2012, a business model was agreed with Walter – ring-fencing periods for creative practitioners, while opening up other parts of the year for public rental to ensure continuous occupancy and help with income and running costs.

Artists started arriving that autumn, alone and in groups, covering a wide range of disciplines – film-makers, painters, poets, musicians, sculptors, photographers. The residency, built on a residency, was now in use as a residency. But Inshriach was always just a starting point, a prototype. Bobby and Iain had envisaged a network of structures, and were already turning their attention towards their next build, their island bothy.

*

I dropped my bags on the floor and sank into a soft maroon armchair set in the middle of the bothy. *What now?*

The view was what now. *The view* is the answer to just about any question you might ask of Sweeney's Bothy. Everything is orientated towards its floor-to-ceiling glass wall (actually four glass panels segmented by three narrow strips of wood, but so slim as to almost fade away after a first look, to seem like a single pane). The armchair, the desk with its own little wooden swivel chair on casters, the snug and bookshelves set in the back wall, the wood-burning stove, the double bed up in the roof space – all put themselves in service of the view. What is the view? Through the window the land undulates down to the sea. Rum appears impossibly close, the Sound reduced to just a few inches of water. You can't see any buildings or any people. But the mountains stare in at you, heavy and implacable: Sgurr nan Gillean, Ainshval, Askival, Hallival, the Nameless Corrie, the Forgotten Corrie. And the rest is sky.

It was just past noon. The interior of the bothy was dim with the sun still so startlingly bright outside – only a sliver of light fell obliquely through the window. It made the view appear over-saturated, like a Technicolor cinema screen. It took a while to get up or to do anything at all. I was suffering from view-induced paralysis – a common affliction, it seemed, for those who stay in the bothy. I sat flicking through the visitors' book and every testimonial came back to the view – a succession of people staring out at the land, the sea, the sky; at Rum disappearing or reappearing out of cloud, rain or mist; at the preponderance of rainbows. 'It's impossible not to be moved by this view' said one entry, written in a neat, spidery hand. Kathleen Jamie wrote a poem about it, when she stayed in the bothy. It opens:

> for too long I haven't
> > glanced at the sea
> > – fully ten minutes!

I could understand those ten minutes now as an achievement of considerable willpower. The poem was called – what else? – 'The View'. The very last entry in the visitors' book, written the day before I arrived, recommended watching the 'ever-changing elements' – and then suggested that 'if it's a clear night, shower under the stars, you won't forget it'. *I won't be doing that,* I thought. I flicked to another entry from a fortnight earlier. It quoted Nan Shepherd's line, 'my eyes were in my feet'. 'Walk as much as you can,' it urged. This roused me.

I heated soup in a heavy cast-iron pan on the gas hob, and took it outside, sitting on the bench and resting my back against the glass. The wind had picked up and clouds had mustered over Rum's peaks. The sun was being switched on and off now like a light. It was good weather for walking. Lucy had described a route up onto the cliffs behind the bothy: 'duck under a clothes-line and then it's a short, steep scramble to the top. Gets the torture over and done with straight away'. I did as suggested, hauling myself up through a rocky gun barrel, and arriving on a wide plateau of heather and soft, spongy grass. For the next few hours I followed the line of the cliffs south to north, moving from precipice to precipice, gaping at the waterfalls tumbling down, always looking for the bothy somewhere below. It appeared as a tiny black dot (three tiny black dots really: the bothy, the wood store with its solar panels, the composting toilet off to one side), set back from the smattering of houses that followed the main road. The landscape was a patchwork of oranges, greens and browns. As the light dipped, patterns began to emerge, lines and curves and circles, the tracery of old abandoned crofts, walls, fields and farms submerged beneath the undergrowth. I touched the trig point at the northernmost stretch of the cliffs, and looked out to Skye, smeared at its centre by a distant, isolated column of rain. The route looped back by a haphazard zigzag path, dipping down a gap between the rocks, then finally rejoining the very end of the island's main road.

Afternoon was tipping into evening when I returned. The bothy was bathed in light now, the low sun reaching into to its back corners, filling the building with a gentle, drowsy heat. The view was back again, insistent and transfixing. The cloud began to thicken, but not too much. Clear pockets of blue and yellow were swaddled in white and grey gauze. The sky over the horizon shifted from gold to bronze. The sun was dipping fast now; it found the gap between the clouds and the sea and burst like a flare, turning the inside of the bothy crimson. Then it was gone.

I lit the fire in the wood burner, cooked some dinner and watched the window turn to black. Now all I could see was the reflection of the desk lamp and the glow of my laptop screen open in front of me. I had recorded my conversation with Bobby in the Pig Rock Bothy, and I wanted to hear it again now.

In the near-darkness, with the fire popping alongside me, I listened to the story of how Sweeney's was made.

*

The project evolved with the creation of the second bothy. Bobby and Iain brought the poet and artist Alec Finlay into the design process, securing investment from Creative Scotland as part of 'Year of Natural Scotland'. As Bobby explained, even at the stage of applying for funding, 'Alec was building a picture around what the bothy could be, both in terms of its physical presence, but also in terms of cultural movements, mythology, sense of place'.

Alec's idea was to take inspiration from Shiubhne – Sweeney – the mad king of Celtic folklore. According to the tale, after killing an old friend at the battle of Mag Rath, Sweeney loses his mind and escapes into the wilderness. He spends some ten years wandering the lands of Ireland and Scotland, looking each night for a new place to rest and sleep, and composing poems on both the beauty and cruelty of nature. At the furthest reaches of his flight, he comes to the Small Isles – to Eigg. But he can never escape the memory of the spears of battle. As Flann O'Brien puts it in his novel *At Swim Two Birds,* time and again Sweeney finds himself enduring, 'the pain of his bed there on top of a tall ivy-grown hawthorn in the glen, every twist that he would turn sending showers of hawy thorns into his flesh'.

The thorn became the bothy's key design motif. Alec's original sketch for the building, submitted as part of the funding application, was a solid blank rectangle, stamped on top of a jagged scatter of overlapping straight lines. 'The bothy begins as a frame in and for the wilderness, as every hut is', said Alec. 'The sketch catches the gist of Sweeney's bed in the thorn trees.' It was captioned 'Sweeney's Bothy: thicket without, shelter within'.

As the building developed, Alec, in the spirit of Sweeney, recorded the design process in poetry.

the thorn finds purpose
as pillar, or pilotis
the thorn turns its points skywards
away from delicate flesh

in our design
the thorn column suggested
extending the angled roof outwards
beyond the bothy walls

...

only when the revisions
are precise
will the bothy stand

square and plumb
on a hill facing
a rugged mountain skyline

the hut-yet-to-be-built
has found its home
in the vale of Cleadale
on the Isle of Eigg

the furthest of the leaps
the outcast Sweeney made
in his mad journey
through the wilds

Sweeney's wee hut
will have its windows
faced to the west

aligned so as to be
filled with the massif
skyline of Rum

'Alec was creating the myth of the structure before it even existed', Bobby said. The *hut-yet-to-be-built* was gaining a public following. And all the while, in his sculpture workshop in an outbuilding of his dad's farm in

Fife, Bobby was bringing the physical bothy to life. As before, the frame was assembled first and then dismantled for transport to its final site: a plot of land cleared out among the bracken on Lucy and Eddie's croft at Cleadale on the north-west of Eigg. In the late autumn of 2013 a flat-bed truck piled high with spruce stud-walling, larch cladding and sheep's wool insulation drove from Fife to the ferry port at Mallaig. The truck made it across on its second attempt, nosed right up against the on–off ramp to fit on the car deck. It was too big, however, to navigate the island's main road. Everything had to be unloaded just a few hundred metres from the pier, above the sands of Galmisdale Bay. A crofter called Alistair then helped move the materials in instalments, wood panels balanced like a Jenga tower on a trailer hooked up to the back of his tractor. Bobby had estimated the build time at six weeks, based roughly on the number of actual construction days at Inshriach. It took far longer. The setting and the environment offered up challenges that he had not anticipated.

'It was brutal,' he said. 'I ended up being on Eigg for five months of the winter. And it was the worst winter they'd had in fifty years. There were only five days with no rain the whole time. The site was a slurry, knee-deep mud round about it.' Access was already difficult because of the steep slope up from the road, and it was made even worse by the persistence of the rain. They had to walk things up piece by piece: wooden panels, window frames, glass. 'We ran out of money. But I was stuck there because I had to complete it.'

For large parts of this time, Bobby was by himself. It was tempting to picture him as a version of Sweeney – the solitary figure wrestling with nature's harsh extremes. He kept a photo diary of the construction. It is a study in saturation, a series of images of mud, wet wood, squalls, snow, pregnant clouds, weak light and watery rainbows. I asked him if Sweeney's felt like more of an achievement than Inshriach because of the adversity, because he had had to do so much of it on his own. But no, most of the time he was just annoyed with himself.

'I felt stupid because I wasn't able to predict how it should have been set up,' he said. 'For people who live on the islands that's just how it goes – and you probably try to do most of your build projects in the summer. For me it was a new thing.' Companionship made a difference. For the first month and a half Bobby's step-brother stayed with him on-site. 'He was at a junction in his life, so he came with his wee dog. He had no building or carpentry experience but wanted to volunteer. It was great hanging out with him. Now he's doing a carpentry course in Australia.' A couple of artist friends from Glasgow also did stints on the island. 'They lit up the place for a couple of weeks, we had a hoot. To have someone visit for a week or a month would help get you through.' With the funds almost exhausted – and Bobby no longer able to pay wages or his rental accommodation – he had to improvise and start pre-selling artists' residencies to institutions, booking up slots in the *hut-yet-to-be-built*. It was this money that allowed him to employ locals on Eigg to help complete the bothy.

The involvement of the community was always important to him. 'A lot of people think of the bothies purely as retreats. That's slightly condescending to the locations. These are not places where there is nothing. What's the periphery for one person is the centre for someone else. It's the communities that bring the bothies to life.' Bobby told me the colourful story of how he first came to bond with the people of Eigg. 'We'd been building for about ten days when we walked over to the tea room one evening for a pint. We didn't really know anyone in the room at all. When we walked in it kind of went quiet, and then there was this chorus. And we couldn't quite work out what they were saying to start with. But basically it was this kind of chorus of abuse, heckling, just heckling as we came in. And then this one loudest voice at the end just shouted "fucking bothy wankers!".' He laughed at the memory of it. 'We had a really nice evening. It was just a heckle to see if you could take it, and if you could then you weren't too serious and you were alright for a chat. I told Lucy about it later and she said "that's a good sign".'

By the spring of 2014 it was almost done. One of the last interior fittings was the mezzanine level in the roof space above the kitchenette, right at the back of the bothy. To hold up the double bed they erected a timber pillar, rising up from the floor and then branching out into three struts. The three-pronged pillar came from one of Alec's first drawings of the thorn motif: it was the hawthorn tree to carry mad Sweeney's bed.

*

I woke in the hawthorn tree, climbed down its ladder and made a trip out to the wood store. The sky was a liquid blue, the sun painfully bright. But the air was brittle, the ground set in a hard frost. I got a fire going in the wood burner to heat the water for the outdoor shower. There was a little digital centigrade thermometer hooked up to a pipe on the bothy wall. When it climbed into the thirties, I dashed out onto the decking and twisted on the shower: a double hit of hot and cold. I made breakfast, then unfolded the big Ordnance Survey map from the bothy's little library and spread it out on the floor. I had decided to climb the Sgurr, Eigg's great skyscraper of volcanic rock.

It was late morning by the time I set off. The sky was still cloudless, marked only by the incessant scribbling of jet contrails. I had to walk back along the main road, almost all the way to Galmisdale Bay, before I turned up a track through the trees. The path opened to a green grassy field, leading up to a house framed beautifully beneath the grey knucklebone of the Sgurr. Beyond the house everything was clad in russet heather. The land was still swollen with rainwater. On up-slopes, the path often deteriorated into a riverbed. On the flats, it disappeared in stretches of murky bog. The route continued into the permanent shadow beneath the lee of the Sgurr. Now I was climbing over snow and ice.

Even at the summit, almost four hundred metres above sea level, there was only the lightest breeze. I hadn't spotted another person since I set out. I watched an eagle ride the thermals below me. It felt like you could see all of Scotland. Looking north there was Rum and Skye. To the east was the mainland, the mountains still encased in snow. South was Muck, then Coll and Tiree. And finally out west was the long tail of the Outer Hebrides, with Mingulay as a last punctuation mark. Beyond that, there's nothing until the coast of Newfoundland.

It was almost six o'clock by the time I got back to the bothy. I'd been walking for seven hours. I quickly ate soup, then made my way down to the beach overlooking the Bay of Laig. The air was perfectly still. Rum was in silhouette, its image reflected in the wide, glassy stretch of wet sands. I sat in the white dunes, listened to the waves breaking and watched the sunset.

I looked in on Lucy and Eddie on the way back to the bothy – taking a proffered can of Guinness eagerly. The darkness came again, and with the fire lit, I poured my drink, sat down in the armchair and started to write. I wrote much of what you are reading here now. At around eleven o'clock I glanced at the digital thermometer. The water temperature had nudged over forty degrees. I closed my laptop, undressed, stepped out into the night, and showered beneath the stars.

*

'There will be loads of huts and cabins popping up over the next few years, which I think is a great thing,' Bobby said. We were talking about the 'Thousand Huts' campaign, an initiative started in 2011 to promote the building of simple structures for living, working and recreation in the countryside. In 2014, the campaign achieved a notable success: a first legal definition of a hut in the glossary of the Scottish Planning Policy. A hut, it says, is 'a simple building … constructed from low impact materials … and built in such a way that it is movable with little or no trace at the end of its life'. A commitment followed from the Scottish Government to exempt huts from building regulations – contingent on developing a Code of Good Practice to ensure adequate health and safety provision. As the campaigners put it, they are attempting to revive a 'hutting heritage' that is in real danger of vanishing. 'Simple, rustic buildings have always been an important part of Scotland's culture,' they say. 'From shielings to mountain bothies and shepherds' huts, they have played a crucial role as temporary bases for people to spend time in the hills, forests, and countryside.'

I asked Bobby if he saw a role for his bothies in the campaign. 'We have a slightly different agenda,' he said. 'The hutting movement has always been about the right of the individual or the family to build and have access to their own hut. It's about the hut in your imagination, and your right and freedom to have it.' All the same, the Bothy Project is offering up a blueprint for the hutters of the future. Soon they will be making prefab bothies available for sale, adapted from the original Inshriach design. 'We'll have two options', Bobby said, 'a volumetric one, that will be delivered to a site complete on the back of a truck; and a panelised flat-pack version for self-assembly. You'll be able to put them anywhere.' Their initial projections for this service are relatively modest: sell ten bothies in their first year, twenty in their second, and forty in their third. It is part of Bobby's plan to turn the Bothy Project into a dedicated charitable organisation – on the one hand developing the creative network by running residencies, on the other selling prefabs and related materials. These include the work of the 'Bothy Stores', an initiative which is challenging designers to develop new products specific to the needs and locations of individual bothies. So far the results have ranged from a terracotta cool box and an 'eco-dyed' apron, to a 20-litre duck canvas shower bag and pulley system. 'One strand is about the imagination and supporting people, the other is practical and tangible,' Bobby said.

The ongoing development of the dwelling bothies remains central, however. The plan is to supplement Inshriach and Sweeney's with another eight residencies within the next five years. Each should be bespoke, Bobby said, the product of further collaborations with artists and architects. 'And we will always be asking ourselves, "what is the need for it, why here, how can it contribute and be a part of the community?" The bothies can't just exist as facilities for people who don't live there.' They may explore building on a bigger scale, establishing some dwellings for groups rather than individuals, and encouraging wider access. This is a project with international ambition. 'We could form partnerships with institutions abroad for a residency exchange project or even a new bothy build,' Bobby continued. 'There's a hutting movement happening globally. And as the Scottish contingent we'd like to do exchanges and share our traditional material and carpentry processes – along with our innovations.'

It may be this last point that has the widest relevance. All of the bothies are developed under the auspices of the project's commitment to sustainability, renewability and low carbon. It's something Bobby doesn't mention overtly because, as he puts it, 'it's intrinsic, there's nothing less inspiring than people telling you the obvious'. Yet what is perhaps not so obvious is the potential for the scalability of the bothy designs. They provide the opportunity to experiment with new materials to showcase how they might be used. They can try things, they can make mistakes and, somewhere down the line, they can make a contribution to the essential conversation about how *we all* should build. 'We don't want to over-promise', Bobby said. 'But on some level it has to be the ambition of the project to achieve that.'

*

After a grey morning, the sun had pushed through. I was back on the ferry, sitting out on the deck, facing backwards to watch Eigg drift away. It occurred to me that one of the most fascinating things about the bothies is that, in the style of the hutting movement, they are *built in such a way that they are movable with little or no trace at the end of their lives.* Both Inshriach and Sweeney's are 'soft touch' builds, erected on two-metre-long concrete pillar foundations. Which means that they can just be pulled out and taken away, and it will be like they were never there in the first place.

'It should be that way,' Bobby had said. The bothies make no claim to legacy or permanence – they are visitors in the landscape, not fixtures. Where so many buildings are fixated on *lasting*, the bothies are preconceived as ghosts. What if, I wondered idly, somewhere down the generations, this becomes the new norm? Just as the digital age seems to offer up the eventual end of the physical archive – no-one actually *writes anything down anymore* – will there be a new wave of buildings, a new generation of builders, that actively avoids inscribing anything in the landscape? What might this mean for our understanding of our past, if we evolve a built environment that leaves nothing behind – no litter, no detritus, no sign? Of course, we are not there yet – we are very far from there. But it is something to think about: that a time may come when what we build will no longer be left behind to tell us who we once were, and who we now are.

And would it be better that way?

Locations

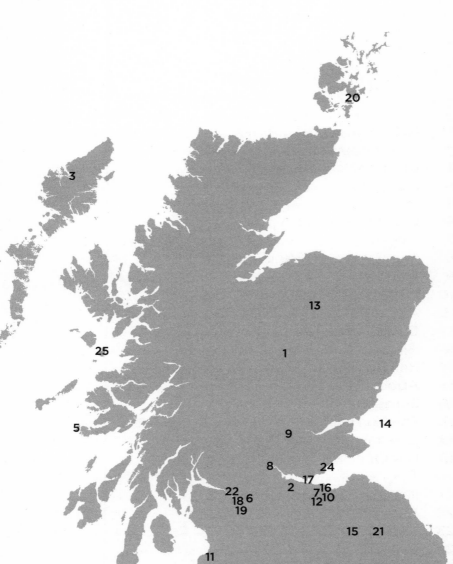

Image Credits – Chapters

Image Credits – Plate Sections

1   Geldie Burn – © Nick Bramhall
2   Cairnpapple Hill – Crown Copyright HES
3   Calanais – Crown Copyright HES
4   Mousa Broch – Crown Copyright HES
5   Iona Abbey – Crown Copyright HES
6   Glasgow Cathedral – Crown Copyright HES
7   Edinburgh Castle – Crown Copyright HES
8   Stirling Castle – Crown Copyright HES
9   Innerpeffray Library – Courtesy Innerpeffray Library © Jo Cound
10 Mavisbank House – Crown Copyright HES
11 Auld Alloway Kirk – Crown Copyright HES
12 Charlotte Square – Crown Copyright HES

Index

on Stirling Castle 93, 99
'Such a parcel of rogues ...' 123
Burns, William 134
Burntisland 73, 206
Burrell Collection 221–222
Burrell, William 221
Bushmills Distillery 163
Bute, 4th Marquess of 153–154
Bute, 5th Marquess of 154
Bute, 6th Marquess of 154
Bute, Earl of 38
Bute House, Edinburgh 153–154
Bynack Burn 14
Byron, Lord 184

Cadell, Francis 59
Caerketton 29
Caesar, Julius 95
Cairngorms, the 13, 38, 160, 302
Cairnpapple Hill 27–33
cairns 28, 29, 32, 44, 284
Caithness 35, 42
Calanais, Lewis 27, 43–47
Calback, Shetland 281
Caledonian Railway Company 206, 231
Callanish see Calanais
Callandar 157
Calton Hill, Edinburgh 195
Calton Street, Edinburgh 195
Cameron, Andy 237
Campsie Fells 29
Candymill 187
Cantors of the Holy Rood 77
Caonachan Ruadha 15, 16
Carlins' Craig, Bridge of Allan 139
Carlisle, stone keep 87–88
Carlyle, Thomas 109
Carnegie, Andrew 110, 111, 112, 113, 116
Cartleyhole 180
Castle Gates, Edinburgh 82
Castle Street
Edinburgh 151, 190
Glasgow 71
Castlehill, Edinburgh 82, 83

Castlemilk, Glasgow 269
Castra Puellarum (Castle of the Maidens) 87
Caterhaugh Ba' Game 235, 236, 240
Cathcart 229
Cathcart and District Railway Company 231
cathedrals
Brechin 40
Dunblane 71, 77, 113–114
Glasgow 71–78
St Andrews 71, 77
St Giles 67, 71
Catterick 87
Central Library
Edinburgh 112
Stirling 112–113
Chalmers Church, Bridge of Allan 136
Chambers, Robert 37
Channel Four 221, 222
chapels
Drummond family 106, 107
Inchaffray abbey 106
Italian 243, 244, 246–248
St Margaret's, Edinburgh Castle 82, 84, 86, 87
St Oran's 66, 68
Charles I, king of Scotland and England 65, 229
Charles II, king of Scotland and England 107, 113, 139
Charles X, king of France 153
Charles Edward, Prince 28, 96, 184
Charlotte Square, Edinburgh 147–155
Charlton, Bobby 241
Chest of Dee 14, 16
Chiocchetti, Domenico 247, 248
Chiocchetti, Maria 248
Chippenham 92
church buildings 133–144
Anniesland, Glasgow 265
Edinburgh 67, 71, 152, 198
Iona 61, 62–63, 64, 65, 67
see also cathedrals; chapels
Church of Scotland
church-building 141

New York 101, 147, 295
Newbery, Francis 217, 218, 222
Newbery, Jessie 217, 218, 222
Newbery, Mary 217–218, 219, 220, 222, 223
Newbigging, Greig 213, 214
Nicholson Street, Edinburgh 193
Nisbet family 260
Niven, Bobby 300–304, 306, 307–309, 310–312
Nor Loch, Edinburgh 85, 148
North Berwick Law 29
North Bridge, Edinburgh 151
North British Railway Company 206, 207
North Queensferry 203, 204
North Roe, Shetland 284
North Uist 44
Northampton, Derngate 220
Northern Lighthouse Board 169, 170, 171, 172
Northmavine, Shetland 279, 286
Northumbria 87
Noup of Noss, Shetland 49
Nunnery, Iona 64, 65

O'Brien, Flann 306
Ochil Hills 29, 299
Olav, King 280
Old College, Edinburgh 193
Old Surgeons' Hall, Edinburgh 195
Old Town, Edinburgh 85, 88, 114, 148, 149, 205
Oman, Mrs Grace 153
Orka, Shetland 281
Orkney 41
   Italian Chapel 243, 244, 246–248
   Knap of Howar 9, 27
   Links of Noltland 290–292, 293–294
   Maeshowe 41
   Ness of Brodgar 31
   Papa Westray 9, 29
   Picts 35, 37, 41
   Ring of Brodgar 41
   Scapa Flow 243, 244, 245

Skara Brae 27, 41
UNESCO 205
Westray 290–292, 293–294
   see also Brown, George Mackay
Ossian 184, 195–196
Oswald, king 87

Paibeil/Paible, Lewis 28
Paisley Abbey 71, 77
Paolozzi, Eduardo 294
Papa Westray, Orkney 9, 29
Paris 122, 147, 204
Park Page 224
Parliament *see* Scottish Parliament
Parthenon Marbles 101
Pasquini, Bernardo 121
Pasteur, Louis 200
Paterson, Robert 188
Pathfoot 137
Paul, George Balfour 197
Paxton, Roland 172
Peers, Charles 99, 100
Pendreich 137
Penicuik 120
   see also Clerk, Sir John, of Penicuik
Penicuik House 122
Pennant, Thomas 65
Penney, Caron 101
Pentland Hills 29
Peploe, Samuel 59
Perth 157, 206
Perthshire 17, 18, 140
   see also Innerpeffray Library
Philip, Prince 280
Picts 35–40, 61, 62
Pig Rock Bothy 300, 306
Pipewell Brae, Inchmyre 260
Piranesi, Giovanni Battista 152
Plaumbo (blacksmith) 247
Playfair, John 195
Playfair, William 155, 195, 196, 197, 198, 200
Plockton, church 142
Pluscarden Abbey 159, 161
Poland, wood for Stirling Heads 101
Pollok, Glasgow 269

St Columba 61–62, 63, 65, 67, 68
St George's Square, Edinburgh 151
St Giles Cathedral 67, 71
St Kentigern 71, 76, 77, 78
St Kilda 205
St Margaret's Chapel, Edinburgh
    Castle 82, 84, 86, 87
St Michael's Church, Edinburgh 198
St Ninian 36, 62
St Oran's Chapel, Iona 66, 68
St Roque's library, Dundee 111–112
St Saviour's Church, Bridge of
    Allan 136
St Vigeans, symbol stone 40
Sandwick, Shetland 49
Sauchiehall Street, Glasgow 219
Scapa Flow, Orkney 243, 244, 245
Schiehallion 38
Scotch Malt Whisky Society 161, 164
Scots Guards 85
Scott, Charlotte 183
Scott, Sir George Gilbert 99
Scott Street, Glasgow 219
Scott, Sir Walter
    Bell Rock 174
    Edwin Muir's opinion 179, 186
    football and 235, 236, 238
    Iona 66
    MacDiarmid's opinion 186
    novels 110, 147, 190
    see also Abbotsford
Scottish Enlightenment 109, 114, 129,
    134, 196
Scottish Football Association 237
Scottish Football Museum 239
Scottish Lime Centre 92
Scottish National Portrait Gallery 171
Scottish Parliament 108, 113, 122, 123
Scottish Poetry Library 114
Scottish Privy Council 96
Scottish Television 217, 219, 220, 221
Second World War see World War II
Selgovae 86
Selkirk, Caterhaugh Ba' team 235
Sgurr, the, Eigg 310
Shankly, Bill 236, 238

Sharp, Archbishop 183
Sharp, James 109
Shepherd, Nan 305
Shepherd, Thomas 196
Sheriffmuir 137
Shetland
    Brae 279
    Calback 281
    Crooksetter 281
    Fethaland 284–285
    Firth 282
    Loch of Burraland 279
    MacDiarmid in 189, 190
    Mavis Grind 279
    Mousa Broch 49–56
    North Roe 284
    Northmavine 279, 286
    Orka 281
    Pictish symbol stones 35
    Rattleton 281
    Ronas Hill 284
    Ronas Voe 284
    Sandwick 49
    Sullom Voe 28, 275, 276, 279–283,
        285, 286
    Sumburgh Airport 276, 278, 284
    Sumburgh Lighthouse 49
    Toft 282
    Whalsay 189
    Yell Sound 284
shielings 17–20
Sidlaw Hills 35
Simpson, Sir James 198
Sir Duncan Rice Library, Aberdeen
    University 114
Skara Brae, Orkney 27, 41
Skibo 113
Skinner, Reverend John 235
Skye 35, 167, 305, 310
Small Isles 167, 306
    see also Eigg
Smith, Charles Joseph 161
Smith, George 160–161, 162
Smith, Col. J G 162
Smith, James 142, 144
Smith, Sydney Goodsir 147

Historic Environment Scotland

We are the lead public body for Scotland's historic environment: a charity dedicated to the advancement of heritage, culture, education and environmental protection.

Our books are telling the stories of Scotland. From landmark works of expert research to creative collaborations with internationally renowned authors, our aim is to explore ideas and start conversations about the past, present and future of our nation's history and heritage.

HISTORIC ENVIRONMENT SCOTLAND | ÀRAINNEACHD EACHDRAIDHEIL ALBA